Methodological Concepts

Methodological Concepts: A Critical Guide clarifies many key terms and issues in social research methodology. It outlines the conventional meanings of these terms, and also addresses their contentious character. The aim is to offer interpretations of them that provide a coherent conception of the nature of social science.

This book is premised on the idea that more clarity about the meaning of major methodological concepts is essential, and that the disagreements which pervade the field must be addressed. Numerous key terms are discussed across 13 chapters, including 'methodology', 'method', 'inquiry', 'research', 'science', 'truth', 'fact', 'rigour', 'bias', 'objectivity', 'data', 'evidence', 'induction', 'deduction', 'abduction', 'understanding', 'explanation', 'reflexivity', 'triangulation', 'theory', and 'researcher integrity'. These concepts have been implicated in fundamental divisions among social scientists that have generated the 'paradigm wars' of the past few decades. The chapters of this book provide an overview of the various meanings given to these terms, whilst also offering distinctive interpretations designed to provide a sound basis for social research.

Methodological Concepts: A Critical Guide should be of considerable value for any student or researcher working in the social sciences.

Martyn Hammersley is Emeritus Professor of Educational and Social Research at The Open University, UK. His research interests include the sociology of education, the sociology of the media, ethnography, and social research methodology. He is the author of numerous books, including *The Politics of Social Research* (1995), *Reading Ethnographic Research* (Second edition, 1997), *Educational Research, Policymaking and Practice* (2002), *Questioning Qualitative Inquiry* (2008), *The Myth of Research-Based Policy and Practice* (2013), *The Limits of Social Science* (2014), *The Radicalism of Ethnomethodology* (2018), *Ethnography: Principles in Practice* (Fourth edition, Routledge, 2019), *The Concept of Culture* (2019), and *Troubling Sociological Concepts* (2020).

Methodological Concepts

A Critical Guide

Martyn Hammersley

Routledge
Taylor & Francis Group

LONDON AND NEW YORK

Designed cover image: Martyn Hammersley

First published 2023
by Routledge
4 Park Square, Milton Park, Abingdon, Oxon OX14 4RN

and by Routledge
605 Third Avenue, New York, NY 10158

Routledge is an imprint of the Taylor & Francis Group, an informa business

British Library Cataloguing-in-Publication Data
A catalogue record for this book is available from the British Library

Library of Congress Cataloging-in-Publication Data
Names: Hammersley, Martyn, author.
Title: Methodological concepts : a critical guide / Martyn Hammersley.
Description: New York, NY : Routledge, 2023. | Includes bibliographical
    references and index.
Identifiers: LCCN 2022038560 (print) | LCCN 2022038561 (ebook) |
    ISBN 9781032395739 (hardback) | ISBN 9781032395746 (paperback) |
    ISBN 9781003350354 (ebook)
Subjects: LCSH: Social sciences—Research—Methodology.
Classification: LCC H62 .H23364 2023 (print) | LCC H62 (ebook) |
    DDC 300.72—dc23/eng/20220815
LC record available at https://lccn.loc.gov/2022038560
LC ebook record available at https://lccn.loc.gov/2022038561

ISBN: 978-1-032-39573-9 (hbk)
ISBN: 978-1-032-39574-6 (pbk)
ISBN: 978-1-003-35035-4 (ebk)

DOI: 10.4324/9781003350354

Typeset in Bembo
by Apex CoVantage, LLC

This book is dedicated to those who find it useful.

The chapters can be read separately, even though they are interrelated; but it would be worth reading the Introduction before any of the others.

Contents

Acknowledgements

Chapter 5 uses some material from 'Objectivity: A Reconceptualisation', in Williams, M. and Vogt, W. P. (eds) *The Sage Handbook of Methodological Innovation*, London, Sage, 2011.

Chapter 6 draws material from 'Rigour', in P. Atkinson, S. Delamont, A. Cernat, J.W. Sakshaug, & R.A. Williams (Eds.), *SAGE Research Methods Foundations*, 2020. www.doi.org/10.4135/9781526421036929656

Chapter 8 is based in part on 'Induction', in P. Atkinson, S. Delamont, A. Cernat, J.W. Sakshaug, & R.A. Williams (Eds.), *SAGE Research Methods Foundations*, 2020. www.doi.org/10.4135/9781526421036757475

Chapter 11 uses some parts of 'Troubles with triangulation', in Bergman, M. (ed.) *Advances in Mixed Methods Research*, London, SAGE, 2008.

Chapter 12 draws some material from 'Troubling theory in case study research', *Higher Education Research and Development*, 31, 3, pp. 393–405, 2012.

Chapter 13 is based on 'Epistemic integrity in social research' in Iphofen, R. (ed.) *Handbook of Research Ethics and Scientific Integrity*, Berlin, Springer, 2020.

Introduction

This book is a guide to some key terms used in social research methodology. The concepts to which these terms refer are crucial for understanding the nature of social research and how it can, and should, be pursued. Yet, in current usage, these meanings are multiple, vague, and contentious; and they are frequently employed, or rejected, without clarification. Their uncertain meaning reflects the fact that there is much disagreement even about what counts as research, as well as about its goal and how it might best be pursued. Some methodological concepts, such as 'truth', are involved in defining that goal, while others (for instance, 'objectivity', 'rigour', and 'reflexivity') refer to essential virtues that researchers must display in their work. Other terms I discuss in this book, such as 'triangulation', refer to strategies that can be employed in carrying out investigations.[1]

There are, of course, many dictionaries and encyclopaedias that deal with methodological concepts.[2] However, to a large extent, these are concerned with outlining current usage. This is certainly an important task, and it will be my starting point in each chapter of this book. But it is insufficient. We must also address the problems surrounding these concepts, and try to work out how to formulate them better, in order to provide a sounder basis for pursuing social inquiry. That is the main aim of this book.

As already noted, fundamental disagreements exist among social researchers about the character and purpose of their work, these reflecting a proliferation of sharply divergent 'approaches' or 'paradigms'. One result of this is that the validity or usefulness of methodological concepts that were previously held to be central has been challenged, and new ones have been put forward. This is the background to my discussion, and it means that I cannot adopt a neutral stance towards the diverse methodological approaches that now exist. Therefore, later in this chapter I will outline the position I am taking, and the reasons for it.

Of course, it could be argued that methodological 'pluralism' or 'diversity' is a positive not a negative feature of the field. Having a wide range of methods available is certainly desirable. There is no 'gold standard', neither the randomised controlled trial nor the in-depth interview, neither participant observation nor the standardised test. Methods always have advantages and disadvantages, whose significance will vary according to the research questions

DOI: 10.4324/9781003350354-1

being addressed and the circumstances in which inquiry is taking place (Hammersley 2015b). Similarly, engagement with different views about methodological issues is essential if progress is to be made in understanding, and thereby dealing with, those issues. However, the sort of diversity in approach that is now prevalent in some areas of social science goes beyond this.

First, it tends to treat differences between methodological perspectives as defying rational deliberation: external criticism is frequently rejected out of hand, rather than engaged with. This tendency has been reinforced by a process of politicisation, in which some approaches are aligned with particular political stances or movements. Second, many influential approaches, especially among qualitative researchers, adopt radical reconceptualisations of the nature and purpose of social inquiry, in ways that tend to turn it into a quite different activity: whether a form of political activism, philosophical scepticism, autobiography, imaginative literature, and/or performance art (for examples, see Denzin and Lincoln 2018 and such journals as *Qualitative Inquiry*, *Cultural Studies ↔ Critical Methodologies*, *International Journal of Qualitative Studies in Education*, and *International Review of Qualitative Research*). In my view, these developments undermine the practice of social research by ignoring restrictions on it that should be respected (Hammersley 2014, 2022a). These restrictions define its task as producing factual knowledge (rather than evaluating the phenomena being investigated or seeking to change them), and as requiring specialist work carried out by a research community whose members are professionally trained for, and devoted to carrying out, that task. It is this orthodox conception of social research that guides my discussion in this book.

Both political and intellectual challenges to this orthodox view have arisen. A historical sketch of how this occurred is essential in order to understand the current state of methodological concepts.

Methodological diversification

The methodological divisions that emerged in the social science community over the past 50 years frequently relate to fundamental questions that are both political and philosophical in character. Of course, there has long been a close connection between the practice of social research and the political concerns and views of researchers, and it has always involved political assumptions. Early on, many assumed that research would directly feed socio-political progress. However, as social science disciplines came to be institutionalised within universities, there was increasing emphasis on the distinction between the goal of producing factual knowledge, on the one hand, and engaging in political argument or action about social issues, on the other. The rationale for social science remained that it could guide practical action, but the distinction between social science and politics came to be widely emphasised, if not always respected.

While there always remained some, on both the political Left and Right, who challenged this distinction, it was not until the 1960s that it came to be widely questioned in Anglo-American social science. This arose initially from the resurgent influence of Marxism, in its 'Western' forms, and especially its insistence on the close relationship between 'theory and practice'. A variety of 'critical' approaches developed within social science under the influence of this, some of these drawing on 'new social movements', such as feminism, that focused on other social divisions than social class: not just sex/gender but also race/ethnicity, sexual orientation, and ability/disability.

These new approaches stimulated research in a variety of areas that had previously been neglected, but my focus here is on their methodological implications. As the label 'critical' implies, central to much of this work was the idea that the task of research is to mount a critique of existing social arrangements, with a view to bringing about change. To one degree or another, researchers were to become political activists. An ethical argument also later emerged, to the effect that the research relationship is itself inherently unequal in terms of who makes decisions, and therefore inequitable; and that this needs to be transformed if research is to be authentically 'progressive', 'democratic', or 'decolonised'. From this there arose various kinds of action research or participatory inquiry, sometimes with the role of researcher being redefined to focus on assisting others to carry out research for themselves, to bring about change in their own situations and on their own terms.

Another significant development was that, during the second half of the twentieth century, social scientists came to draw on a wider range of philosophical traditions than hitherto. Where, earlier, positivism and pragmatism had probably been the most influential, others now played an important role: phenomenology, hermeneutics, structuralism, post-structuralism, critical realism, and new materialisms (see the Glossary for the meanings of these terms; new materialisms are discussed later in this chapter). At the same time, ideas from these sources were transmuted through contact with particular forms of research practice. An illustration of this is the way in which phenomenology, itself an internally diverse philosophical tradition, often came to be reformulated within social science as in-depth investigation of other people's experience through interviews (see Giorgi 2010).

One effect of these new philosophical ideas was the emergence of a general trend of thought that is often given the label 'constructionism' (or 'constructivism'), this taking a variety of forms. In its more radical versions, constructionism rejected a concern with how social phenomena shape human behaviour in favour of a focus on how those phenomena are constituted through human action or by dominant discourses. To take an early example: where, previously, criminology had been concerned with identifying the causes of crime, the sociology of deviance in the 1960s focused on how particular activities come to be socially defined as crimes, and on the contingent processes involved in whether or not people are labelled as deviant and processed by the legal system (see, for instance, Becker 1963).[3] This sort of approach later came to be applied in other fields, including the sociology of science, with investigations of how physical phenomena are constituted in and through the discursive or practical work of natural scientists.

A major philosophical influence on the deepening methodological disagreements among social scientists in the second half of the twentieth century was Thomas Kuhn's (1962) book *The Structure of Scientific Revolutions*. He rejected the usual image of natural science as gradually accumulating a body of knowledge that corresponds to physical reality, with each study building upon previous ones and providing a foundation for further investigation. He also challenged the commonly accepted idea that what counts as scientific knowledge is solely derived from observable or experimental evidence. He argued that natural science necessarily relies upon metaphysical assumptions, in the form of 'paradigms', whose validity cannot be proven by scientific research itself; as a result, he denied that scientific knowledge captures the character of independently existing phenomena. Moreover, he claimed that, historically, 'scientific revolutions' had occurred which involved dramatic changes in metaphysical assumptions, for instance he suggested that this was true of the shift within physics from Newtonian science to relativity theory. So, Kuhn argued that the history of science was one of discontinuity, not of continuous growth, change occurring between 'paradigms' that were 'incommensurable', in the sense of not being easily comparable with one another. In short, his enormously influential book undermined the idea that natural science involved continuous progress towards true understanding of the physical world.

Kuhn's philosophy of science was particularly appealing to social scientists because their work had frequently been found wanting in comparison with natural science, whereas he showed (they believed) that there were strong similarities between the two. His arguments were taken to explain why there were conflicting approaches within social science that relied upon divergent philosophical assumptions. Moreover, they challenged the positivism that had previously informed much social science, and appeared to legitimate the alternative approaches that were emerging: these could be regarded as distinct paradigms that should be evaluated in their own terms, not against positivist criteria. In addition, Kuhn's work appeared to suggest that natural science could only be understood through sociological analysis, since the changes in paradigms he documented relied on social factors rather than being the result of rational assessment based on logic and evidence. Subsequently, the sociology of scientific knowledge built on Kuhn's analysis, later morphing into Science and Technology Studies; and central to this has been rejection of any distinction between the social and the rational.

Social scientists' use of Kuhn's work frequently involved significant misinterpretation. He had drawn a sharp distinction between prescientific and scientific forms of thought, and viewed the social sciences as belonging in the first category. One of his reasons for this was precisely that they were characterised by the presence of multiple parallel approaches, whereas (he argued) mature scientific fields are dominated by a single paradigm, apart from during relatively brief periods of scientific revolution. Indeed, he insisted that, most of the time, scientific work takes the form of what he called 'normal science', which is devoted to solving puzzles that arise within the framework of a dominant paradigm. Yet little social scientific work was of this character. Furthermore, while Kuhn emphasised that science relied on metaphysical assumptions, he did not treat these as simply a matter of prior commitment; they were assessed indirectly for their productivity in stimulating scientific work; and they were only changed when serious anomalies occurred and a more promising alternative paradigm was available. While he insisted that there were radical discontinuities in the development of sciences, he did not imply that all paradigms are true in their own terms and could not be evaluated against one another. His main point was that it was not possible to choose rationally between them at the point of revolution *solely on the basis of empirical evidence*; not least because, very often, paradigms define differently what will count as evidence.[4]

The 'paradigm wars' (Gage 1989; Guba 1990) that occurred within social science from the 1970s onwards left central methodological concepts enveloped in 'the fog of conflict'. Andrew Tudor (1982:1–2) graphically described the misuse of philosophical ideas in the context of sociology:

> Having rightly concluded that philosophy was of some importance to the sociological enterprise, sociologists (and I am one) have used that discipline much as the military might use a guided missile. Safely fired in the conviction that it will seek and destroy, the soldier need know little of the missile's true workings and consequences. Likewise for the sociologist. Recognising the incipient power of labels borrowed from philosophy, sociologists have strewn them about with little regard to their detailed significance. Indeed, if armies were so irresponsible (and they may yet be) I should not be writing, nor you reading, this essay. We would have long since vanished in drifting clouds of nuclear fallout.

This warning is even more relevant today than when it was given 40 years ago, and the danger is by no means restricted to sociology, but extends across the social sciences.

The main philosophical weapons used in the 'paradigm wars' were various forms of relativism and scepticism, selectively employed, as well as what came to be referred to as standpoint epistemology. Scepticism about the very possibility of knowledge, or severe methodological criticisms directed at particular kinds of data, were used to undercut the claims of other paradigms. Relativism was also used in this way, others' arguments being dismissed as simply reflecting their paradigmatic commitments or social positions. Relativism was also employed *defensively*: appealing to Kuhn's notion of incommensurability, it was argued that each 'paradigm' must be judged in its own terms, since there can be no overarching perspective by which they could be assessed against one another (see, for instance, Smith 1989).

By contrast, on the basis of standpoint epistemology it was often claimed that one paradigm had epistemic privilege, while others suffered epistemic deficit. The history of this idea can be traced back to the work of Marx: he claimed that the working class had the potential for unique insight into the character of capitalist society because of the way it exploited them. And, given that Marxism built on this standpoint, the claim was that it was superior to bourgeois thought. Subsequently, this form of argument was applied to the case of women by feminists (Hartsock 1987; Harding 1993, 2004). And it was later generalised to insist that those in subordinated, exploited, or marginalised positions within a society have a greater capacity for understanding the nature of that society. This is because they are likely to have little commitment to current social arrangements, and must find ways of countering the effects that these have on their lives; whereas, it was argued, those in power are blinded by their own interest in preserving the status quo. It was concluded from this that those social science paradigms which champion subaltern groups have epistemic privilege, whereas the dominant paradigm has ideological blinkers. Another implication sometimes drawn from standpoint epistemology is that testimony from people belonging to marginalised or oppressed social categories should be treated as more likely to represent reality accurately than accounts from other sources; and indeed perhaps should be accepted at face value. In more recent times, this argument has gone beyond treating the substantive knowledge available to marginalised groups as superior, to claim that their distinctive ways of knowing must also be adopted (Santos 2014; Smith 2021). This is on the grounds that, for example, patriarchal or neocolonialist bias operates right down to the epistemological level.

Under the influence of these political and philosophical trends, methodological diversification of social science continued throughout the twentieth century and into the twenty-first century. A key factor from the 1980s onwards was the influence of that diverse array of philosophical ideas frequently given the label 'postmodernism'. An important aspect of this was rejection of the idea that historical development is progressive, whether in its liberal or its Marxist version. As with Kuhn, there was an emphasis on discontinuity rather than continuity, of a kind that stretched down to disagreement over fundamental philosophical assumptions. There was also a strong element of scepticism, deriving from an insistence on the instability of meanings, as well as on what language obscures or cannot express. Equally important, knowledge was interpreted as performative, rather than being defined in terms of a capacity for representing phenomena independent of it – here there are strong parallels with what I have referred to as constructionism. Thus, there was a focus on the role of discourses, or modes of expression more generally, in *constituting* social reality in one way rather than another. Indeed, it was argued, notably by Foucault, that bodies of scientific knowledge had played, and continued to play, a key role in the reproduction and legitimation of existing social institutions. The implication of this was often taken to be that social scientists are complicit in the social forces that structure the world, and have a responsibility to resist and destabilise those forces. This further encouraged both radical forms of constructionism and activist conceptions of social research.

If we jump forward to today, we find that many of the approaches to social scientific work established in the second half of the twentieth century continue to be influential, while new ones still emerge. One recent example is what has been referred to as 'the ontological turn' in anthropology and Science and Technology Studies (Holbraad and Pedersen 2017; Heywood 2017; Jensen 2017). This involves rejection of the assumption that there is a single experiential world that all people share, and therefore of the idea that people from different cultures simply have different perspectives on the same reality. Instead, it is insisted that there are ontologically distinct, and incommensurable, realities. From this perspective, it may be possible to study other realities than one's own, but this requires suspension of prior assumptions, especially those characteristic of Western science and secular thought. While this is not an entirely new idea – somewhat similar positions had been put forward before by the philosopher Peter Winch (1958, 1964), the anthropologist Benita Jules-Rosette (1978), and the writer Carlos Castenada (see Silverman 1975) – recent developments of it have taken distinctive forms.

A parallel development has been calls for the 'decolonisation' of research (Bishop 1998; Chalmers 2017). It is argued that the very character of social science has been shaped by Western imperialism, extending to the fundamental ontological, epistemological, and axiological assumptions on which it relies. (For the meanings of 'epistemology', 'ontology', and 'axiology', see the Glossary). Challenged here, in particular, are positivist conceptions of the research process in which the researcher must measure and exercise control over variables. This is portrayed as corresponding to the underlying function of Western scientific knowledge as enabling the exercise of social control, not just over non-Western populations but also over subordinated and marginalised groups within Western societies. A sharp contrast is drawn here with indigenous and Africanist views of inquiry and knowledge, and 'epistemologies of the South' (Santos 2014) more generally. These recommend drawing on traditional 'ways of knowing' characteristic of marginalised groups, and adopting a respectful stance, perhaps with learners waiting patiently for understanding to come, rather than demanding answers in the manner of modern science.

In tandem with this have been arguments that social research must be democratised, in the sense of becoming more inclusive as regards who can participate in decisions about what to investigate and how. This sometimes extends to the idea, mentioned earlier, that the task of those officially designated as researchers should be to facilitate others to do their own research (including children, see Kellett 2005). In part, this reflects concern about the underrepresentation of members of marginalised and oppressed groups among researchers; though it is, of course, not the only potential solution to that problem. The concept of democratisation is also sometimes extended to include the exercise of control over research by the local communities where it is taking place. For instance, this is commonly built into ethical protocols for research in indigenous communities, but has also sometimes been applied in other contexts too (see, for example, Benjamin 1999).

A final example I will give of a new approach that became widely influential in the present century is various kinds of 'new materialism' (see Coole and Frost 2010). These inherit some assumptions from postmodernism but also react against it, particularly its emphasis on discourse. Here, the argument is that material objects and processes must not be conceived as passively constituted by discourse, or viewed merely as human constructs, but rather should be regarded as playing an active role in making the world. This argument has been closely associated with 'post-humanism', a reaction against the assumption that humanity is of central significance in the world, and that it is unique. Attention is therefore given to the role of other forms of life in remaking the environment and indeed in shaping human lives. One result of this has been the declaration of a new 'post-qualitative' phase in social research methodology (see Lather and St. Pierre 2013; St. Pierre 2021). This explicitly rejects the 'humanism' of previous qualitative work, with its emphasis on the need to understand human social life in a different way from how we explain the behaviour of animals and physical objects. Also rejected, frequently, is the secular orientation characteristic of much Western science, which denies the validity of non-naturalistic interpretations of the world (see, for instance, MacLure 2022). In place of this what is proposed is a post-secular understanding of social life that often draws on indigenous peoples' ideas, according to which nature and culture are not separated but intertwined or even blended, so that animals and material objects, as well as human beings, are treated as spiritual as well as material in character (or this very distinction is erased). There are obvious links here with the notion of decolonisation.

As can be seen, then, a wide range of intellectual and political tendencies have shaped social science methodology over the past 50 years or so; and these have led to a proliferation of approaches that are very different in character from one another. There are shared ideas among some of them, but also fundamental conflicts. For example, the notion of a right to engage in research as a feature of democracy may not be compatible with some traditional 'ways of knowing' championed in the name of decolonisation. Equally, where advocates of decolonisation valorise the experience of marginalised groups, there are significant differences in outlook among these groups; and much potential for conflicts between them. Furthermore, both radical constructionism and new materialisms insist that all experience is socially constructed rather than having intrinsic authenticity. Finally, while all of these approaches claim to produce knowledge of the social world, many of them also flirt with relativism and scepticism, both of which raise questions about the very possibility of knowledge, at least in the conventional sense of that term as correspondence with reality. Despite their significance, these conflicts are frequently overlooked.

Relations among these diverse approaches rarely involve much attempt at sustained mutual understanding, ranging instead from superficial cooperation, through reciprocal ignorance or toleration, to occasional acrimonious disputes. It is hardly surprising that methodological concepts have been among the main casualties. Some that had been regarded as core elements of a scientific orientation – such as truth/validity, error/bias, and objectivity – came to be questioned, reformulated, or rejected. Others gained new influence, such as abduction and reflexivity, but were subject to divergent interpretations.

The view adopted in this book

Given the situation I have described, the need for attention to the meanings of central methodological terms should be clear. However, as I explained earlier, clarification of these concepts cannot avoid taking a position on issues that have come to be matters of dispute. In subsequent chapters I will need to address the criticisms that have been made of older methodological concepts, and the arguments supporting newer ones. But, prior to this, here I must sketch my attitude towards the disputes over what axiological, epistemological, and onto-logical assumptions should underpin social research. As already indicated, mine is a rather orthodox view that is at odds with some of the trends I sketched in the previous section.[5]

My starting point is that the only legitimate operational goal of research can be the production of factual knowledge (in other words, descriptions and explanations of social phenomena), thereby ruling out 'critical' forms of inquiry and others that treat its goal as going beyond the production of such knowledge (for instance, to challenge existing practices, policies or institutions, and bring about change; or, for that matter, to preserve the status quo). However, here it is important to recognise the distinction between the motives we have for being researchers, or for engaging in research on particular topics, and the goal we are pursuing in doing it. Most researchers quite reasonably hope that their work will contribute to social improvement of one kind or another, this is often the main reason they engage in it. But this is very different from *carrying out research in such a way as to bring about social improvement*; doing *this* involves subordinat-ing the pursuit of knowledge to a quite different goal, and distorting it in the process. The danger of coming to erroneous conclusions is increased, and con-clusions are put forward that exceed the intellectual authority of social science.

The position I am adopting here also excludes many forms of epistemo-logical relativism and scepticism. The reason for rejecting these is that they amount to abandoning a key assumption that necessarily underpins the activ-ity of research: that producing knowledge about social phenomena is possible. Thus, these positions do not so much redefine the goal of social inquiry as relinquish it. At the same time, as I indicated, those who employ these radical epistemologies rarely do so consistently: very often they themselves claim to be putting forward knowledge, of one kind or another. This reflects the fact that, as has long been recognised, such radical epistemologies are self-undermining.[6]

I also reject forms of standpoint epistemology that assign epistemic privilege or deficit on the basis of people's membership of particular social categories. While it is true that different social positions generate different experiences, and that all of these can provide insight into the nature of social phenomena, none is uniquely privileged or disqualified (or, usually, sufficient in itself). Fur-thermore, the argument for standpoint epistemologies is also self-undermining. The key question is: On what basis is a particular viewpoint to be assigned epistemic privilege? The answer to that question either involves circularity, standpoint epistemology being justified in its own terms, or requires appeal to some other epistemological position that claims to transcend all standpoints, thereby undercutting standpoint epistemology.

The position I have outlined here does not amount simply to dismissal of all the methodological developments within social science that I outlined earlier. There are many disagreements – such as about the nature of sociocultural phenomena, or the extent to which cross-cultural understanding is possible – that I believe should be treated as open to resolution by exploring the capacity of alternative approaches to produce worthwhile knowledge. Similarly, some disagreements relate to matters that, in my view, ought to be resolved pragmatically in the context of particular studies. An example would be how far to involve the people being studied in making decisions about what is to be researched and how this is to be done: there are both ethical and pragmatic reasons why such involvement might be desirable in particular circumstances; as well as ones that make it undesirable. However, radical attempts to redefine the goal of research or the role of the researcher, to reject the conventional understanding of knowledge, or to deny the possibility of achieving it, cannot be accepted, in my view. This is because they amount to a redefinition of 'research' that erases its distinctive features by comparison with other activities, and thereby undermines its very rationale and institutional position. If social research is to be abandoned, this must be done explicitly, and the costs of doing so paid by those making this move.

The foundation of my discussion in this book is a view of social research as a refinement and development of the forms of inquiry that are employed more widely in social life. I suggest that, while departures from the assumptions underpinning those other types of inquiry may be necessary, these need strong justification, given that such inquiry has undoubtedly already produced knowledge. For example, like academic researchers, various other occupations (journalists, social workers, police officers, etc.) use documentary material, observation, and/or interviewing successfully as a means of gaining knowledge about social situations. However appealing we may find radically alternative methodological or theoretical assumptions, they should not be adopted without very strong epistemic grounds for doing so. In philosophical terms, this is in line with the sort of philosophical pragmatism advocated by Charles Peirce (Almeder 1980; Hookway 1985). False radicalism has been encouraged by the adoption of Kuhn's notion of incommensurability, interpreted as implying that new ideas cannot be assessed in existing terms, by 'constructionism', 'postmodernism', and 'new materialisms', and by what might be called the idolatry of the new, which now seems to pervade contemporary societies.

The sort of position I am adopting here has sometimes been labelled 'post-positivism' (see Phillips and Burbules 2000). I have no objection to this label, even though it has increasingly acquired negative connotations. It captures the idea that we should not simply reject previously influential methodological assumptions (on the grounds that they are 'positivist') but rather must reflect on, refine, and develop them in light of new experience and ideas. This is very much the spirit in which this book has been written.

The concepts examined

I have not attempted to discuss all of the methodological concepts that are employed by social scientists. The coverage is highly selective. For the most part, I have concentrated on those that I regard as most central to the research enterprise, in the sense that they provide the framework within which it must operate. Given the history and current state of social science methodology I have sketched in this Introduction, it is perhaps not surprising that, as currently formulated, these concepts do not constitute an agreed and coherent set. Nevertheless, there are relationships amongst them, even if these are sometimes suppressed. For instance, despite widespread nervousness on the part of social scientists about using the words 'true' and 'truth', the concept of research itself depends upon their conventional meaning: its core aim is to produce knowledge; and, as the standard philosophical view has it, this is 'justified true belief'. Similarly, 'bias' is a form of error, and this is the opposite of truth, so that use of this term implicates the concept of truth as well. Furthermore, the concept of objectivity relies on the notion of bias. Much the same is true of the other methodological concepts I will discuss.

Truth is what Wittgenstein (1969) referred to as a 'hinge' concept: it bears the same relationship to inquiry as hinges to a door. It is, of course, possible to deny that accounts may be true or false, that we can ever know whether they are true or false, and even that knowing whether they are true or false is important. However, such denials are not compatible with the pursuit of any form of inquiry; and, indeed, are incompatible with most other activities, since these usually depend upon knowledge of some kind. Truth/falsity is a concept that is woven into the very character of human social life. In practice, it cannot be abandoned, however hard we might try; and it should be interpreted in ways that are compatible with the role it necessarily plays in our lives.

Some of the terms I discuss are often regarded by qualitative researchers as associated with quantitative method, or as 'positivist', and may therefore be rejected by them. And it is true that interpretations of these terms have been shaped by the forms of empiricism that influenced much early social science (On positivism and empiricism, see the entries in the Glossary). However, it is a mistake to *dismiss* them on these grounds. One reason for this is that, despite its appalling reputation today, positivism has positive features (Hammersley 1995: chapter 1). Another is that usage of these methodological concepts is by no means restricted to adherents of that philosophical persuasion. Indeed, as I have already indicated, many of them are essential to the very practice of research. At the same time, I am not suggesting that quantitative methodologists have been correct all along, and that supporters of qualitative inquiry are entirely wrong in their criticisms. I believe there are fundamental failings with both much quantitative and much qualitative work, and that these are extremely challenging (Cooper et al. 2012: chapters 1 and 2).

In this book, I have also discussed some terms that are frequently associated with anti-positivist positions, such as 'understanding', 'reflexivity', 'induction', 'abduction', and 'triangulation'. These, too, point to important aspects of the research process. However, as will become clear, on the interpretations I develop they are by no means at odds with more traditional concepts. I also examine the meanings that should be given to the most basic methodological terms of all: 'research' and, of course, 'methodology' itself.

Conclusion

Decades of philosophical debate among social scientists about methodology have resulted in vagueness, ambiguity, and plurality in the meaning of key methodological terms. In this Introduction, I have sketched the background to the detailed discussions of them that follow in subsequent chapters – in particular, the proliferation of methodological approaches and the fundamental disagreements that now plague the field.

In my view, despite commonalities, it is essential to draw a sharp distinction between social research, on the one hand, and, on the other, socio-political commentary, the provision of political or practical advice, journalistic reporting, the production of propaganda, imaginative literature or art, and practical or political activity. For me, academic social research has a quite specific, but nevertheless important, role: to provide factual knowledge (as opposed to normative evaluations or recommendations) about perennial issues that are of human significance. There was a tendency in the past to assume that the provision of factual knowledge would automatically bring about desirable personal or social change (see Hammersley 2000: chapter 3). And it is almost certainly true that most people engage in social research, and investigate particular topics, because they believe or hope that their work will have progressive consequences. But this is not the same as making those consequences one's goal in carrying out inquiries; and doing so increases the risk of coming to false conclusions because evidence and conclusions will tend to be judged for their practical or political implications not just their validity.

As I noted, the relatively small number of terms examined in this book does not exhaust the methodological lexicon, but many of them determine the very character of social research as an activity distinct from others. This book is dedicated to the task of clarifying appropriate meanings for these central terms, and some associated ones. The concepts concerned apply to both quantitative and qualitative approaches.

I explained that, underpinning my interpretations, is a particular view of the nature of social science. So, while the chapters can be read separately, the ways in which the concepts are related to one another, and the perspective I have adopted towards them, need to be borne in mind. Nevertheless, I trust that readers will find the discussions of key concepts in this book of value irrespective of whether they agree with my beliefs about the shape that social research ought to take. Of course, I hope, even more, that it will persuade them of the cogency of those beliefs. But, either way, I want to insist on the need for clarification of central methodological concepts: social science cannot operate successfully without this.

Notes

1　Throughout this book, I often use inverted commas around words to indicate when they are being mentioned rather than used. They are also sometimes employed to clothe commonly used labels, such as 'new social movements', or definitions of terms I mention. Very occasionally I deploy them to indicate that what a term refers to is problematic, as for example in the case of 'critical' research; here they amount to what are generally referred to as 'scare quotes'. Sometimes, of course, inverted commas are simply quotation marks. The context should indicate which meaning they are intended to carry.

2　These include: Payne and Payne's *Key Concepts in Social Research*, Jupp's *Sage Dictionary of Social Science Methods*, Miller and Brewer's *The A-Z of Social Research*, Lewis-Beck et al.'s *The Sage Encyclopedia of Social Science Research Methods*, Atkinson et al.'s *Sage Research Methods Foundations*, Schwandt's *Dictionary of Qualitative Inquiry*, and Riazi's *Routledge Encyclopedia of Research Methods in Applied Linguistics*.

3　See Pollner 1974, 1978 for an insightful analysis that lauds this radical constructionism.

4　Kuhn's work has been subject to considerable criticism even as an account of the development of natural science, and he developed and changed his views somewhat over time (see Hoyningen-Huene 1993; Bird 2000; Kuhn 2000; Sharrock and Read 2002). Nevertheless, in the second half of the twentieth century it came to be generally accepted within the philosophy of science that no empirical conclusion can be proved, or for that matter falsified, with absolute certainty.

5　I have provided the justification for this position elsewhere: see Hammersley 1995, 2000, 2008b, 2014a, and 2017c.

6　For a sophisticated account of epistemology that takes relativism and scepticism seriously, while nevertheless rejecting them, see Williams 2001. For a history of scepticism, see Popkin 1979.

1 Methodology and method

Since this is a book about methodological concepts, it seems appropriate that it should begin by dealing with what the term 'methodology' can and should mean. The words 'methodology' and 'method' are sometimes employed as synonyms but are usually differentiated in meaning and need to be. Each of them has come to be used in a range of ways. I will outline these and try to clarify their most useful meanings.

It is also important to note that there have been sharply discrepant attitudes towards what these terms refer to. On the one hand, there are those who insist on the essential role that methodology and method play in social research, for example, suggesting that this indicates its scientific status. On the other hand, some social researchers have not only criticised particular forms of research methodology, for example those that privilege quantitative method, but also occasionally questioned the value of the entire methodological enterprise; perhaps dismissing it as 'methodolatry' (Gouldner 1965; Janesick 1994; Emke 1996; Chamberlain 2000; Mattern 2013). Attention to methodology and method has also been questioned on the grounds that it fails to take account of the 'messiness' of social reality (Law 2004), or of the 'social life' of methods (Law et al. 2011). Sometimes, methodology and method seem to be treated as only of relevance for novice researchers, the implication being that once one has carried out some research there is no need to learn any more about how to do it, except perhaps for reading up on new techniques.[1] In my view, while reflection on methodology and method can be excessive or misguided, it is required continually if social research is to achieve its potential.

Methodology

The original meaning of the term 'methodology' was 'the study of method', and this sense is still in use today. Here what it refers to borders on the philosophy of science and sometimes overlaps with it.[2] It is important to stress that methodology, in this sense, is both a descriptive and a normative enterprise: it is concerned with what researchers do *and* with what they should do.

Of course, 'methodology' is also used to refer to the body of knowledge and knowhow that has resulted from researchers reflecting on their research

DOI: 10.4324/9781003350354-2

practices and writing about the issues arising from these. This knowledge is embodied in a now huge, and still growing, literature. This literature is made up of several types of contribution. There is what can be called methodology-as-technique, concerned with outlining particular methods, when, where, and how they should be used. A second is methodology-as-philosophy, focused on the ontological, epistemological, and axiological issues (see the Glossary for the meaning of these terms) surrounding social research. A third common form of methodological writing was a reaction against the first, and consists of what I will call methodology-as-autobiography: first-hand accounts of the experience of carrying out particular projects, and reflections on various methodological or ethical problems that were faced. While particular contributions to the literature tend to focus on one or other of these forms of methodological writing, they are often mixed together in varying degrees and ways.

All three kinds of methodological writing serve important functions.[3] For example, while methodology-as-technique has been much criticised, especially by qualitative researchers, a concern with the technical effectiveness of the methods we use is essential, it seems to me. Similarly, while methodology-as-philosophy is often dismissed as superfluous, especially by quantitative researchers, there are undoubtedly challenging philosophical issues that social scientists must address if they are to do their work well. Finally, methodology-as-autobiography has sometimes been regarded as of little value because it consists of 'subjective' accounts of individual projects, but the concrete illustration of methodological problems and how they were dealt with in particular cases (successfully or otherwise) is an essential complement to the other two genres of methodological writing.

A third sense of the term 'methodology' is closely related to methodology-as-philosophy: its plural form, 'methodologies', is sometimes used to refer to the diverse approaches that now exist within social research. Here 'methodology' is synonymous with words like 'approach' and 'paradigm'. Use of this third meaning signals the fact that the many competing methodological approaches are believed to rely on fundamentally discrepant assumptions about the purpose of research, the nature of the phenomena investigated, and/or how these can best be understood (see the Introduction). Employed in this third way, there can be references to quantitative and qualitative methodologies, to mixed method methodology, and to a whole variety of qualitative methodologies up to and including the 'post-qualitative' (despite the fact that the latter 'refuses method and methodology': St. Pierre 2021: Abstract). Thus, 'positivism', 'postpositivism', 'interpretivism', 'critical research', 'phenomenology', 'post-structuralism', 'postmodernism', and 'new materialisms', are all occasionally referred to as methodologies. As this list indicates, there is overlap here with differences in *theoretical* stance, since these also tend to involve methodological assumptions. For instance, phenomenological theory implies a rather different approach to carrying out research from, say, both Activity Theory and Actor Network Theory.

In my view the third meaning of the term 'methodology' is linguistically redundant, the core reference of the term must be to the process of reflection in which researchers engage before, during, and after their investigations: continually revisiting questions about what they are doing, why they are doing it, what problems it involves, as well as whether and how these can be resolved. This is close to what Fitzgerald (2019:206) means by the term 'methodologist-in-action', which he uses to describe Harvey Sacks, the inventor of conversation analysis. What this makes clear is that methodology as the study of research methods must not become too separated off from the practice of research itself. Furthermore, this kind of methodological reflection is not simply an individual, even less an idiosyncratic, matter. Academic social research is pursued with a view to building on and contributing to a body of knowledge shared by a research community (see Chapter 2); and what can be learned from the experience of carrying out particular projects must also be shared within that community so that the practice of its members becomes more effective over time. In this respect, the second sense of the word 'methodology' I identified is complementary to this first one.

Therefore, while methodological discussion should draw on direct research experience, it should also make systematic use of the existing methodological literature, even in the case of methodology-as-autobiography. It is also essential that any discussion does not take place solely among adherents of a single approach but must take account of diverse views, without this degenerating into the exchange of stock arguments between those supporting different positions. Current discussions of social research methodology are often some way from meeting both of these requirements. There is a tendency to treat methodological issues that have arisen in current research as if they were novel, which they rarely are, and a resulting failure to engage sufficiently with previous accounts. Furthermore, fruitless debate between advocates of opposing views is much more common than discussions where the parties engage with each other's views in a sustained way. This reflects the fact that, very often, there is a predisposition to regard the adoption of methodological approaches as a matter of commitment or choice, rather than as being open to reasoned consideration.

Equally important, while methodology as the study of method must be grounded in the individual and collective experience of carrying out research, it must also draw on the resources offered by external specialist disciplines, not least philosophy. There is, of course, much scope for discussion here about how, and how much, methodological reflection ought to draw on these external sources. In practice, there are quite severe limits to this; and, for instance, care must be taken that a preoccupation with philosophical issues is not substituted for reflection on how to pursue empirical research questions. The task of the methodologist, it seems to me, is to use philosophical ideas to understand problems faced in doing social research and to find ways of dealing with those problems *within that context*. There is also the danger, as I pointed out in the Introduction, that philosophical ideas are used simply as weapons in 'paradigm wars' (Gage 1989). One effect of this has been to facilitate the proliferation of competing methodological approaches that are largely insulated from one another. Nevertheless, the philosophical literature has an important role to play in clarifying methodological problems, and this contribution has rarely been fully deployed.

One further point that perhaps needs to be made is that I am drawing a sharp distinction between methodology and ethics. In my view, the goal of research is defined by epistemic rather than ethical (or political) values, since it is concerned solely with the production of factual knowledge (see the Introduction). Ethical values – such as a concern with minimising harm, as well as respecting people's autonomy and privacy – are important constraints on how research should be pursued, but they are external to it, they do not define its goal (see Hammersley and Traianou 2012).

In summary, methodology – in the sense of reflection on the process of social research, what it can produce, and how it should be pursued – is a core component of social science. Furthermore, it has technical and philosophical aspects, and can vary in whether it is pitched at the level of general discussion or focuses on particular studies. While it is essential, it is also subject to potential distortions that can be counterproductive. The concern with technical effectiveness may diverge into attempts to proceduralise aspects of the research process that cannot be treated in this way, perhaps ultimately pursuing the quixotic aim of eliminating all 'subjective judgement' (Dunne 1993; see Chapter 5). Equally, methodology-as-philosophy may degenerate into the substitution of a philosophical for an empirical focus, and it has certainly encouraged excessive growth in the number of competing approaches and in deepening divisions between them.

Method

The meaning of the term 'method' is somewhat less variable but suffers from similar problems (see Swedberg 2021). As I noted at the start of this chapter, while a distinction is usually drawn between methodology and method, there can also be some overlap in the meanings of these words. One reason for this is that it is frequently argued that methods involve ontological and epistemological assumptions (see Chapter 12).

Generally, though, 'method' is used to refer to specific ways of carrying out data collection or analysis, rather than to underlying methodological approaches. In this usage, the meaning of 'method' borders on that of 'technique' or 'procedure'. However, there is often resistance, especially amongst qualitative researchers, to the idea that research involves deploying techniques or procedures, on the grounds that this reflects a positivist conception of inquiry. They insist that research cannot be reduced to blindly following a set of rules. And this is sometimes extended to the rejection of any rules, echoing philosophical rejections of the idea of 'scientific method' (see Chapter 9). It is certainly true that 'method', like 'technique', may carry the implication that what is involved is a closely specified procedure that must be followed precisely if its use is to be effective. It is also the case that, while there are a few aspects of the research process that can be conceptualised in this way, such as calculating the results of a statistical test, most of it cannot be proceduralised; and any attempt to do this is likely to be counterproductive. Judicious assessment is required about when specification and standardisation are beneficial and when they are not.

The objection to method is sometimes rather broader than this: it may be insisted that what is required in some kinds of research is not so much following a plan or method but, rather, being responsive to situations and people. In the case of participant observation, for example, the aim may be to put oneself in more or less the same situation as those being studied, so as to try to align one's own experience with theirs. Similarly, in relatively unstructured interviewing the advice may be to open up a conversation, to listen to what the other person is saying, and to respond to this in such a way as to explore their feelings and views in a manner that builds on what one learns about them in the course of the interview. In the field of hermeneutics, Gadamer (2004) argued for this sort of approach even in understanding documents – such as, in his case, the writings of past philosophers. He contrasts this responsive attitude with the application of a *method*, arguing that such responsiveness is essential for producing interpretations that are true and have 'revelatory power' (Gadamer 2001:42). Something similar has been proposed more recently within anthropology, under the heading of the 'ontological turn'. Holbraad and Pedersen (2017:5) write:

> How do I enable my ethnographic material to reveal itself to me by allowing it to dictate its own terms of engagement, so to speak, guiding or compelling me to see things that I had not expected, or imagined, to be there?

We might reasonably ask, though, whether what these authors are recommending is not, itself, a kind of method. Indeed, Holbraad and Pedersen go on to ask: 'Through what analytical techniques might such an ethnographic sensibility be cultivated?'.

There is no good reason to associate the word 'method' with a proceduralist conception of inquiry, or even with the idea of sticking to a pre-established plan. Following rules need not be slavish: they can be used as guides rather than as absolute injunctions. And plans can be flexible. Conversely, adopting a responsive, creative or innovative approach does not usually involve abandoning all rules or all planning, it generally amounts to a more selective and adaptive orientation: some rules may be observed, while others are re-interpreted, suspended, or rejected; an initial plan may be continually revised in light of what is being learned. Furthermore, no rule or plan *applies itself*, there is always a degree of judgement involved in its application. So, we must take care not to adopt a false contrast between method, on the one hand, and an interpretation of responsiveness or creativity as spurning all guidance, on the other.

In this spirit, we can think of being 'methodical' as conscientiously taking account of the best guidance available. Here there is overlap with the idea that research should be carried out in a 'systematic' or 'rigorous' fashion, where the contrast is with a haphazard or careless approach (see Chapter 7). We should also note that rules and plans are *enabling* as well as constraining (Bohlin 2016). Much methodological advice usefully indicates how certain sorts of data or analytic outcome can be achieved, points to problems that can arise, and how these may be dealt with, and so on. What is involved here is similar to the guidance that is available for carrying out other sorts of activity. There, too, we must recognise both the dangers of following rules slavishly and, equally, the consequences of ignoring what has been learned by those who have carried out this activity previously.

If we suspend concerns about proceduralisation, then, we can use 'method' to refer to quite specific ways of doing social research that can be distinguished from one another. Along with 'approach' and 'technique', it allows us to recognise degrees of specificity in the categories we use to make sense of research practice. In the previous section I mentioned a range of methodological *approaches* to be found within the field of social science today. These can be differentiated from *methods*, such as observation, interviews, or the use of self-administered questionnaires (online or offline). However, these categories of method themselves involve considerable internal variation. For instance, both observation and interviews can take 'structured' and 'less structured' forms. Indeed, there are even more options than this; for example, while all interviews involve questions designed to elicit data, there can be variation in how long interviews last, whether they are repeated, the number of participants involved, and where they take place. Given this sort of variation in what a method can involve, the term 'technique' may be used to register more specifically defined research strategies. In these terms, both 'fixed-choice questionnaires' and 'participant observation' could be labelled as techniques; so long as we remember that this word does *not* mean that they amount to following a set of rules blindly.

However, this set of distinctions does not enable us to make clear sense of all the methodological labels used in social science to capture differences in how research is done. For instance, we could reasonably ask whether grounded theorising is an approach or a method, and some have even suggested that it has become reduced to a technique. It seems to me that it is best treated as an approach, because it carries implications not just for how data will be analysed but also for research design. At the same time, it is more specific in meaning than describing one's research as 'interpretive' or 'postmodernist'. A further complication is that, while grounded theorising is usually regarded as a qualitative approach, in their initial presentation Glaser and Strauss (1967) suggested that quantitative data could also be used: this means that its relationship to the quantitative–qualitative distinction is uncertain. What this indicates is that what I am referring to here as specificity is a *dimension*, and the words 'approach', 'method', and 'technique', do not represent fixed points on that dimension; their meaning is relational, and perhaps context-specific.

A key question that arises when thinking about the relationship between approaches, methods, and techniques is the extent to which the approach adopted determines the methods and techniques that should be used. Some approaches appear to involve quite strong implications for how research is done. This is true, for instance, of 'critical discourse analysis' which in some of its forms implies the use of publicly available documents as data and specifies a form of analysis derived from linguistics (see, for instance, Fairclough 2003). In other cases, the relationship between approach, method, and technique is much looser. For instance, both Marxist and feminist research can employ qualitative or quantitative techniques, and of various kinds. Generally speaking, it seems to me that the relationship between approach and method is much weaker than is sometimes assumed; in other words, there is considerable scope for variation within any particular approach as regards how research is actually carried out.

It should be clear, then, that the word 'method' needs to be handled carefully. There is no point in treating it as synonymous with 'methodology', nor should it be rejected on the grounds that research cannot be fully proceduralised. We can recognise the impossibility of this while still using the word. Indeed, this term can play an important role in guiding social research when it is differenti-ated from both 'approach' and 'technique'. The distinction between method and technique, in particular, has the virtue of reminding us that, for example, 'observation' and 'interview' have many variants, and that *which* of these is to be adopted in particular investigations, and why, must be given consideration. Also highlighted is the fact that adopting a particular 'approach' by no means resolves all the questions about how an investigation should be carried out: a variety of methods and techniques may still be options.

Conclusion

In this chapter I have considered some of the meanings given to the terms 'methodology' and 'method', and have suggested how they might most use-fully be employed. I tried to draw out distinctions which vague and variable usage of these words obscures. I proposed that the root meaning of 'methodol-ogy' should be a process of learning by researchers through continual reflection on how they do their work. In the case of 'method', I suggested that this term can best be used, as it sometimes is, along with 'approach' and 'technique', to clarify the relationships amongst the various descriptive labels that identify different ways of doing research, and to highlight the full range of options available.

I also noted how the meanings of 'methodology' and 'method' have been caught up in debates within social research. These debates certainly point to dangers, for instance associated with the idea that carrying out research can be reduced simply to following a set of rules or a fixed plan: it is essential to be responsive to the phenomena one is studying. At the same time, we must remember that research is, to a considerable degree, a technical form of prac-tice: researchers must capitalise on their own and others' experience in carrying it out so as to do it better in the future.

Notes

1 Surprisingly, this position appears to be adopted by Lazarsfeld and Rosenberg (1955:12) in an early, landmark, methodological text.
2 For a classic, but rather neglected, illustration of this conception of methodology, see Kaufmann 1944.
3 For a more detailed discussion of these, and of the whole nature of social research methodology, see Hammersley 2011b: chapter 1.

2 Inquiry, research, and science

What counts as research is a key question, perhaps among the most fundamental ones of all for social scientists. However, it is often left unanswered in methodological texts. Even in Alan Bryman's (2016:3) excellent introduction to *Social Research Methods*, in a chapter on 'The nature and process of social research', while there is a brief section entitled 'What is social research?', in answering that question the author largely takes for granted what the word 'research' means, focusing instead on distinguishing *social* inquiry from other kinds.[1] Similarly, the various dictionaries and encyclopaedias dealing with research methodology do not usually have any entry on 'research' itself. Yet what should be included under that heading is a contested matter.

In this chapter my aim is to clarify this concept by identifying its distinctive features. I will begin by distinguishing between the meaning of 'inquiry', treating this as the most general term, and 'research' as referring to a specialised form of inquiry. I will also draw distinctions among different types of social research, and discuss how they are distinct from journalism and literature. Finally, I will consider what meaning can be given to the term 'science', and what this contributes to an understanding of social research. While many social researchers use the label 'social science' to refer to their work, if only as a flag of convenience in seeking funding, there is little agreement about what the term means, and attitudes towards it vary sharply.

Inquiry

'Inquiry' and 'research' are often used as synonyms, but it is worthwhile differentiating them. I will treat 'inquiry' as referring to any kind of search for knowledge. Clearly, this can take a wide variety of forms. At its simplest, inquiry may involve seeking information one needs from others, or from textual sources, online or offline, but it can also involve pondering questions to which there are not widely accepted answers, out of curiosity. It is an activity anyone can engage in, and indeed everyone does in some form, to some degree, on some occasions. We can also leave open the issue of the precise nature of what is sought: whether this is empirical facts, diagnoses of problems,

DOI: 10.4324/9781003350354-3

evaluations of situations and people, predictions, or whatever. All of these can be the aim of inquiry. It is important to emphasise, however, that there is a sharp distinction between inquiry, on the one hand, and, on the other, collecting information in order to make a case in favour of, or against, some position. The aim of inquiry is always to discover true answers to questions (on truth see Chapter 3).

As the pursuit of needed information, inquiry is not just a ubiquitous feature of human social life, it can also be a significant component of occupational activities whose aims go beyond the production of knowledge: such as police or social work, medicine, and law. In this way, a great deal of inquiry is subordinated to other activities. The need for inquiry is particularly likely to arise when a problem is encountered. Some pragmatist philosophers, notably John Dewey, viewed problem-solving inquiry as the prototype for all research and science (Dewey 1938). While there is much to be said for this view, it is important to reiterate that in everyday life we sometimes engage in inquiry out of curiosity. Indeed, Aristotle seems to have believed that curiosity about the surrounding world, and about ourselves, is an essential characteristic of humanity (Lear 1988). And such curiosity-driven inquiry is, perhaps, a better model for academic research and science, much (though not all) of which is not tied *directly* to practical problems.

There is an important distinction here, then, between what I will call inquiry-subordinated-to-another-activity and inquiry-driven-by-curiosity. The key differences are that in the former what information is pursued is determined by the activity being served, and what that activity requires can change during the process of investigation. Furthermore, inquiry will be terminated when the necessary information has been obtained, or if it is decided that it is not providing a solution to the problem. Equally, if the problem is resolved while the inquiry is still ongoing, the pursuit of knowledge will probably be abandoned. There may also be little interest in knowing *how* the problem was solved, since the original activity can now carry on.

By contrast, everyday inquiries motivated by curiosity tend to occur in the interstices of social life, in periods of relaxation or leisure; though they may be prompted by problems encountered in activities. Furthermore, the same inquiry can recur over time, being taken up afresh whenever the opportunity arises, as for example with local history or astronomy as hobbies. And, while curiosity-driven inquiry sometimes begins from a quite specific question, very often it will lead to further ones that the inquirer will also follow up. In other words, there is no automatic terminus, in the way that there often is with inquiry-subordinated-to-another-activity.

These various kinds of inquiry are the ground out of which what I will refer to as research emerged. As this indicates, it is not a form of activity that is completely alien to, or separate from, ordinary social life. Nevertheless, in the way I am interpreting the term here, research does have some important differentiating features (see Hammersley 2002: chapter 6).

Research

I suggest that the term 'research' should be treated as referring to a form of inquiry with all the following features:

1   It is devoted to the production of knowledge as its prime task, rather than this being subordinated to other purposes.
2   It is a sustained enterprise rather than one taking place in the interstices of other activities.
3   It is carried out by a specially qualified workforce that employs collectively developed methods.
4   Researchers engage in collective criticism of both research findings and methods, and this requires these to be made public, at least within the research community.
5   It is aimed at producing knowledge that is not currently available to anyone, rather than simply collating what is already known, or adding to the personal knowledge of inquirers.
6   The knowledge aimed at is intellectual rather than practical: it is concerned with what is the case not with deciding what is right or wrong, what should be done, who is to blame, etc. Some philosophers deny that there can be knowledge about such practical matters, but – however that may be – I am excluding inquiry concerned with them from the field of research. Note, however, that my definition does not rule out philosophical research into what such words as 'good' and 'right' can be used to mean, on what grounds praise or blame might be assigned, and so on.
7   Research operates with a relatively high and consistent threshold as regards what is to be treated as well-established knowledge, rather than this threshold varying according to the likely practical costs of particular sorts of error (see Chapter 3; Hammersley 2011b: chapter 5).
8   Findings are only presented as well-established knowledge if adequate reliable evidence can be found for them, as judged by the relevant research community: *if this is not available, then reaching a conclusion is suspended.*

In these terms, it is characteristic of research that it is the pursuit of knowledge carried out as a, more or less, full-time occupation, a sustained activity in its own right. This contrasts with both inquiry-subordinated-to-another-activity and part-time, curiosity-driven inquiry. The growth of specialised occupations has been an essential aspect of the development of modern societies, bringing considerable benefit in the quantity and/or quality of what is produced. In the case of research, specialisation allows for more intensive and effective investigation, and for development of the knowledge and skills necessary for this. Where specialisation occurs, the result should be that the findings produced are more likely to be true than information from other sources. However, this does not mean that they are *guaranteed* to be true. Furthermore, specialisation is not all gain: specialised activities prioritise one set of goals over others that, on some occasions, may be viewed as of greater value from a broader perspective. Thus, social research can come into conflict with both political and ethical concerns (Hammersley 1995; Hammersley and Traianou 2012). More than this, though, it is open to the charge of 'fiddling while Rome burns': for instance, seeking to document and explain social problems but doing nothing directly to solve them. There are, then, two sides to the process of specialisation, but the benefits cannot be obtained without incurring the costs.

Of course, what I am putting forward here is an idealisation. If we look at universities today we find that, to a large extent, full-time devotion to research is more characteristic of PhD students and junior staff on research contracts than of senior academics: even those who are practising researchers usually also spend much time on teaching and various administrative and managerial duties. And these other demands have increased in recent decades, squeezing the time available for research. Indeed, there has been a considerable increase even in the managerial activity surrounding research itself. However, the fact that what I have outlined is an ideal, and one whose realisation is becoming more difficult in many quarters, does not undermine its importance.

Indeed, the value of research, as I have defined it, needs to be underlined in a world where the label 'research' is often stolen by organisations and groups whose goal is to further particular causes. For example, among Conservative MPs in the UK Parliament in recent times there has been a 'European Research Group' devoted to promoting 'Euro-scepticism' and Brexit, and a 'Northern Research Group' designed to serve the interests of the Conservative Party in the north of England. And, outside Parliament, there are pressure groups which dress themselves up as if they were committed to research when they are concerned with promoting a particular cause or set of ideas: the Institute of Economic Affairs is, arguably, an example of this. Even research agencies that are not tied to any particular ideological commitment, such as the Institute for Fiscal Studies, nevertheless produce research reports that put forward evaluations of problems and policies, and even recommend solutions.[2] Another relevant feature of the world today is that public discourse has come to be degraded, so that there is often little careful attention to the question of what can be relied on as facts, as well as tendentious questioning of factual claims and expertise that are found to be inconvenient for political purposes, not to mention blatant lying in the face of counter-evidence. To a dangerous degree, this serves to blur the distinction between research findings and ill-formed opinions in the public sphere.

Any downplaying of the distinctiveness of research as a specialised activity is, I suggest, very undesirable in this context. But it is not uncommon. One reason is the growing influence of an instrumentalist conception of knowledge, which assumes that research is only of value for the immediate impact it has in serving practical purposes. This tends to lead to a blurring of any distinction between the findings of inquiry and what practical conclusions can be drawn on the basis of them: as a result, it is frequently assumed that academic research can and should produce such conclusions, and perhaps even contribute to putting them into effect. In line with this, the funding of research has increasingly come to be viewed by funders and publics as a process of investment that is to be judged on the basis of the returns that it is expected to provide or has provided, these conceived in terms of 'impact' (Hammersley 2011b: Introduction).

However, this instrumentalist viewpoint is also to be found amongst researchers themselves, many insisting that, for it to be worthwhile, research must 'make a difference'. This has led to an increasing tendency to view research as being aimed at achieving practical as well as epistemic goals, for example improving some occupational practice or countering social inequalities. There is an important distinction to be drawn here between the goal of research and the motives that researchers have for engaging in it, and for investigating particular topics. It is quite reasonable for those motives to include a desire to make a practical difference in the world. However, this cannot be the operational goal of research activity without distorting it. Making it serve two goals (producing knowledge and bringing about practical change) can lead to serious dilemmas and a failure to serve either of them well. In particular it can involve bias and result in false research findings being presented as if they were true (see Chapter 5).

Other developments within the academic world have also blurred the distinction between research and other forms of activity. An example is pressure for research to be 'democratised' or 'decolonised' (see the Introduction). Democratisation requires that relations between researchers and researched are 'equalised', in the sense that participants should be included in the decision-making process as regards what should be investigated and how, or that the role of the qualified researcher ought to be restricted to aiding participants in carrying out their own research. This is an idea that developed in the context of feminist inquiry and development studies, but it has spread to other areas, such as Childhood Studies (see Hammersley 2015a, 2017b). Decolonisation of research frequently involves giving local communities, especially indigenous groups, control over research that relates to them, often with the requirement that the methods adopted are in line with what are taken to be their distinctive cultures or interests. Both these moves amount to a de-professionalisation of social research, tending to erase any distinction not just between research and inquiry but between inquiry and other forms of activity.

To a large extent, these developments are based on a spurious appeal to the principle of equity. A two-party relationship is assumed: researchers being on one side, participants (and perhaps also the local community to which they belong), on the other. Furthermore, research is treated as a form of benefit to which there should be equal access for the two sides. Both of these assumptions are false. First, research is aimed at producing knowledge that is of value to everyone, not simply to researchers. Furthermore, it should not be assumed that the interests or cultures of research participants and members of their communities are homogeneous; very often, there are diverse perceived and actual interests as well as significant cultural differences among participants and within communities. The second point is that, while there is an issue about how research topics are selected, and who they are most relevant to, research is not some sort of benefit that ought to be equally divided, it is an activity involving work that may be a success or a failure; and there are conditions that must be met if it is to be successful. One of these is that it is progressively guided towards answering some set of factual questions effectively. Given that there are likely to be conflicting interests, and varying degrees of relevant knowledge and skill, both amongst participants and within communities, democratic control is unlikely to provide effective guidance, to say the least.

Types of social research

Social research can take diverse forms. Here, I will distinguish between practice-focused and academic research.[3] The first term is close in meaning to the more commonly used (but rather misleading) phrase 'applied research', where the aim is to produce knowledge that is of immediate practical value for some other activity. Examples would include the work of political polling agencies in supplying information about voting intentions, or market research aimed at documenting consumers' buying preferences. Such practice-focused research is distinct from inquiry-subordinated-to-another-activity because, while the goals may be set by the needs of the client, once the contract has been signed the research will continue until the knowledge specified in it has been achieved, or it is decided that this is not possible. And the aim is to produce *new* knowledge, not simply to gather information that other people already have, even if the latter is one component.[4] While the boundary here is a fuzzy one, and the character of practice-focused research can vary considerably, the broad difference from inquiry-subordinated-to-another-activity should be clear enough in analytic terms.

What I mean by 'academic research' is that which is usually initiated by a researcher working in a university, academy, or institute, who sets the research questions, and designs the investigation so as to contribute to the body of knowledge which defines a particular field – it is part of a long-term collective academic endeavour. This orientation has implications for the sorts of question that can be addressed: these must be of persistent or perennial, rather than short-term, interest, given the amount of time this kind of research takes. Furthermore, a research topic that is only relevant to a particular local audience is likely to be judged of little academic value.

Academic research is a collective pursuit in another sense too: while particular investigations may often be carried out by individuals working largely alone, they draw on others' work and what they produce is evaluated by colleagues before it is accepted into the body of established knowledge (Hammersley 2011b: chapter 7). New knowledge claims are evaluated against what the research community already takes to be established knowledge, and on the basis of the evidence offered in support of these claims – this being judged in terms of methodological considerations relied upon by this community (see Chapter 3). Moreover, the process of assessing knowledge claims tends to operate in such a way as to err on the side of rejecting as false what may be true, as against accepting as true what is in fact false. While this mode of operation maximises the chances that the conclusions reached will be true (though it cannot guarantee this), the disadvantages are that the answers to some questions will remain uncertain, and the process of knowledge production is relatively slow, with the result that it cannot usually meet the deadlines which surround policymaking and practice.

An implication of the collective character of academic research is that its immediate and most important audience is fellow members of the research community. While the questions addressed must ultimately have relevance beyond the academy, lay audiences should not be the target for reports from particular investigations. Communication with those audiences ought to operate through reviews of research findings on particular topics, as well as via the production of textbooks and trade books that draw on findings from multiple studies. This is one of the areas where it is perhaps clearest that I am outlining an ideal, since authors of individual studies are often keen to communicate their findings to lay audiences, and are encouraged to do so by universities and funders, in order to maximise impact (Hammersley 2014b).

Of course, academics may carry out practice-focused, as well as or instead of academic, research. Indeed, the border between the two has become blurred because, as I noted earlier, the justification for academic research has come to be questioned, with researchers increasingly being required to demonstrate the immediate practical relevance of their work. Also, there are academics who regard academic research, as I have defined it here, as of little value in itself: they too insist that research should serve political or practical goals, in the belief that these are more important than producing knowledge (Hammersley 1995; see the Introduction). Thus, much social science today purports to answer evaluative questions about what is wrong, and what should be done; and sometimes even claims to be directly engaged in bringing about practical results. However, in my view these external and internal pressures on academic social research must be resisted if it is to function well. And maintaining clear differentiation not just from practice-focused research but also from inquiry-subordinated-to-other-activities is an essential part of this.

There is, of course, internal differentiation within academic social research, in terms of different disciplines – politics, economics, sociology, and so on – and various substantive fields – such as education, health, and crime – as well as diverse theoretical and methodological approaches within each, of the kind outlined in the Introduction. However, the concept of academic research is intended to apply to all of these. There are also relationships between social research and the various areas of natural science, including medicine, as well as with the humanities, notably history and philosophy. Natural science is usually focused exclusively on producing answers to factual questions, as are some of the humanities; whereas others, including philosophy, are concerned with conceptual or even evaluative issues.

Another relevant boundary concerns the relationship with journalism. Some journalistic work amounts to inquiry or even research, under the definitions I have used here, but much does not. To take an extreme example, when the recent UK Prime Minister Boris Johnson is described as having been a 'political journalist', this does not imply engagement in research or even inquiry, but rather the expression of his opinions in newspapers and magazines. Social researchers have often been keen to distinguish their work from that of journalists, and one would certainly hope that it is very different from some forms of this; but there is a much closer relationship to other kinds, notably what is often referred to as investigative journalism. A difference may still remain, in the latter's tendency to focus on particular events, and usually quite recent ones, but there can be overlap in topic, and some journalists draw on academic studies in their work.

Science

Research is frequently labelled as scientific, and the term 'science' is clearly of central methodological significance. This is true whether the attitude adopted towards what it represents is positive or negative. While much research trades under the heading of 'social science', many social researchers have become uncomfortable with that label, and there are a significant number who reject it (see, for instance, Hutchinson et al. 2008). Indeed, there are those who employ contrasting designations, for example calling their work 'arts-based research' (Barone and Eisner 2011; Cahnmann-Taylor and Siegesmund 2017; Leavy 2015, 2018).

The most influential model for the meaning of 'science' has, of course, been a notion of scientific method based on the practice of physics, chemistry, and biology. Historically, social research developed in the shadow of natural science and, given the latter's impressive progress in understanding physical processes, its influence is not surprising. However, this influence has never been unequivocal. It has long been recognised that the sciences vary in the methods they use, for example physics and biology shared relatively little in common in the nineteenth century. Furthermore, there have been competing interpretations of the nature of scientific method even in relation to physics (Losee 2001). Indeed, some philosophers of science came to deny that there is any such method (Feyerabend 1975). In addition, in more recent times there has been a tendency to conflate science with technology, as with the notion of 'technoscience' (Haraway 1997), this reflecting changes in key parts of natural science since at least the mid-twentieth century (see Ziman 2000). Finally, social scientists claiming to adopt scientific method have drawn different conclusions about what it meant for their own practice, differing for example as to whether experimental controls were essential; whether data must be derived solely from observations of physical behaviour; and whether discovering universal laws was the aim, as against statistical regularities within particular populations, or detailed accounts of particular cultures or settings.

Equally important, there have long been conceptions of 'science' that did not treat modern natural science as the model; in fact, that were based on criticisms of it. For example, in the nineteenth century both Goethe and Hegel viewed the practice of natural scientists negatively as empiricist, and believed that the knowledge they produced was inadequate even for understanding physical phenomena. Goethe insisted that, as the source of true knowledge, science must penetrate to the underlying meaning of phenomena, not just document their surface features; and that this meaning was to be found in original forms from which particular instances of phenomena had developed (see Heller 1961). Hegel's conception of science placed primary emphasis on the need for a comprehensive, philosophical system of interpretation, based on understanding how ideas had developed in the past. He drew on an element of the meaning of the Latin word 'scientia' that emphasised the idea of a *systematic* corpus of knowledge, a body of propositions organised in a hierarchical structure. Euclid's geometry was a model for science of this kind that was adopted by some, but Hegel's conception of the organised nature of knowledge was dialectical: for him, it developed historically through internal contradictions, in a way that paralleled, indeed embodied, the dialectical development of both human history and nature itself. The scientific task was to discern the character of the world as a systematic whole. Later, Marx adopted and adapted this dialectical conception of science as the foundation for a forward-looking unity of theory and practice, as against Hegel's backward-looking reconciliation of reason with reality. And, as a result of the development of Marxism in the twentieth century, this dialectical notion of science has had considerable influence.

Other conceptions of science were to be found in nineteenth-century German historicism and hermeneutics, and these went on to influence Anglo-American anthropology, and work in other disciplines as well, throughout the twentieth century and into the twenty-first century (Hammersley 1989b: chapter 1; see Chapters 8 and 9). Husserl's phenomenology and Saussure's structuralist linguistics provided further models, these later transformed by various kinds of post-structuralism (Luckmann 1978; Lundy 2013; see the Glossary). All of these developments shaped social research, so that today multiple meanings of the term 'science' persist, and are often mixed and blended implicitly in common usage.

The differences in meaning relate, for instance, to whether the aim of research is evaluative or just factual, and if the latter whether it involves description or explanation, what form of description or explanation is sought, the role of theory, the function of evidence and what counts as this, and what shape the products of research ought to take. Furthermore, as I noted earlier, some social researchers have rejected any conception of science in favour of models from literature and art. One example of this is a shift from explicit argumentation designed to engage readers in the pursuit of knowledge, and providing the resources for this, to modes of presentation aimed at capturing lived experience in its own terms, or generating particular sorts of effect on the part of readers, whether this is a shock of recognition, feelings of sympathy or anger, or the motivation to act in a particular way.

It is of significance, of course, that 'science' has often been used as an honorific title. In the past, especially, fields claimed scientific credentials in order to boost their status, both within the academy and beyond. However, over the course of the twentieth century, the reputation of 'science' became tarnished by the role of natural science in the development of technologies of destruction and in the exploitation of fossil fuels that cause pollution and climate change. There have also been claims that its practice has involved significant biases, in relation to both gender and race. Even more fundamental challenges have asserted that it claims a false objectivity or a spurious detachment from society; that it embodies a false, inhuman, or irreligious perspective; and/or that it is implicated in Western imperialism.

Despite all this, there are some benefits to thinking of social research in terms of how it might be scientific – so long as we make clear what we mean by that term. If employed in what probably remains the dominant sense today, where natural science is taken as the model, the term can be used to clarify the nature of the social researcher's task: to mark a distinction between the investigation of factual issues and attempts to address other sorts of question that are also of importance, but not part of that task; in particular, to answer evaluative questions about what is good or bad, right or wrong, or who is to blame. It can also be used to highlight the difference between careful investigation, along with the restriction of knowledge claims to those that can be empirically justified, as against claims about highly speculative matters for which little evidence is available.[5] In my view, natural science serves as a worthwhile model in these respects, with its exclusive focus only on factual questions that can, in principle and practice, be answered with a reasonably high level of confidence on the basis of empirical evidence that is accessible to others. Adopting this model does not require us to assume that social science must employ exactly the same methods as physics or chemistry (hardly anyone has suggested this), that its task is to discover universal laws, or that it must rely for data on standardised measurements of observable behaviour. But it does place emphasis on a preparedness to question assumptions and to test both these and research findings against evidence, rather than simply putting forward plausible or appealing ideas. Moreover, this must be done in a way that ought to be accepted as convincing by anyone else who adopts this scientific orientation, whatever their background.[6]

Adopting a scientific stance of this kind does not implicate us in Western imperialism, or in the degradation of the planet, any more than most of us are already implicated in these matters. There is no deep and tight relationship between this conception of science and such deplorable aspects of modernity. Nevertheless, it is true that much can be learned from other views of science. For instance, Marxism, phenomenology, and structuralism all usefully emphasise the value of searching for underlying generative structures rather than being satisfied solely with documenting the character and distribution of particular social phenomena.

But, ultimately, whether to adopt the label of science is a pragmatic matter, it does not affect the question of whether social research is worthwhile or what it demands if it is to be pursued well. Natural science is a useful model for social researchers in some respects, but a misleading one in others; and much the same could be said about investigative journalism, imaginative literature, or art as models (all of which have sometimes been employed to make sense of social research practice). It is the task of any particular social research community to determine what questions it can reasonably claim to address, and how best to pursue answers to those questions. But it must do so in ways that promise to live up to the claim that is built into the mandate of all research: to provide knowledge that is more likely to be true than that from other sources.

Conclusion

In this chapter I have sought to clarify how the terms 'inquiry', 'research', and 'science' can best be interpreted in order to identify a distinctive and worthwhile mission for social research. I argued that this required maintaining clear boundaries, as well as being aware of similarities and interrelationships, with other activities: practical thinking in social life; politics; natural science; the humanities; journalism; and art or imaginative literature. I drew a distinction between inquiry and research, treating the first term as referring to any kind of search for knowledge, and the second as referring to specialised forms of inquiry designed to produce factual or conceptual knowledge that is of collective value. I also distinguished between practice-focused and academic research. I ended by discussing the meanings of the term 'science' and some of the issues surrounding its application to academic social research. Here I emphasised the obligations associated with a scientific commitment, in terms of limitations on what can be investigated and requirements concerning how knowledge should be pursued (see also Chapter 13).

All of the boundaries I have mentioned must be maintained, not in order to eliminate or deny any connection between social research and other kinds of inquiry and activity, but to distinguish its goals, and thereby to provide a sound basis for its pursuit. Yet, today, many of these boundaries are weak or eroded, and (as I have noted) there have been efforts to erase several of them, on the part of both researchers and external agents (governments and other powerful interest groups). Some social scientists have celebrated such 'blurring of genres', or at least treated it as an inevitable feature of the postmodern world (Geertz 1980), but there are good reasons to believe that it is neither inevitable nor desirable. It is essential to identify the sort of inquiries social researchers should, and should not, engage in as part of their work, *and to do so in a way that respects key boundaries without denying the commonalities across human activities and human beings.* Furthermore, this must be done in a manner that neither unjustifiably privileges nor deprivileges social research.

Notes

1 The same is true of the latest edition, produced posthumously with new authors: Clarke et al. 2021:4.
2 For a contested example of their work, see Riordan and Jopling 2021.

3 For a slightly more complex typology, see Hammersley 2002: chapter 6.

4 Here there is a contrast with the 'research' done by civil servants in seeking the information available that a policymaker requires in order to make a decision.

5 While a considerable amount of social science appears to transgress this boundary, there are good reasons for respecting it: see Hammersley 2014a.

6 This is to rely on a somewhat idealised conception of natural science, underplaying the rise of what Ziman (2000) calls 'real science'. However, we should not assume that all natural scientific work takes a degraded form, and there is no reason to treat the real as rational. For a vigorous defence of the conception of science that my discussion here presupposes, see Haack 2003.

3   Truth

Today, the words 'truth' and 'true' are used hesitantly, if at all, by many social scientists.[1] Even when they *are* employed they are frequently clothed in inverted commas that serve as 'scare quotes', to signal that the author does not wish to be committed to the concept. At best, euphemisms are deployed, such as 'validity' or 'accuracy'. One reason for timidity about 'truth' is that many researchers believe (wrongly) that use of the term necessarily implies the possession of knowledge whose epistemic status is proven *beyond all possible doubt* and is therefore *absolutely certain*; and they think (quite rightly) that this can never be achieved. However, while it is true that there are some deep philosophical problems surrounding the concept of truth, this is no reason to abandon the term, especially since synonyms do not avoid the problem but simply cover it up.[2] Indeed, reliance on these synonyms indicates that it is impossible to avoid employing the *concept* of truth in practice, even if the *word* can be avoided. It is essential not just in the context of research, where it defines the goal of this activity (the pursuit of knowledge), but also for our everyday practical dealings with the world: we are recurrently concerned with whether or not information is accurate – in other words, whether it should be treated as true.

The importance of truth has, if anything, increased in an age when the prevalence of advertising, political spin, and 'fake news' has grown considerably. Furthermore, all sides in the increasingly vehement political debates that occur across deep ideological divides today appeal to this concept, labelling their own beliefs true while denying that status to opposing positions. But in this process what it means to say that some statement is true is either largely taken for granted or degraded through sceptical or relativistic criticism of other views which sows doubt about whether we can ever really know anything. In public debate, very often, whether a belief or statement is true seems to be decided in large part by what are taken to be its political implications, and this is even true to some extent in the academic world as well. However, I suggest that in this purportedly 'post-truth' era researchers have a heightened responsibility to uphold the importance of truth, and to guard against the danger of error and bias (Hammersley 2022a). But this requires clarity about what the term means (see Haack 2019).

DOI: 10.4324/9781003350354-4

In the methodological literature concerned with quantitative methods distinctions are drawn among various 'types of validity'. Perhaps the most common distinction is between internal and external validity, but in addition there are those among various kinds of measurement validity, such as 'face validity', 'content validity', 'construct validity', 'predictive validity', and 'criterion validity'. All of these distinctions are of value in identifying various threats to the truth of research conclusions, both those relating to the effects of rival causal factors and those arising in the operationalisation of concepts. However, it is misleading to view these as types of *validity*, the implication being that a particular finding can be, say, internally valid but externally invalid, or have high predictive validity but low construct validity. This would be to suggest that research conclusions can be, simultaneously, true and false.[3]

There have been discussions of types of validity in qualitative research too. Sometimes these have paralleled those in quantitative methodology, simply involving modifications to take account of differences in the kinds of data and analysis used. But, here too, these are not *types of validity* but either conditions that must be met if findings are to be treated as true, or means by which we can judge whether findings are likely to be true. At the same time, some typologies of validity put forward by qualitative researchers cannot be interpreted in this way. An influential example is Lather's (1993) distinctions among 'ironic', 'paralogical', 'rhizomatic', and 'voluptuous' validity, these apparently all forming part of 'transgressive validity'. Here, the term 'validity' is being used in a sense that is quite different from the concept of empirical truth I will be discussing in this chapter. Indeed, she rejects that concept as 'foundationalist': for her, the meaning of 'validity' is closer to a notion of authenticity, conceived in political and/or metaphysical terms. In my view, this notion is irrelevant to social science, and its adoption is damaging in that context (and most others).

Meanings of 'true'

There are several quite different senses of the term 'true', only some of which are relevant to social research findings. For example, people occasionally claim that a particular belief is 'true for me', by which they imply that it carries significance, or serves a purpose, for them, rather than that it corresponds to relevant features of a shared reality. Equally we need to distinguish between what is true by definition (logical truth) and what is true as a matter of fact (empirical truth). Definitions only tell us the meanings being given to words, whereas empirically true statements tell us about things to which they refer that exist independently of them.[4] There is also literary truth, which concerns whether what is portrayed in a novel or short story is believable and relates to characteristic features of human life (even though imaginative literature does not report actually occurring instances of these features). Empirical truth is the focus of academic social research (see Chapter 2), and this is my primary concern in this chapter. I will argue that it necessarily involves the idea of a correspondence

between what is stated and the scene, objects, and so forth to which the statement refers; but, as we shall see, this is a difficult and contentious matter.

Another challenging issue concerns whether we can apply the concept of
truth to evaluations of what is good or bad, right or wrong. I suggest that
what is involved here is very different from matters of empirical fact: in such
evaluations, an action, situation, person, organisation, and/or institutional
arrangement is being judged against some value standard. Whether what is
being judged has been described accurately is a factual matter, and therefore
can be assessed in terms of empirical truth, but evaluation also involves selection of an appropriate standard of assessment followed by application of it to the
object described, and these are not factual matters, nor ones about which social
research can legitimately claim any intellectual authority. There are many values that we employ in making such evaluations (justice, authenticity, autonomy,
privacy, self-esteem, pleasure, efficacy, etc.), and deciding what value or combination of values should be employed depends upon an underlying conception
of how the world ought, and ought not, to be. We cannot decide this by logic
and empirical investigation alone, even though both can help us in coming to
such a conception and in deploying the evaluations that derive from it. It is
for this reason that I regard evaluations of what is good or right as beyond the
scope of social scientific research, though it is possible for it to provide conditional evaluations. These state what evaluative conclusion would be reached
about some object, situation, and so on, if we adopted a particular, coherent
set of values, while recognising that others could be adopted (see Hammersley
2017c).[5]

In the next section, I will look at arguments that are frequently believed to
disqualify the use of 'truth' in a factual sense. In the course of this, I will outline
an interpretation of this concept that can serve the purposes of social research,
despite difficult philosophical questions that remain unresolved. Finally, I will
look at how the truth of knowledge claims ought to be assessed in social science.

Challenges to truth

There are several philosophical problems that can lead to hesitancy about
relying on the concept of truth. These concern the essential fallibility of all
empirical claims; the framework dependency of such claims; the problem of
correspondence between any knowledge claim and the phenomena to which it
refers; and various political and ethical issues surrounding the concept of truth.

The fallibility of all knowledge claims

As already indicated, to say that some statement or belief is true is *not* to imply
that its truth is beyond all possible doubt: we can never prove the truth or falsity
of any empirical proposition beyond all question (by contrast, this *is* possible,
arguably, with logical truths). In other words, all of the empirical propositions
we take to be true are fallible: this means that, at least *in principle*, they may be

false. However, as I will explain, this does not imply that we should assume that they are all equally likely to be false; and judgements about what is false are just as fallible as those about what is true. Nor does this fallibility mean that we must always suspend judgement about whether knowledge claims are true; what is required is only that we should keep their fallibility in mind, and assess the likelihood that they are true or false, in terms of some threshold – I discuss this later.

One reason for the fallibility of knowledge claims is that their truth depends upon how the terms they contain are interpreted. For example, if we say 'no human being comes alive again after dying' this is generally speaking true, but in some cases its truth will depend upon how we interpret 'alive' and 'dying'.[6] While for most purposes the use of these words is unproblematic, in the context of medicine they can be more troublesome: Do we count someone who is in a coma from which they are very unlikely to emerge as alive or dead? If someone's heart stops beating, does that mean she is dead, or is brain death the key criterion? After all, people sometimes survive heart attacks (and perhaps even crucifixions). Problems of meaning are probably rather more widespread in the case of the terms used in social science than they are in medicine, so attention to them is particularly necessary (see Hammersley 2020: Introduction).

A second reason to emphasise the fallibility of knowledge claims in social science is that we rarely have access to evidence that is very strongly conclusive. Normally, we must rely on weaker evidence than that available in natural science or even in many everyday matters; and any inference from this evidence to a conclusion about the truth of a knowledge claim may itself be questionable. Furthermore, new evidence can always arise, or we may discover that evidence we thought was reliable is not. Equally, what seemed like the most conclusive inference from the evidence to an accurate description or explanation may come to be challenged by an alternative that is even more cogent. To take a mundane instance from the physical world, it may look as if the sun travels round the earth, just as does the moon, but we now know that it does not. In much the same way, appearances can also be deceptive in the social world.

However, as already emphasised, the fact that all knowledge claims are fallible does *not* mean that they are all equally likely to be false, or that we cannot have good reasons for believing that some of them are true. Nor does it mean that we cannot legitimately treat some of them as *almost certainly* true – in the sense that, if they turned out to be false, then there would be little else we could reasonably take to be true. For instance, I think we can take it as true that there are currently large differences in income and wealth among households or individuals in both the UK and the US; though there are, of course, various ways of measuring these differences that will give somewhat different results. The conclusion that all knowledge claims are equally likely to be false would only be reached if we assumed that, for a claim to be treated as true, our judgement about this must be absolutely conclusive. But there is no good reason to adopt this radical assumption: doing so would require us to accept that we can have no knowledge at all, in social science, in physical science, or even in everyday life. We could not even rely upon any of those assumptions about the world that we routinely depend upon to do the most basic things (for instance, that gravity will keep us pinned to the earth's surface). We could not live like this.

One reason why we might be inclined to assume that we can only use the words 'truth', 'true', 'know', and 'knowledge' when we can be *absolutely certain* of the epistemic status of the statements or beliefs to which they are being applied is that they are achievement words, not task words (Ryle 1949:216). So, for example, it makes no sense to say 'It was true that Tiddles the cat was sitting on his mat, but it turned out he wasn't', or 'I knew Tiddles was sitting on his mat, but I was wrong'. This linguistic feature may appear to imply that all knowledge is true by definition. But we must distinguish between semantics and epistemology, between the meanings we give to words and our knowledge of the world. All that is required in using words like 'true' and 'knowledge' is that we must be *justified in believing* that the statements to which we are applying them are true; we cannot know they are true with absolute certainty, but this is not necessary for us to use those words.

This indicates that there is an important distinction to be drawn between truth and justification. We can be justified in believing what is in fact false. Equally, we may not be justified in believing what is actually true (because we do not have sufficient evidence to be properly confident that it is true). It is usually assumed that, if someone claims knowledge of some kind, he or she must be able to provide convincing evidence for why it is likely to be true; in other words, the claim must be justifiable. This is correct, in my view, but there are difficult questions surrounding the notion of what is *sufficient* evidence and how we assess this. These will be examined later.

Of course, it could be argued that, since the idea of truth is a cultural construct, there might be cultures in which there is no such concept, or at least in which it is understood in a very different way (see Holbraad 2009). However this flies in the face of what we usually assume we know about other cultures, and throws severe doubt on whether we could ever understand them. It also treats all assumptions as culturally arbitrary, *and as entirely determining our experience*, with the implication that people can live in multiple cultures that generate *completely* different 'worlds'. This links directly to the next challenge to the concept of truth I will discuss.

The idea of framework dependence

The second type of argument against the concept of truth insists that all knowledge necessarily relies on a framework of assumptions that could be questioned, with this taken to imply that contradictory 'truths' will be recognised by different frameworks, these deriving from disparate theoretical and methodological paradigms or even different cultures. The key point being made here is that there is no overarching position from which competing frameworks can be assessed, since all assessments are themselves framework-dependent.

This often implies a form of relativism: that there are 'multiple realities', corresponding to different cultures, or each reflecting the social location of different social classes, genders, races/ethnicities, and so on, within a society. This is an argument to which some protagonists have explicitly appealed in the paradigm wars which have plagued social science in recent times (for instance, Smith 1989; Guba 1992; see Hammersley 1998). However, while it is true that there is some systematic variation in beliefs about the world between cultures, and among those occupying different social locations, this is not total; and therefore does not in itself imply relativism (see Moody-Adams 1997). Furthermore, relativism involves a performative contradiction: if it were true, it could only be true (on its own terms) for some particular culture or social position, and therefore could be false for others.

Of course, instead of treating what different frameworks produce as conflicting 'knowledges', it can equally be argued that none of them offer knowledge at all, just different perspectives on a supposed external world about which we can know nothing. In other words, the move may be made from relativism to epistemological scepticism. In one of its forms, this argues that if all claims to knowledge rely on assumptions, there can be no knowledge because we can never know whether all these assumptions are true. Indeed, it may be suggested that we have no adequate grounds for believing that there are any real phenomena independent of our beliefs. The problem, here again, is that we have no place to stand: in assessing any set of assumptions we must rely upon other assumptions, taking *their* validity for granted at least temporarily; and alternative assumptions would always be possible. Yet, any attempt to question all of our assumptions simultaneously would be impossible. According to scepticism, then, while we can be aware of how phenomena appear to us, we can have no knowledge of reality.[7]

This argument is a version of the ancient sceptical device known as 'the problem of the criterion' (see McCain 2014). It starts from the idea that establishing the truth of any statement depends upon an appeal to some criterion that distinguishes between what is true and what is false. But it can be asked: by what criterion has this criterion been selected? And, when this second criterion has been specified, it can then be asked: by what criterion was that second one selected; thereby demanding a third one. And so on. There is no ultimate criterion, no foundation, that can be beyond all question. A different way of putting this would be to say that, in order to distinguish what is true from what is mere appearance, we need a *means by which this can be done*. But to know whether our means of doing this is successful, we must already know which appearances are *true* and which are *false*: we are apparently caught in a vicious circle.

However, as I have already explained, we do not require an ultimate foundation to justify our use of epistemic terms like 'true', 'truth', 'knowledge', etc. There is no requirement that claims must be *beyond all possible doubt*. Instead, what is required is that they are beyond *reasonable* doubt (and judgements about this can, of course, be revised), *as well as that we have a process whereby errors can be discovered and corrected.* What is involved here is not some logically determinate procedure by which absolutely certain knowledge can be produced but, rather, a learning process. I will outline later what that process involves.

The sort of fallibilist philosophy I am putting forward here is often felt to be unsatisfactory because we tend to assume that we either have logical procedures that produce infallible knowledge *or* we can only rely on 'subjective' judgement that is entirely arbitrary and therefore gives us no purchase on whether answers to our questions are true or false. The fact that we could always be mistaken is taken to mean that, in the absence of absolute proof, we must assume that we *are* always mistaken. In other words, the suggestion is that we are condemned to the realm of opinion, and all opinions must be assumed to be as good as one another in epistemic terms, since what is a criterion of truth can itself only be a matter of opinion. Yet, as I have pointed out, this scepticism is not the basis on which we do, or could, live our lives. It is also a fact of experience that we can learn that we were mistaken with reasonable surety, and that we can identify better and worse ways of setting about the task of inquiry (see Peirce 1877). Furthermore, the challenge of the sceptic, like that of the relativist, is self-disconfirming: the statement that we can never have any knowledge is itself a knowledge claim. If it is true then by that very fact it negates itself. Once again, there is a performative contradiction.[8]

Given these problems, in practice relativist and sceptical arguments are usually applied selectively as a way of challenging others' claims to knowledge. But this amounts to a form of bias, and involves a lack of integrity that ultimately undermines any rational enterprise, including inquiry (see Chapters 5 and 13).

The problem of correspondence

Another area of philosophical uncertainty leading to hesitancy about using the term 'truth' concerns the idea that, for a statement to be true, it must correspond with reality. I will suggest that this idea is correct, while acknowledging uncertainties surrounding what 'correspondence' means.

The idea of correspondence could be taken to imply that we must have direct access to the world in order to compare it with the statement we are assessing, so as to check whether the correspondence holds. It may appear that we can do this in some cases. To return to an example I used earlier, if I say 'Tiddles the cat is now sitting on his mat' this assumes that in the relevant part of the world at the relevant time this particular cat was indeed sitting on that particular mat. In short, there is a correspondence between what the statement claims to be true and the state of affairs to which it refers: Tiddles is not out chasing birds, he is not sitting on the sofa watching television, some other cat has not usurped his place on the mat, he is not sitting on some other cat's mat, and so on. Moreover, we can check the truth of the statement by looking and seeing.

However, this is not the same as gaining direct access to the world: all perception of phenomena involves processes of sense-making, even if we are not aware of them; and, as a result, we can be wrong. I may mistake another cat for

Tiddles (my eyes are not as good as they once were, and perhaps the other cat is almost identical); I may mistake Tiddles' mat for another one (perhaps I have more than one cat, each with its own nearly identical mat!); I may only imagine seeing Tiddles on his mat because that is where he usually is; or perhaps I got the time wrong (I forgot to reset the clock after a time change, or perhaps it has stopped). So there is a potential for error even in this simple case. At the same time, it should be clear that looking and seeing can give us quite strong evidence as to the whereabouts of Tiddles, especially if we look very carefully (check that it definitely is him, that it is his mat, that the clock is telling the right time, etc.).

The key point is that, even though in this simple example we cannot have direct access that is error-free to the phenomena to which the statement refers, we can gain evidence that provides strong grounds for believing (until further notice) that the statement is true, or that it is false. And the same applies to many statements whose correspondence to reality we cannot check by looking to see. Take, for instance, the claim that 'social mobility in England is currently declining'. One problem here, again, is the meaning of the key terms involved. Unless we are philosophers, we are unlikely to be much troubled in defining 'Tiddles', 'sat', 'on', or 'the mat', but 'social mobility' is a different kettle of fish. It depends upon a set of categories specifying social positions among which people can move, into which every individual or household in a population can be assigned at a particular point in time, along with some specification of the time period over which movement is being assessed. And these positions are not like the physical location of Tiddles: the categorisations on which they depend are much more complex, and contestable.[9] It follows from this that we cannot simply look to see people's social positions, even less their social mobility. Nevertheless, we can search for and assess evidence about the social mobility of particular people, and on the basis of this come to some conclusion about whether the amount of social mobility within a population is increasing or decreasing; thereby determining whether the statement 'social mobility in England is decreasing' is likely to correspond to what is happening in England at the moment. This is by no means a simple task, but it is doable (indeed, it has been done – and the best answer we have is that social mobility is neither declining nor increasing significantly at the moment: see Buscha and Sturgis 2018).

Therefore, we can retain the idea of truth as correspondence despite the fact that even in the easiest of cases, such as the location of Tiddles, we do not have direct access to reality so as to decide whether it corresponds to what is implied in the statement whose truth we are assessing. In both the case of Tiddles and the more challenging sociological example of social mobility, we cannot gain direct access to reality to check the correspondence, but we can draw inferences about the phenomena we are concerned with from what we can see and hear, and from what others report in documents and interviews. That these data and inferences are fallible is true enough, but this does not mean that the idea of truth as correspondence is undercut; and we can check for, and discover, errors.

More fundamentally, the assumption that use of the notion of correspondence requires direct access to the world confuses the *concept* of truth, how that word is defined (in terms of correspondence), with the means by which we determine what is true (evidence of various kinds). This is to conflate truth with justification, a distinction whose importance I emphasised earlier.

Another problem with the idea of correspondence is that it may be taken to mean that a knowledge claim must exhaustively reproduce the phenomena to which it refers; in other words, it must 'correspond' in every detail, much in the way that a sculpture may be said to reproduce the outer surface of the object it represents. However, this analogy is misleading when applied to knowledge, even if we accept that sculptures are reproductions. A knowledge-claim is always an answer to a question or set of questions about the phenomena concerned, and these relate only to *some* aspects of those phenomena and not to others. Knowledge never reproduces phenomena, *and does not need to do this.* This can be obscured in some forms of social research, as for example when anthropologists claim to have described particular cultures. They may well have described some aspects of those cultures, but the ethnographies they produce are not reproductions of them but are structured by questions that reflect particular concerns about how cultures operate and the differences between them.

A final problem that is sometimes raised about the notion of truth as correspondence concerns how there can be a correspondence between linguistic objects (words and sentences) and the (often) non-linguistic phenomena to which they refer. Given their quite different character, how can the one correspond with the other? However, what is assumed is not a correspondence between words and things but between what a particular combination of words implies or assumes about the state of the world and how the relevant part of the world is at the relevant time. While there are certainly philosophical puzzles about meaning and implication, these should not lead us to reject the notion of truth as correspondence. And this is good news because, in practice, we cannot avoid relying on it.

The politics and ethics of truth

There are also sometimes ethical and political objections made to the concept of truth. It may be argued that what counts as truth is largely determined by those who hold power in society, so that the very notion of truth, perhaps especially as embodied in the concept of scientific knowledge, upholds social hierarchy. What is required, instead, it might be suggested, is to recognise and amplify the views of those who are oppressed or marginalised, in the name of social justice.

At face value, this argument does not reject the concept of truth; rather, it is a complaint about how knowledge claims are made and justified within a particular context. Moreover, sometimes it relies upon a distinctive conception of how knowledge about society is most likely to be produced: that the true nature of society is revealed to the marginalised and oppressed but obscured from those in power and those who serve them. This is what is often referred to as standpoint epistemology. In its original Marxist form, the industrial working class were treated as epistemically privileged in this way. But this type of argument has subsequently been applied to various other social categories, notably women (Harding 2004).

However, there are fundamental problems with standpoint epistemology. In its Marxist form it relied upon a teleological meta-history inherited from Hegel that has been largely discredited. This was not, in any case, easily applicable to the category of 'women', so feminists relied on alternative grounds for attributing epistemic privilege. However, these are no more convincing in my view (Hammersley 1995: chapter 3). And, aside from this, there is the more fundamental problem that those putting forward any standpoint epistemology must validate it without appealing to the epistemic privilege that their version of it ascribes. It cannot be convincingly justified in its own terms, since that would be circular; and to justify it in more conventional epistemological terms undermines it by suggesting that it is dependent upon what it rejects (Hammersley 2011b: chapter 4). This problem is highlighted if it is asked: why should we adopt one standpoint epistemology rather than another; how are we to decide *which* 'marginalised group' has epistemological privilege, given that their perspective may well be in conflict with those of others? Do all marginalised groups enjoy such privilege? (see van den Berg and Jeong 2022).[10]

There is, however, a more radical political argument which *does* challenge the concept of truth. Relying on relativism or epistemological scepticism, this contends that any claim to knowledge is no more than a claim to spurious authority, and that it amounts to an injustice. From this point of view, because of its very character in claiming superior knowledge, science reinforces forms of social inequality that are inequitable. It may be argued, instead, that there can only be imaginative interpretations; and that, since accounts cannot be judged in epistemic terms, political, ethical, or aesthetic criteria of assessment must be used. For example, what becomes important is whether research leads to conclusions that are believed to have progressive political implications or consequences (for an early statement of this position, see Lather 1986).

Yet, as noted earlier, relativism and scepticism suffer from performative contradiction if applied consistently: they themselves make knowledge claims while simultaneously denying that such claims can be known to be true. Furthermore, claims about political consequences necessarily rely on knowledge, and questions about what is politically, ethically, or aesthetically desirable are even more open to disagreement than those about what is true. Finally, as I have emphasised, we all rely on the concept of truth in our everyday dealings with the world, whether we acknowledge this or not.

What I have sought to establish in this section is that, while there are certainly difficult philosophical issues surrounding the concept of truth, none of these undercut its use. We can recognise the fallibility of all knowledge claims, their dependence on assumptions, the complexities of a correspondence theory of truth, and the politics of knowledge, without abandoning that concept.

Furthermore, in practice, reliance upon it is unavoidable, and we should be explicit about this.

Assessing and justifying knowledge claims

Having dealt with the challenges that have been made to the concept of truth, the next step is to clarify the process by which the truth of a knowledge claim is assessed. This is a process that human beings have long deployed, with greater or lesser effectiveness, but researchers can employ it in a more refined way because they specialise in inquiry (see Chapter 2). As already noted, what is central here is reliance on a notion of 'beyond reasonable doubt', rather than 'absolute certainty'. In everyday life, we accept as true (until further notice) what seems very likely to be true. And, in judging what is beyond reasonable doubt, we rely on two considerations: what I will call 'plausibility' and 'credibility', using these terms in rather more specific senses than is normal. By the first, I mean 'how well a statement fits with what we currently take to be existing knowledge relevant to that statement'. By 'credibility', I mean 'how likely is it that there was significant error in producing the statement'. Researchers employ this same general approach, even though they may apply it in a more careful and self-conscious fashion; indeed, they are obliged to do this.

Providing a little more detail, three steps can be involved in assessing the validity of research claims, though the final one may go through several cycles:

1   We must start by asking how *plausible* a knowledge claim or assumption is: that is, whether we judge it as very likely to be true, very likely to be false, or of uncertain validity, given what we take to be existing knowledge. Some claims will be so plausible that we can reasonably accept them at face value (until further notice), without needing to know anything about how they were produced or what evidence could be offered in support of them. (Current examples might include that a substantial number of children worldwide engage in work that contributes to their households' incomes, or that some religious authorities disapprove of gay and lesbian relationships.) However, very few if any research conclusions will be so plausible that we can reasonably accept them at face value; after all, any that met this requirement would have little news value.

2   If a knowledge claim or assumption is insufficiently plausible to be accepted at face value, the second question we must ask is whether it was produced in such a way that error is unlikely. This will require us to think about the nature of the phenomena to which it refers, the manner and circumstances in which any process of inquiry involved was carried out, the characteristics of the inquirer, and so on. This is the issue of *credibility*. In assessing credibility we make a judgment about the likely threats to validity involved in the production of a knowledge claim, and the likely size and direction of their effects. As with plausibility, there are claims whose credibility is such that we can reasonably accept them without further ado (unless and

until we discover new doubts about them). To return to our feline friend, we are likely to assume, quite reasonably, that someone who knows Tiddles and was observing his mat at the appropriate time can and will give us an accurate statement about whether he was sitting on it. However, once again, most social science findings are more complex and rely on using indicators of various kinds. So, a third step is almost always necessary.

3   Where we conclude that a claim is neither sufficiently plausible nor sufficiently credible to be accepted at face value, we do not simply reject it but look to see what evidence is offered, or available, as to its truth. However, when we examine this evidence we will have to employ the same means to assess *its* validity as we applied to the knowledge claim itself: we will need to judge the plausibility and credibility of that evidence. And, of course, we may require further evidence to support this first set of evidence, which we shall again judge in terms of plausibility and credibility, and so on. This process must continue until we get to the point where we have sufficient evidence that validates or falsifies the claim, beyond reasonable doubt; or until we run out of evidence, at which point we will have to suspend judgement about the truth of the original knowledge claim.

It is important to emphasise that this process necessarily relies on judgement, and is itself fallible, so that we must accept any conclusion reached only 'until further notice'. Sceptics are right that there is no prospect of empirical knowledge claims whose validity is beyond all possible doubt. But, as I said earlier, this does not mean that any judgement is as good as any other: that is certainly not an assumption we normally make, or could make, in relation to everyday matters that are of significance to us. And it is not one that researchers could make either. Instead, we assess the validity of knowledge claims on the basis of plausibility and credibility, in order to determine whether they are beyond reasonable doubt.

An important aspect of checking the likely truth of knowledge claims is to assess whether false assumptions have led to a conclusion that appears plausible or credible but is not. We rarely have every piece of information required, and we tend to fill in any gaps with what we take to be existing knowledge; yet in doing this we may be mistaken. An example is provided by Duneier (2000:216), discussing his study of book vendors on the streets of New York, many of whom were homeless. He notes that he often saw these men urinating at the back of a nearby building, but thought nothing of it. He comments that it reminded him of 'my upper-class male friends who do the same thing when they are in the middle of the golf course and are too lazy to go back to the club house take a piss'. He only realised that his interpretation was mistaken, and appreciated the significance of what he had seen, when he heard one of the men reporting that he had been excluded from going to the restroom in the local McDonald's. Duneier recognised that, for these black men living on the streets, finding somewhere to urinate was a problem, one that reflected a significant aspect of their lives.

Judgement cannot be avoided, then: the idea that the whole process of assessing knowledge claims could be reduced to a matter of procedure, for example by applying a check-list, is mistaken. Furthermore, it is false to assume that all judgement is 'subjective' and therefore erroneous (see Chapter 5). As I indicated, judgements in the context of inquiry rely on a notion of reasonableness, but the obvious question that arises concerns what is *sufficient* plausibility or credibility for us to accept a knowledge claim as true or false? This reliance on a notion of reasonable doubt derives from Peirce's rejection of the Cartesian idea that genuine knowledge can only be derived from premises that are beyond all possible doubt (see MacDonald 2020). In everyday life we make judgements about what is beyond reasonable doubt in a flexible way according to the likely costs of error of different kinds. For example, most of the time, whether or not Tiddles is sitting on his mat is unlikely to be consequential, and we would probably accept any evidence about his location more or less at face value. However, if there is some suspicion that he has attacked next door's prize parakeet, determining whether he was actually on his mat at home at the relevant time is a matter of rather greater importance, and we will insist on stronger evidence about his whereabouts. Indeed, should we be taken to court by the neighbour in a demand for compensation, we may need to have very strong evidence to show that Tiddles was not the culprit, given that he has a record of bird murder. By contrast, in the case of research, the threshold of what is beyond reasonable doubt should be the same whatever the costs of error. Furthermore, this threshold must be relatively high, if researchers are to be able to make a legitimate claim to produce findings whose likely validity is greater than that of those from other sources. And such a claim is essential for the justification of research (Hammersley 2011b: chapter 5).

There is a parallel here with legal judgements, where the evidence must indicate guilt beyond reasonable doubt in order to convict someone. A relatively high threshold is essential to minimise the risk of false convictions; there is a commitment to err on this side, at the risk of the guilty going free. A similar policy is also essential in science if its authority is to be maintained. Here, the most serious danger to be minimised is including a false conclusion in the body of scientific knowledge. This is important to avoid because, as we have seen, existing scientific knowledge is employed to assess the likely validity of new claims to knowledge; and, if too much of what is taken to be knowledge is false, scientific progress becomes impossible – the body of scientific knowledge has been corrupted.

It is also worth pointing out that we do not usually engage in the process of assessing knowledge claims on a purely individual basis. In academic research there is an obligation to make public our findings to colleagues and to try to resolve disagreements through rational discussion within the research community. In doing research we anticipate the likely reactions of colleagues, and adapt our decisions about what conclusions should be reached, what evidence is sound and sufficient, and so on, accordingly. Furthermore, academic discussion may reveal to us that what we have accepted as adequately plausible or credible should not be accepted; or it may reveal errors in the presuppositions on which we have relied. It is the function of the research community to act as a corrective to the beliefs of individual researchers in this way (Hammersley 2011b: chapter 7). While this will not always be successful, over time it should bring us closer to the truth about the matters being investigated. In other words, a self-correcting learning process is involved.

Conclusion

In this chapter I began by examining some of the reasons why social scientists are hesitant about using the words 'true' and 'truth'. I showed that, while these relate to genuine philosophical problems surrounding the concept, they do not warrant abandoning it. Indeed, I argued that it cannot be abandoned because it defines the goal of research – to produce knowledge – and is implicated in much essential human activity more generally. Furthermore, the alternative epistemological positions that some social scientists have adopted to avoid the problems with truth are not defensible. In response, I sought to outline a conceptualisation of truth that is reasonably cogent and can provide a basis for social research.

I then went on to consider the process by which we should determine whether we are justified in believing that particular research conclusions are true. I suggested that, fundamentally, this is the same basis on which we all judge the validity of knowledge claims in everyday life, albeit with researchers adopting a more careful and self-conscious approach than is common on the part of others much of the time. The issues addressed by social science are challenging ones, and the conclusions it produces are almost always more complex and uncertain than the knowledge claims involved in dealing with everyday matters: they require evidence that is not easy to produce or assess. I also noted that research needs to operate with a higher and more consistent threshold as regards accepting claims as true than is the case in many (though not all) everyday decisions. Finally, I emphasised the important role that research can play in correcting false assumptions, that it is (or should be) a collective learning process.

A commitment to addressing threats to the truth of knowledge claims is an obligation for researchers (see Chapter 13). Yet not only is there hesitancy about the concept of truth, there is also a tendency on the part of many social scientists to underestimate the likelihood and severity of threats to validity in their work (for examples, see Foster et al. 1996, McSweeney 2022a, 2022b; Gomm 2022). This endangers the effective practice of social research.

Notes

1 Hesitancy and distrust about the concept of truth are not restricted to social scientists: see Campbell 2011: chapter 1.
2 For discussions of the philosophical problems surrounding truth see, for example, Allen 1993; Williams 2002; Blackburn 2005, 2017; Campbell 2011; Glanzberg 2021.

3 They can, however, be closer to or further away from the truth. This is sometimes labelled verisimilitude. It should be noted that there are problems with the very distinction between internal and external validity: Hammersley 1991.

4 There is an associated, and contested, issue about the nature of mathematical truth, but it is not central to my argument here.

5 It is perhaps necessary to emphasise that I do *not* regard evaluative judgements as necessarily irrational: see Hammersley 2022c. Even less do I believe them to be unimportant.

6 Of course, if we defined 'dying' as 'no longer being alive' this statement would be *logically* true. This highlights the need for clarity in the meanings being given to terms.

7 This was central to the arguments of some ancient sceptics: see Burnyeat and Frede 1998.

8 Burnyeat and Frede (1998) document the contortions involved in trying to escape this contradiction.

9 For a discussion of the complexities associated with categories like social class, gender, and ethnicity, see Hammersley 2020.

10 This is not to deny, of course, that some people may be better placed than others to discover particular truths. What I am rejecting is the claim that one group has all the advantages, or suffers all the disadvantages, in understanding society.

4   Fact

'Fact' is a term that is used unselfconsciously by some social scientists, employed hesitantly by many, and rejected by others. Like 'truth' – with which it is, of course, closely related – it is (I will argue) indispensable, but it touches on challenging philosophical issues. For example, some commentators have been preoccupied with the fact that facts are socially constructed, which is sometimes taken to imply that they could therefore always be constructed differently. This appears to carry dramatic implications for the practice of social science, suggesting that what is required is imagination rather than rigour, and that the model should be art and literature not science. A first requirement in addressing these issues is clarification of the meanings that can be given to the word 'fact'.

Different senses of the term

'Fact' can have several meanings, formed through various contrasts:

1   *Fact versus value*. Here 'factual' refers to knowledge claims about what phenomena exist or do not exist (in particular contexts at particular times, or more generally), their properties and propensities, how these have changed (or remained the same), why they exist when and where they do, and so on. By contrast, value claims relate to what is good or bad, right or wrong, what ought to be done, who is responsible or to blame for what, and so on, as judged in terms of one or another set of values.
2   *Fact versus opinion*. In these terms a fact is a statement that can reasonably be taken to be true, as compared with an opinion that is much more open to question as regards its validity. Very often the contrast implied is between what can be known to be true with great confidence versus what is mere speculation or is believed because of a desire for it to be true. However, it is better to think in terms of a continuum, with few if any claims falling under the heading of absolute truths, and many ranged between the extremes. As I argued in the previous chapter, empirical knowledge claims are all fallible, but this does not mean that they are all as likely to be true as one another. Sometimes 'fact' in this sense is taken to refer to what is generally accepted as true within a given community, as opposed to the beliefs

DOI: 10.4324/9781003350354-5

of individuals. But *descriptions* of what is believed, collectively or individu-
ally, are not the same as epistemic assessments of the truth of knowledge
claims; after all, conventional wisdom may prove to be false.

3   *Accurate versus false claims.* Here the contrast is between what is taken to be
true, with justifiable confidence – 'it is a fact' – and what is believed to
be false. There is an important difference from the contrast with opinion,
since opinions are not by definition known to be false (though in some
usage falsity is implied), their validity is simply uncertain to a significant
degree; whereas in this third sense of 'fact' its opposite is definitely regarded
as false.

4   *Fact versus fiction.* Here, factual accounts are aimed at documenting reality, as in sense 1, but are contrasted with fictional accounts that relate to
imagined situations, people, and events. These do not purport to represent
what happened in some real situation, though they may sometimes claim
to represent more general truths about what commonly occurs, or might
reasonably be expected to occur. Imaginative literature is predominantly
fictional, but fictions are also sometimes used in scientific inquiry as aids to
thinking. The function of fictions in social science can be representational –
as with composite types indicating the typical features of some class of
person, situation, etc. – but often they are designed to aid recognition of
some set of facts. In the case of Weber's (1949) ideal types, for instance,
these are a means of determining explanatory facts: they serve as a template
with which facts can be compared, in order to determine where they correspond to and where they deviate from the type.

5   *Fact versus theory.* This is sometimes simply a formulation of point 2 or 4,
depending on what meaning is given to 'theory' (see Chapter 12). However, it can also refer to a functional distinction between explanatory claims
(a theory) and the evidence (the facts) that allow us to judge the theory's
validity. On this interpretation, facts may be restricted to descriptions
rather than explanations (the distinction between descriptions and explanations is addressed at the end of this chapter).

Given this range of meanings, it is important that, whenever the word 'fact' is
used, the particular sense intended is clear. In this chapter I will focus primarily
on the third sense of the term. And I will be concerned with *empirical* facts –
true descriptions or explanations of actually existing phenomena – rather than
logical or evaluative facts, if such there be.

Hesitating over fact

The concept of empirical fact is implicated both in the idea that research
builds on data and evidence and in the assumption that it produces 'findings'
that count as knowledge (Becker 2017; see Chapter 7). In practice, both are
treated as potentially having the character of facts, of being true. However,
there is often reluctance on the part of social scientists, especially qualitative

researchers, to use the word 'fact' in this way – it is dismissed as 'positivist' by some. This parallels a similar hesitancy over use of the words 'true' and 'truth' (see Chapter 3). In both cases, the problem arises from a belief that these words imply that there can be empirical knowledge claims whose validity is beyond all possible doubt. And, given that there cannot be such claims, the conclusion is often drawn, with Nietzsche (1967:§481), that there are no facts 'only interpretations'.

However, use of the word 'fact' does not imply infallibility, or an absence of interpretation. One source of this error is that, like 'truth' and 'knowledge', 'fact' is an achievement word (Ryle 1949:216; see Chapter 3): we cannot sensibly speak (except humorously) of an erroneous fact, any more than we can talk of erroneously knowing something. Yet, use of these words does not imply absolute certainty about the validity of the claims made; simply that, until further notice, those claims are being treated as true, in other words as stating facts.

There is an additional, closely related, problem with the meaning of 'fact'. Like 'experience' and 'data', it is a term that operates at the interface between our making sense of things and the things themselves. As a result, there is an ambiguity about whether 'fact' refers to a *true statement about the world* or to the *feature(s) of the world* to which that statement relates. In other words, are facts linguistic or ontic in character? If we say that, at the time I am writing this, it is a fact that the cost of living in the UK is currently increasing even more sharply for families on low incomes than for other families (see Karjalainen and Levell 2022), are we referring to the statement itself as being the fact or is it the cost of living increases that are the fact? That this ambiguity should arise is not surprising because if a factual statement (in sense 1) is true it corresponds (in relevant respects) to the related state of affairs in the world (see Chapter 3). What we should conclude from this is that 'fact' is a relational term: it implies correspondence between a statement and the state of affairs to which that statement refers; it must relate to both. But whether this correspondence holds is an empirical, not a semantic, matter.

It should be clear, then, that this relational conception of 'fact' does not imply that the state of affairs to which a factual statement refers is brought into existence simply by making the statement. Stating that 'the cost of living for poorer families is higher than for better off ones' did not make it true; it was true already. But there is a deeper issue here that could lead us to think that we determine how the world is by what we think or say about it. This arises from a longstanding philosophical argument about whether the world is structured independently of the categories we use to understand it, or whether those categories themselves produce whatever structure there is. This argument gains added complexity in the case of social phenomena, since here researchers are using categories to understand people who themselves use categories to understand the world (this is sometimes referred to as a double hermeneutic). All this can encourage adoption of the idea that there are no phenomena, no states of affairs, independent of our statements about them; and the door is thereby opened to relativism or scepticism. But, for reasons I have already tried to explain, this is a false path to take (see Chapter 3).[1]

Given these complex issues, it is perhaps not surprising that many researchers hesitate over using the word 'fact', put it in scare quotes, or even reject it. As we have seen, they may do this because they believe that the term implies that there can be absolute proof of the truth of empirical statements, when they know there cannot be; whereas, as I have indicated, this implication does not follow at all. Meanwhile, others put 'fact' in scare quotes or reject the word because they believe that how we formulate the world, what discourses we use, 'constructs' how it is. In short, they insist that the world is psychologically or socially constituted, rather than existing and having particular character-istics independently of the sense we make of it. This is one form of what is referred to as social constructionism (see Introduction), and requires further consideration.

Are facts still facts when they are socially constructed?

It is worth spelling out this notion of the social construction of facts, in order to assess it. In its most radical form, the claim is that the inquiry pathways by which facts are produced involve choice points, with these potentially leading to divergent outcomes, to different 'factual' conclusions; and that this simulta-neously makes the world one way rather than another. In other words, what are facts depends upon this process, not on the nature of phenomena inde-pendent of it. From this point of view, there are not just different versions of reality but 'multiple realities'. Indeed, here the term 'reality' is an empty signifier – there is, in fact, nothing lying behind 'factual' accounts to which they might or might not correspond. Yet we can recognise that facts – in the sense of true statements about the world – are psychologically and socially produced without adopting this radical form of constructionism. The one does not automatically imply the other (see Chapter 7). We do not usually take the idea that there could be multiple realities seriously when we are making everyday inquiries about, say, the times of trains or the location of loved ones. This is even true of constructivist philosophers when they are off-duty. Given this, it is unclear why we should take the idea seriously when we are engaged in social research.

How we understand the world does indeed depend, in part, on our catego-ries, but these only provide the frame within which answers to questions about the nature of the world make sense, the categories do not determine what answers fit the evidence; alternative answers are allowed for. Furthermore, these categories are not fixed, and they do not come out of nowhere but rather out of prior learning in dealing with the world. We routinely (and necessarily) draw a distinction between categories and judgements that 'work', in the sense of allowing us to pursue our purposes effectively, and those that do not. In other words, we need to recognise the pragmatic character of categories: that they come out of our engagement with phenomena that exist independently of us, and that they are shaped by that process. While this does not, of course, guarantee that our categories and beliefs will be true, it introduces a process of self-correction which can lead in that direction.

In line with this, we need to exercise caution over what we take the phrase 'social construction' to mean. Some senses apply as much to physical as to social reality. For example, in identifying a piece of rock as sedimentary I am relying on a set of categories that have been socially generated, notably by geologists. However, the characteristics of that rock are not in any sense created through my describing it as sedimentary, nor were they created by invention of the concept of sedimentary rock. Rather, those characteristics are a product of the geological history of the earth. Geological knowledge about those characteristics could be wrong, of course, but it has been confirmed in many different ways over a long period of time, so that we are justified in accepting it as true (until further notice).

It may seem that social facts are different from physical ones in this respect. For instance, the fact that some pieces of metal in my pocket are money is clearly socially constructed in a sense that goes beyond the fact that we recognise them as being made of copper, nickel, and zinc. Outside of the relevant money economy they would be virtually worthless (other than to a coin collector). However, it is important to recognise that I did not construct them as money by labelling them as such; indeed, they would have this character whatever attitude I took towards them. Nor is what counts as money determined by economists or, for that matter, bankers. Thus, despite the way its socially constructed character differs from that of physical phenomena, money also exists independently of any investigation of it (see Hammersley 2019b). We can even recognise that the very notion of a fact is a socio-historical construction (Poovey 1998) without denying the independence of matters of fact from our interpretations of them. While the categories we use are cultural constructions, and while we decide what belongs in them, nevertheless whether particular phenomena have the characteristics that warrant their inclusion within a category (whether they are facts) is neither simply a cultural construction nor an arbitrary result of researchers' decisions.

The unavoidability of fact

You may have noticed that, in much of this chapter, I have myself used the term 'fact' quite liberally. As already stated, it is impossible to do without the idea that there can be statements that refer accurately to phenomena that exist independently of them. Even those social researchers who explicitly deny that there are facts cannot avoid reliance on this concept. Of course, this leaves plenty of scope for disagreement about what is and is not a fact. For example, while some trans-activists and feminists deny that there are biological facts which differentiate females from males, they insist that discrimination against trans-people and women is a fact (as, indeed, it frequently is). Similarly, while anti-racists rightly deny that there are biological races, and insist that race is a social construction, they treat racial discrimination as a fact (as, indeed, it frequently is).

If we can use the word 'fact' even though our knowledge is never infallible, and despite the fact that the phenomena we study are socially constructed, an obvious question concerns when, and on what basis, we should treat a knowledge claim as true and therefore as referring to a factual state of affairs: one which exists, and has the characteristics attributed to it, independently of any claims about it. As I explained in Chapter 3, in doing this we operate on the basis of judgements about plausibility and credibility, employing a threshold of likely validity above which we treat knowledge claims as stating facts, in other words as likely to be true (until further notice). We regard them as beyond *reasonable* doubt, *even though they are not beyond all possible doubt*. And we revise our judgements later if new evidence arises, correcting errors that we discover. Or, at least, this is what we ought to do.

Types of fact

Factual statements can take at least two forms: descriptions or explanations. Both of these play an important role as evidence in social research, as well as potentially comprising its findings.

Descriptions are especially important as evidence. They document specific aspects of particular sets of objects – for example, features of a person or situation, or of a collection of people or situations. However, descriptions never exhaust all aspects of the phenomena they refer to, instead they only focus on relevant ones. This is because factual statements, in the sense I am using the term here, are always answers to questions, and there are always multiple questions that could be asked about any set of phenomena. For instance, we would produce different descriptions from observing people in a supermarket according to whether we were interested in the social class of the clientele, how those we observe decide what to buy, or how they navigate their way around the aisles without bumping into one another (most of the time). It is also worth noting that descriptions can vary in their complexity. There are those that simply assign some object or property to a category, for example 'these customers are working class', but there can also be more elaborated descriptions, such as 'these working class customers are elderly women, and they frequently examine products very carefully before putting them into their baskets'. What is mentioned will depend on what is judged to be relevant to the questions being addressed.

By contrast, *explanations* are concerned with *why* some set of phenomena and their features exist or occurred, or varied in the way that they did, proposing that this is a product of particular factors operating directly or indirectly upon them. In other words, explanations are concerned with identifying a causal process that has brought about the existence of some phenomenon or the occurrence of an event, its possession of particular properties or variation in these. For instance, why is it that the elderly, female, working-class customers observed in the supermarket tend to evaluate their purchases more carefully than others?

Explanations always rely on descriptions, at least in the minimal form of phenomena having been assigned to categories. Sometimes descriptions may serve as explanations, in that the categories to which objects are assigned may imply certain causes (for example, to describe a death as a murder is to imply that it was caused by the deliberate actions of someone). However, it is important to recognise that two quite different cognitive functions are involved here: while all explanations rely on descriptions, they go beyond them in explicitly claiming that some feature, event, or outcome was a product of some set of causes. If the explanation is true then that causal relation exists or existed: it is a fact.[2]

Conclusion

In this chapter I began by distinguishing different senses that can be given to the word 'fact'. However, my main focus has been on the contrast between true statements about the world (facts) as against false ones. I examined the main reasons why many social scientists are reluctant to refer to facts: for instance because they believe this implies that statements of fact must be true beyond all possible doubt. But this implication does not follow from use of the word 'fact'. I also noted how there is an ambiguity in using this word: it may refer to a statement about the world or to a state of affairs existing in the world. I argued that this ambiguity arises because the word 'fact' is relational: it refers to a correspondence between the two.

I went on to examine those forms of epistemological radicalism, often listed under the heading of social constructionism, which assume that reality is discursively constituted. I argued that we can recognise that our understanding of facts is psychologically and socially constructed without taking this to imply that there are no phenomena existing independently of factual statements that correspond to them if they are true. I also examined the notion of social construction itself, again insisting that this does not necessarily lead to the sort of epistemological radicalism – relativism or scepticism – that it is often taken to imply; and that there are good reasons not to adopt those positions.

Finally, I distinguished between descriptions and explanations as different types of fact, these both playing a crucial role in the research process, whether as evidence or as findings.

Notes

1 Anyone who wishes to get a sense of the complex philosophical issues surrounding 'fact' can gain this by consulting Mulligan and Correia 2021. Perusal of the opening few sentences should be sufficient confirmation. Their account both outlines and exemplifies the complexities.

2 While some social scientists baulk at the idea that there can be causes of social phenomena, they are only right to do so if the term is used in a very narrow sense. See Hammersley 2014a: chapter 1; Chapter 10.

5   Bias and objectivity

The terms 'bias' and 'objectivity' each have multiple senses, but many of these are closely related, with bias treated as the problem for which objectivity is the remedy. However, both these terms are frequently used without being clearly defined, and their main senses have been subject to increasing challenge in recent decades. In this chapter I look at the meanings given to each of them, and examine criticisms directed at them. I conclude by arguing that what these words refer to must be a central concern in the pursuit of social science, if it is to flourish.

Bias

Accusations of bias are a recurrent event in social science. They may be made by social scientists themselves – a classic example is the acrimonious dispute within anthropology over Freeman's (1983, 1998) critique of Margaret Mead's (1928) account of adolescent life in Samoa (Ember 1985; Bryman 1994). But outside groups also sometimes criticise academic work as biased, especially when it does not fit with their preconceptions, or does not serve what they see as their interests. Interestingly, in many cases, the reaction to an accusation of bias is a counter-charge; this illustrates the fact that it is not just research itself but also evaluations of research that can be accused of bias (for examples, see Hammersley 1995: chapter 4, 2016).

As should be clear from this, bias is usually viewed negatively, as something that can and should be avoided or eliminated. There is variation, though, in the meaning given to the term, and there have been disagreements about the main sources of bias, as well as about whether (or how) bias can be remedied. Furthermore, in recent times the concept has been rejected by some qualitative researchers, or even treated as referring to something positive (see Roulston and Shelton 2015). In this section, I will begin by examining different meanings of the term 'bias', before focusing on one of these, what can be referred to as researcher bias.

The meanings of 'bias'

In most usage, 'bias' refers to a form of error, and this indicates that its meaning is dependent upon the concept of truth (see Chapter 3). However, there is an

DOI: 10.4324/9781003350354-6

important ambiguity that needs to be mentioned. This concerns whether 'bias' applies to the *process* or to the *outcome* of research: in other words, to errors in researchers' decision-making or to errors in the conclusions presented as findings. Obviously, the two are related, in that the first often causes the second; though bias in decision-making does not *automatically* lead to error in conclusions; and sound decision-making does not *guarantee* that the conclusions will be true. Here, I will treat 'bias' as referring to a form of *systematic* error *in how research is carried out* that is likely to lead to the distortion of research findings *in one specific direction*. An analogy would be loaded dice, where some numbers are always more likely to come up than others. The contrast is with 'haphazard error'; in other words, error which approximates to being random, the errors in different directions tending to cancel each other out.

Several potential sources of systematic error are commonly identified. One is 'sampling bias', for example resulting from use of a sampling frame that excludes or under-represents a particular section of the target population. A second is measurement bias, where features of measurement procedures tend to result in systematic error, for instance the use of leading questions in questionnaires. Similar sorts of bias can, of course, occur in qualitative interviews. Another source of systematic error is reactivity, where people's knowledge that they are being researched, or reaction to the research method or to characteristics of the researcher, may lead to error in a particular direction. For instance, people may answer questions in such a way as to present themselves in a socially acceptable fashion; or when being observed they may modify their behaviour to avoid what could be viewed as immoral or illegal. But perhaps the most common meaning given to 'bias' is what I will call 'researcher bias': a tendency for researchers' background preconceptions, preferences, or commitments to produce decisions in research design, data collection, and analysis that confirm those preconceptions or serve those preferences or commitments.

In the past, guarding against all these kinds of bias was regarded as central to sound research practice, and this is still true today in many quarters. However, as I noted earlier, the concept has been challenged, particularly that of researcher bias, and I will focus on this here.

Researcher bias

To recap, the core idea is that because of their background preconceptions, preferences, and commitments, researchers may make decisions in ways that are likely to produce false conclusions, or to rule out true ones. This can be done deliberately, where the aim is to produce evidence in support of a case, but the most common form of researcher bias is an unconscious (or, at least, less than fully conscious) tendency to err in one particular direction. While little social research is simply propaganda, there is quite a lot that appears to be biased in this second way (for examples, see Foster et al. 1996; Gomm 2022; McSweeney 2022a, 2022b).

There are at least two mechanisms potentially involved here, though they frequently operate in tandem, and are not easily separated in practice. First, the social location of the researcher may provide more direct access to some ideas, forms of understanding, and sources of information than others. For instance, it has been argued that the characteristic experiences of males and females differ in ways that make it difficult for researchers of one sex to understand the attitudes and behaviour of the other; and the same argument has been applied to members of different ethnic or 'racial' groups. The second mechanism is the tendency for the prior beliefs, perceived interests, and value commitments of researchers to lead to more ready acceptance of some assumptions or conclusions; and to rejection, or more reluctance to accept, others.

Sources of researcher bias can also arise from within the research process itself. For example, it may result from a desire on the part of the researcher to produce novel or startling findings, or alternatively ones that confirm previous results that have been questioned. It has also been pointed out that once a particular interpretation, explanation, or theory has been developed or adopted by a researcher, he or she may tend to interpret data in terms of it, be on the lookout for what would confirm it, or may even shape the data production process in ways that tend in this direction; while overlooking counter-evidence. In the context of data collection, this can arise in interviews, for instance not just through the questions asked, or not asked, but also through the *way* they are asked and through interviewers' responses to what informants say. Researchers' expectations about the findings of an inquiry are also a potential source of systematic error, one that has been recognised in experimental investigations, with various precautionary strategies recommended (Rosenthal and Rosnow 1969; Rosenthal 1976). Very often, the solution proposed is to employ highly structured methods that are designed to proceduralise the role of researchers, so as to reduce the risk that their social and personal characteristics will lead to bias. This reflects a particular conception of objectivity, what I will refer to as objectivism.

Qualitative inquiry is often thought to be particularly prone to researcher bias, not least because here, as is often said, 'the researcher is the research instrument'. It is suggested that this makes the research process much more vulnerable to the influence of the social and personal characteristics of the researcher than in more structured forms of data collection. There is also the danger, particularly highlighted in the context of ethnography, that if a researcher 'goes native' he or she will interpret events solely from the point of view of the people being studied, taking over any biases that are built into their perspectives (see Hammersley and Atkinson 2019:91–92). Here again, in the past at least, the remedy often proposed was an effort to maintain objectivity; though with this term interpreted in a different way from objectivism, one that is closer to reflexivity (see Chapter 10).

Objectivity

Like 'bias', the word 'objectivity' also has several meanings, and these are by no means always clearly distinguished in methodological discussions. One refers to an unbiased orientation in carrying out research, but 'objective' is also some-times employed as a synonym for 'truth', so that an objective account is one that accurately portrays the objects it is designed to represent. There are fur-ther complications arising from the fact that, while the opposite of 'objec-tive' is 'subjective', this latter word carries a whole range of meanings, deriving from the following contrasts: mental/physical; internal/external; private/pub-lic; implicit/explicit; judgement/procedure; idiosyncratic/shared; variable/fixed; particular/universal; dependent/independent; relative/absolute; as well as erroneous/true.[1] In much usage in the past, many of these various distinc-tions were blended together, reflecting the influence of a particular conception of objectivity that emerged within psychological and social inquiry during the early twentieth century, what I will refer to as 'objectivism'.

Objectivism

Objectivism treats the word 'objectivity' as combining many if not all of the meanings that contrast with the various senses of 'subjective' I listed. It amounts to a particular conception of the nature of scientific inquiry, how it should be pursued, and what it produces. Its starting point is the idea of researcher bias that I outlined earlier; that as researchers we are often led into error by false preconceptions and prior preferences that result in our tending to 'find' what we expected or wished for, rather than what is actually there. In short, subjec-tive factors of various sorts (mental, internal, private, idiosyncratic) are treated as leading to false conclusions. From this it is concluded that we must try to engage in inquiry in a manner that is unaffected by our personal and social characteristics.

Several strategies are proposed for avoiding such 'subjective' error. One is that we should restrict what we treat as evidence to that which is directly observable, and to what can be inferred *logically* or via *calculation* from such data (on the meaning of 'data' and 'evidence' see Chapter 7). Of course, there is an important sense in which nothing is directly observable with *absolute* certainty (see Chapter 3), so this tends to turn into the idea that researchers should rely only upon the sort of observational capabilities that every human being has, or that anyone could be easily trained to employ, rather than on spe-cialised forms of interpretation, intuition, or connoisseurship. More broadly, there is the insistence that we must commit ourselves to a research design that specifies in procedural terms what will be done through all stages of the process of inquiry; not just in data collection but also in drawing conclusions from the data. In this way, it is assumed, the inquiry process can be largely insulated from the effects of subjective factors, and thereby rendered transparent; an ideal that is sometimes referred to as procedural objectivity (Eisner 1992). For instance, in the case of interviews, these must be carried out according to a schedule that specifies the exact words of each question, and the order in which ques-tions are to be asked. Furthermore, there will be standard instructions regarding how to react to respondents' queries, or their failure to answer.

Such proceduralisation is viewed not only as of value in itself, in that it minimises error deriving from subjectivity, but also as facilitating the use of checks on validity via replication: the same procedures can be followed by others to discover whether they produce the same results. By contrast, so the argument goes, if researchers do their work in a more flexible and variable fashion, as is true of most qualitative investigations, it is impossible to test the reliability of their conclusions. Furthermore, this flexible approach is likely to be affected by all manner of hidden threats to validity deriving from the distinctive subjective characteristics of the researcher.

Objectivism has been particularly influential among quantitative researchers, and often forms the basis for criticism of qualitative inquiry. However, it has itself been challenged, on a number of grounds:

- While it is true that we may be led astray by subjective factors (whether conceived of as mental, inner, inexplicit, particular, or whatever), it is also the case that we are inevitably dependent upon personal knowledge, capabilities, and motivations in producing *any* evidence or conclusions. For instance, we necessarily rely upon our senses in making observations, and what we perceive cannot be completely separated from expectations, habits, and cultural tendencies. Much the same applies to the processes of inference involved in producing evidence from data and drawing conclusions from this. Here, we cannot operate in a strictly logical or calculative manner, we cannot avoid employing assumptions, ampliative inference, and imagination. Even in physical science, it is impossible to reduce research to the following of explicit procedures (Polanyi 1958).

- It may be true that evidence coming from the use of ordinary everyday perceptual capabilities is less open to potential error than that which relies upon specialised knowledge and skills; or, at least, that it is easier to check the results. However, this does not mean that reliance solely on those capabilities is more likely to lead to sound knowledge of the kind desired. What needs to be observed may not be accessible to ordinary capabilities, so that the questions we are addressing cannot be resolved by appeal to evidence of this sort. Similarly, drawing the kind of conclusions required, in a sound manner, will also often depend upon specialised knowledge and skills. We should not choose the research questions we address solely on the basis of which ones are open to objectivist investigation, since this risks turning social research into a trivial pursuit.

- Subjective factors are not the only cause of error in observation and reasoning. For example, we may accurately note that the sun rises in the sky each morning, but to describe it as moving over a fixed earth is still a misleading description of what is happening. Similarly, we may correctly document the similarities between two pieces of rock and infer, on the basis of their easily observable characteristics in comparison with other types of object, that they must have been produced by a common causal process when, in fact, one rock is igneous while the other is a product of sedimentation. In other words, we may employ careful observation and uncontroversial modes of inference yet still reach false conclusions. It could even be that the questions we are asking are based on false assumptions: the effect we are seeking to explain may not exist, our hypotheses may be misconceived, and so on. What this indicates is that being objectivist in how we carry out inquiries does not guarantee that our conclusions are objective, in the sense of true.

- It is never possible to ensure that different researchers will apply a procedure in exactly the same way, however closely it is specified. This is particularly true in social research because much depends upon how the people being studied respond to the procedures employed. It is in the nature of human social interaction that the actions of each side will be shaped by the other. Moreover, since what people experience in the data collection process will inevitably depend partly on their background expectations, cultural habits, social interaction with the researcher, and so on, there is always considerable danger that what they *actually* experience will be different from what was *intended* in the research design. For example, even if experimental subjects are all presented with the same instructions they may interpret these in discrepant ways, and behave differently as a result: two subjects may interpret the experimental instructions in divergent ways and as a result produce the same type of response; whereas, had they interpreted the instructions in the same way, their responses would have been different. Furthermore, and of particular importance, proceduralisation of the research process increases reactivity, in the sense that the people being studied will behave in ways that are very different from how they would in normal circumstances.

- Applying a procedure may rule out the use of some personal capability that is essential if error arising from its use in particular circumstances is to be avoided. Procedures and guidelines can serve a useful function in reminding us of what needs to be taken into account, but they can also result in our failing to notice what could be relevant and important in particular cases. There are issues too about what is and is not measurable by means of fixed procedures, which relate to the nature of the world being investigated. Some have argued that social phenomena are complex, in the technical sense that they are systems subject to influence by a very large number of variables that themselves influence one another. If this is true, it may not be possible to capture them via standardised procedures.

For all these reasons, the fact that two or more observers using the same procedure agree in their observations, or that two or more researchers using the same analytic procedure come to the same conclusion in working with the same data, does not in itself indicate that their reports are true, even where they have operated independently of one another. Instead, their work may be affected by errors, including those built into the procedures employed, that lead in the same false direction. Objectivism points to some strategies that may reduce researcher bias, but these do not guarantee this, and they may carry distinctive threats to validity of their own.

While it is probably the case that most social scientists have never adhered completely to objectivism, much methodological thought and research practice has been strongly affected by it. And it continues to have influence today. However, among qualitative researchers in recent times there has often been rejection not just of objectivism but of the concepts of bias and objectivity too, as I noted earlier.

Radical challenges

Criticism of the concepts of bias and objectivity has taken two quite different forms. Some critics have argued that conventional approaches to achieving objectivity are inadequate, that they fail to deal with the most significant forms of bias, and that a 'stronger' interpretation of it is required, based on what has come to be called standpoint epistemology. Meanwhile, others have rejected the concepts of bias and objectivity completely, on the grounds that these presuppose a conception of truth as correspondence to independently existing phenomena; and this is often labelled 'positivist' and rejected by positions that draw on epistemological relativism or scepticism (see Chapter 3). I will outline each of these lines of criticism in turn.

Standpoint epistemology

It has been argued that, even in natural science, the procedures that are supposed to eliminate bias fail to detect and deal with fundamental systemic forms of it that arise from the unequal structure of society, for example deriving from the fact that, predominantly, scientists are white Western males. And this can be seen as a particularly severe problem in social science, given that it involves much greater reliance on researchers' own background experiences and knowledge in collecting and analysing data. The solution usually proposed to deal with this deep-seated form of bias relies on the argument that marginalised and oppressed groups within Western society – the working class, women, or subordinated racial groups, for example – or those subject to colonialism or neocolonialism in other societies, have, by virtue of their position (their 'standpoint'), better access to a true understanding of the world than members of the dominant group.[2] The rationale put forward for this varies, but an influential version is the idea that those who are oppressed develop a capacity to understand the world from both their own position and that of their oppressors; whereas the latter are restricted to their own perspective. Another is that in suffering oppression one witnesses how society really operates, this being hidden from others. At the same time, most versions of standpoint epistemology have recognised that members of marginalised and oppressed groups may be influenced by the dominant ideology, and thereby could perpetrate unconscious bias in how they make sense of the world. The proposal is that researchers work with these groups, and that, through a dialectical process, the potential insights provided by a subordinate standpoint can be identified and developed. Here, the concept of bias is retained, but transformed: its main, if not exclusive, application is to the way that dominant groups misperceive the world because of their social location, by contrast with the 'strong objectivity' (Harding 1993, 1995) available to oppressed or marginalised groups.

The relativist and sceptical challenge

Other qualitative researchers completely reject the concept of bias, or at least its applicability to qualitative inquiry (Galdas 2017:1). This may be based on the idea that this type of research involves a different epistemology from quantitative work, one which denies the distinction between subject and object, on which the conventional conception of bias is presumed to rely. Instead, qualitative research accounts are treated as, primarily, expressions of the background assumptions and personal characteristics of researchers. In these terms, what otherwise might be referred to as bias can be seen as a positive feature, through appealing to some notion of personal authenticity. Meanwhile, quantitative inquiry, and the objectivism to which it frequently appeals, may be dismissed as committed to an epistemology that is not only indefensible but also has negative political effects, ones that are characteristic of modernity more generally: domination by impersonal, supposedly rational organisational forms.[3] Objectivism requires researchers to separate themselves from all inherited assumptions, from the particular circumstances in which they are located, and from their other background characteristics: all passion and personal involvement are to be removed. In effect, they are to turn themselves into robots.

However, what is rejected here is not just objectivism but the concept of objectivity itself. The relativist version of this argument insists that any research can only produce a partial perspective on a reality that is not directly accessible. The truth of any knowledge claim is necessarily relative to the framework of assumptions on which it relies, and there are multiple such frameworks, so that what is treated as true or biased will depend upon which framework is adopted. The concept of objectivity is rejected because it implies that research can capture phenomena in their own terms, as they exist independently of any investigation, and this is dismissed as presupposing a 'view from nowhere'. On this basis, the concept of bias is rejected, or given a positive interpretation.

The sceptical version of the argument is that research simply *constructs* what counts as reality; nothing exists independently of this process. This is frequently given the label 'social constructionism' (see Introduction and Chapter 4). Here, there is even less room for the concepts of bias and objectivity, since there is nothing for research accounts to correspond to or deviate from. There are simply multiple constructed 'realities'.

In short, rejection of objectivity stems from denial of the possibility or desirability of knowledge, as conventionally understood (see, for instance, Lather 2007). From both relativist and sceptical points of view, the distinction between scientific truth and imaginative fiction is erased. Also involved may be the idea that any claim to objectivity amounts to inauthenticity, since it involves an attempt (inevitably futile) to escape the distinctive personal characteristics, or unique social location, of the investigator. What is required, instead, it is often argued, is that accounts be explicitly presented as just one *construction* amongst others. Some insist that it should be a construction that openly acknowledges its constructed character: the fact that it necessarily draws on particular resources in particular circumstances for particular purposes. What is also frequently demanded is recognition that there can always be other, even contradictory, accounts of any scene; with choice amongst these being in an important sense undecidable or arbitrary, or a matter of personal self-expression or ideological commitment.

For relativists and sceptics, there is a sense in which no-one is biased, or everyone is biased (and a good thing too). It is argued that research cannot be objective because all researchers have interests and value commitments of one sort or another that shape their work (see, for example, Gitlin et al. 1989). Indeed, the production of diverse, even conflicting, accounts may be valued. For example, some qualitative researchers appeal to the model of art, rather than science: the aim is to connect with diverse emotional sensibilities, rejecting science's concern with universal cognitive validity (Leavy 2015); the emphasis, instead, is on creative diversity. However, there is also, frequently, a political aspect to the argument, with research accounts being judged according to whose interests they are taken to serve. Mainstream social research is frequently portrayed as a form of domination that reproduces the socio-political status quo. This is contrasted with research that creatively generates diverse perspectives, or amplifies the voices of those in subordinate positions within, or on the margins of, society, thereby (it is hoped) bringing about progressive change.

In the next section, I will assess these criticisms. Following this, I will argue that it is quite possible to recognise the importance of objectivity, in the sense of minimising the risk of researcher bias, as defined earlier, without adopting the 'solution' proposed by objectivism. Indeed, one of the most influential statements of objectivity as a principle, that of Max Weber (1949, 2012; see Bruun 2007), took a very different line: the task was not to *eliminate* the effects of 'subjective' factors but to try to ensure that they do not distort research findings. In other words, these factors were not regarded as *inevitably* causing bias; in fact, they were also seen as potentially generating important new ideas. Moreover, minimising their negative effects was to be achieved by clear recognition of the limits of social science and through a reflexive process of monitoring the risk of bias, rather than the adoption of standardised procedures.

Assessing the challenges

There are undoubtedly problems with objectivism, these were noted earlier; but it points to genuine potential sources of error and the need to counter them. In my view there is no warrant at all for rejecting the concepts of bias and objectivity, as traditionally understood. This is because the radical epistemological positions on which criticism of them relies are unsustainable.

Standpoint epistemology tends to assume that the pressure for bias comes entirely from a single (previously neglected) source: from the interests and ideology of a dominant group. Here there is reliance on a crude, dichotomous conception of society, with different forms of standpoint epistemology prioritising different subordinate groups: the working class; women; sexual, racial or ethnic minorities; and those with disabilities. Once the complex structure of modern societies is recognised, however, it is clear that bias can come from, and go in, a variety of directions. For example, most people occupy several positions within society, not just one, and the relationships of these with one another are multi-stranded. Each of these positions will give them access to some kinds of information while making it less likely that they will obtain other kinds; and it will also open them up to some sorts of potential bias, and reduce the risk of others. There is no standpoint that is free from the threat of bias, any more than there is any position in society which entirely prevents recognition of the truth. Another problem concerns how we are to identify who does and does not belong to the epistemically privileged category of person; only a small proportion of the Western working classes have ever been communist, and not all women are feminists, for example. Finally, as I noted in Chapter 3, standpoint epistemology is internally inconsistent: its claim that one standpoint is epistemologically privileged while another lacks the basis for understanding society is either circular or depends upon the conventional epistemology it purports to reject (Bar On 1993; Hammersley 2011a; van den Berg and Jeong 2022).[4]

Equally serious problems arise with epistemological relativism and scepticism. These, too, are self-undermining because they claim universally valid knowledge about the relativity or impossibility of knowledge. As a result, they cannot be adopted as coherent positions. Furthermore, they undermine not just the idea that knowledge claims can be assessed epistemically but also that they can be judged in ethical, political, or aesthetic terms. They undercut evaluations of what is good or right, sublime or ugly, that purport to go beyond sheer expression of opinion, just as much as claims about what is and is not true. While there can be no view from nowhere – we all necessarily have starting assumptions which we take for granted until further notice – this does not mean that we cannot learn to recognise errors and correct them. The scepticism which insists that there is no foundation for knowledge, *and that therefore nothing can be known*, is the alter ego of the discredited foundationalism it rejects: both assume that we must have an indubitable foundation if we are to achieve knowledge. However, what we require, instead, is a self-correcting (albeit always fallible) learning process, and this is precisely what inquiry can provide (see Chapters 2 and 3). Of course, approaches to research can (and do) vary in how dogmatic they are: in how far they allow for discovering mistakes. But, even though the danger of unconscious bias is ever-present, we can take precautions designed to identify and overcome this, thereby opening the way for learning.

It is also important to note that all of these radical epistemological positions themselves have a tendency to encourage bias. This is most obvious in the case of relativism and scepticism, since they deny its existence and thereby allow it to operate freely. Furthermore, in practice, relativism and scepticism are applied selectively, and this (too) amounts to a form of bias. Meanwhile, though standpoint epistemologies usefully point to sources of bias that may previously have been overlooked, they too encourage bias arising from their own particular political commitments, on the mistaken assumption that these cannot lead to error.

Re-assessing bias and objectivity

It is important to note that the concepts of bias and objectivity are not unique to the context of research: in everyday life we routinely recognise that some sources of information, news outlets, and perhaps even some of our friends, are subject to systematic error of particular kinds, as a result of commitments or preferences they have, or their social location: for instance, they may tend to give us a rosy picture of some things and an overly negative account of others. Similarly, we sometimes suspect that match referees or high court judges are biased, and we regard this as a breach of an objectivity they have an obligation to maintain. What is involved in this mundane notion of bias is simply the idea that there has been deviation from the path required to serve the appointed task, *and deviation that was motivated by considerations that ought to have been treated as irrelevant*. In these terms, objectivity can be defined as taking account of everything that is relevant to a decision, and of nothing that is irrelevant. I suggest that there is no more reason to reject this idea of objectivity in relation to research than in these other contexts (Rescher 1997).

Indeed, the concepts of bias and objectivity are of particular importance to research because of its distinctive rationale: that it is capable of producing knowledge claims that are more likely to be true than those coming from other sources (see Chapter 2). Achieving this requires a vigorous and sustained attempt to eliminate error in the course of carrying out investigations, including that which may come from the effects of the researcher's own preconceptions, attitudes, and commitments (however laudable). Any tendency to downplay the need for this, or to obscure directions from which bias may come, threatens epistemic integrity (see Chapter 13).

It is especially important to recognise that we ourselves can be biased, not just other people whose views we do not share. Furthermore, accusations of bias must only be made judiciously and on the basis of evidence. It is worth noting that Freeman (1983, 1998) spent a considerable amount of time and effort in showing why he believed that Mead's research was biased. The sheer fact that a researcher has particular views or interests does not, in itself, tell us that their research findings are a product of bias, even when the findings seem to serve those views or interests. Such a correlation is grounds for *suspicion*, but not for *conviction*. Too often, accusations of bias are used simply as weapons in pitched battles among researchers who tend to treat their own positions as beyond question; indeed, they may immediately reject any questioning of these specifically as a product of bias on the part of the critic.

Thus, researchers have an obligation to scrutinise their own practices for any signs of bias, as well as those of others, and to do so judiciously. Where necessary, checks need to be carried out, for example by comparing the information coming from diverse sources, along with the results produced by different modes of analysis (see Chapter 11). Equally important is to engage with viewpoints other than our own, whether through thought experiments or via discussion with people holding them. In carrying out any research, it is necessary to offer evidence that ought to convince any member of the research community, irrespective of their perspective, commitments, or social background. Equally, it is important to engage with any criticism that is directed at our own work, since this may reveal hidden biases, whether our own or those of others (Hammersley 2011b: chapter 7). Needless to say, this does not require us to accept the views of critics, but we must have strong grounds for rejecting them and be prepared to spell these out. These are important components of a commitment to objectivity.

Conclusion

In this chapter I have sought to clarify the meanings of the terms 'bias' and 'objectivity' as these apply to social research. I explored an influential approach to these concepts that I labelled objectivism. While recognising problems with this, I insisted that these do not count against the importance of a concern with bias and a commitment to objectivity.

In the middle part of the chapter I examined criticism of the concepts of bias and objectivity that relied upon various forms of epistemological radicalism – standpoint epistemology, relativism, or scepticism. I explained why these alternative positions are unsustainable: above all, they suffer from internal incoherence. Furthermore, their effect is to allow or promote particular kinds of bias, and in some cases to undercut the very possibility of social research.

I argued that a defensible conception of researcher bias treats it as deviation from the best path for finding true answers to one's research questions. And the meaning of 'objectivity' is following that best path, which requires taking into account all that is relevant, but *only* what is relevant, to the task of producing empirical knowledge. Of course, in practice, it is not easy to identify the right path, but seeking it, and trying to stay on it, are essential (see Chapter 13).

Notes

1 Barone (1992) also recognises the mutual semantic dependence of 'objective' and 'subjective'. However, he takes a very different position from the one adopted here, declaring that the concept of 'objective truth' is dead, and pointing out that, if this is true, then the idea of subjectivity as a form of error must also disappear.

2 For the feminist version of the argument, see Flax 1983 and Hartsock 1983. As I noted in Chapter 3, the original source of standpoint epistemology seems to have been Marxism.
3 For discussion of such a critique in the context of health care, see Porter and O'Halloran 2009.
4 This is not to deny, of course, that some people may be better placed than others to discover particular truths. What I am rejecting is the claim that one group has all the advantages, or suffers all the disadvantages, in understanding society.

6 Rigour

The word 'rigour' is closely associated with conceptions of scientific method that are modelled on the natural sciences, ones that have shaped much quantitative social research. In these terms, rigour is a virtue: it is concerned with carrying out research in such a way as to minimise known and unknown threats to the validity of the results.[1] Qualitative researchers have sometimes also applied this concept to their work, but they have usually emphasised that the requirements of rigour here are different from those involved in quantitative investigations (see, for instance, Rolfe 2006 and Morse 2015). However, in recent times there has been an increasing tendency for qualitative researchers to reject the concept of rigour as implying inflexibility, in the sense of sticking to a fixed plan rather than adapting to circumstances, or as stultifying the research process, thereby preventing creativity and innovation (Sandelowski 1993). These critics have questioned what they take to be the positivist philosophical assumptions on which this concept relies, and sometimes even rejected any commitment to the model of science.

In this chapter I will begin by outlining how 'rigour' has been interpreted in the context of quantitative research, and then consider the question of whether it is also applicable to qualitative work. I will argue that it is a requirement in both, and so the chapter ends with a discussion of issues that need consideration in assessing the rigour of a study, whether quantitative or qualitative.

Rigour in quantitative research

The words 'rigour' and 'rigorous' have been caught up in disagreements about whether social research can be scientific, and what counts as science (see Chapter 2). In the first half of the twentieth century, 'rigour' in social science generally came to mean employing techniques to measure and control variables, and was closely associated with quantitative method, in the form of experimental or survey research. In large part, this reflected the influence of positivist interpretations of the nature of science, which tended to treat *physics* as exemplifying scientific method (Halfpenny 1982; Bryant 1985). The control of variables was regarded as essential to rule out the effects of confounding variables, which could lead to correlations being treated as indicating causal relationships when they did not. Nevertheless, this model for scientific method was modified and

DOI: 10.4324/9781003350354-7

supplemented to take account of distinctive features of psychological and social inquiry. The main additions included random assignment to treatment and control groups in experiments; the use of sampling techniques and statistical control in surveys; as well as questionnaire design aimed at obtaining objective data from respondents. One elaboration of this notion of rigour has been to treat it as a property of research *designs*, so that these can be arranged in a hierarchy, usually with experimental method, for instance randomised controlled trials, at the top, these serving as a 'gold standard' (see Hammersley 2015b).

Additional features of this notion of rigour are the requirement that hypotheses must be specified at the start, along with the methods to be used in testing them; that there must be no appeal to private sources of knowledge; and that the research should be carried out in a fashion that minimises the effects of the individual characteristics of researchers. These led to attempts to proceduralise the research process, to what is referred to in Chapter 5 as objectivism. So, as far as possible, the way in which data are collected and analysed must be designed to avoid any influence by the researcher(s) that could cause bias. There is some variation in what this has been taken to entail, but in the context of survey research, for example, it involves systematic attempts to standardise interviews or the administration of questionnaires, so as to minimise both random and systematic error in the data collection process.

The notion of rigour also had implications for the assessment of research findings: very often it was assumed that this must take the form of replication. In the case of experimental research, it should be possible for others to repeat the investigation, thereby checking that the findings had not been generated by some uncontrolled source of error in the original study.[2] In order for replication to be possible, the data collection had to be carried out in an environment largely controlled by the researcher, and in a manner sufficiently specified that others could repeat it. While it was not usually possible for social surveys to meet this requirement closely, they could be repeated (in principle, at least), and the reliability of the instruments employed (for example, attitude inventories) could be tested prior to their use, to check whether they produce consistent results.

These are what were regarded as some of the essentials of rigour in the context of quantitative research, and this conception of rigour was often treated as if it should apply to all research, thereby sometimes leading to criticism of qualitative work as lacking rigour. In short, research findings should be assessed in terms of such criteria as internal and external validity, reliability, and measurement validity.[3]

Does the concept of rigour apply to qualitative research?

At face value, it would seem that qualitative researchers ought to be as concerned with minimising the risk of error in their investigations as quantitative researchers. And, indeed, as I noted previously, some early advocates of qualitative methods were keen to establish that their work could be just as rigorous as that of their quantitative colleagues, albeit usually via somewhat different means. However, over time, many qualitative researchers came to reject the concept of rigour in favour of alternatives that were felt to be more appropriate in the context of qualitative inquiry, such as reflexivity (see Morse 2015; see Chapter 10).

Sometimes, this stemmed from opposition to the assumptions about science on which the concept of rigour appeared to rely, in favour of an alternative that was taken to be a more realistic characterisation of how scientists actually do their work. Here, appeal could be made, for example, to the writings of Michael Polanyi (1958), a physical-chemist-turned-philosopher who pointed out that scientists necessarily rely on tacit knowing (which he sometimes formulates as 'personal knowledge'), insisting that it is not possible *fully* to explicate and therefore to proceduralise even natural scientific investigations, in the way that the concept of rigour is often taken to require. Another source that could be used to support scepticism about the concept of rigour is philosopher of science Paul Feyerabend's (1975) insistence that, in practice, there is no such thing as scientific method, that scientists employ whatever means seem likely to be successful; indeed, that methodological specifications can get in the way of this (see also Phillips 1973; Lakatos and Feyerabend 1999). Here he was echoing the physicist Percy Bridgman, who had declared that 'the scientific method is doing your damnedest, *no holds barred*' (Bridgman 1955:535).

However, it should be underlined that, generally speaking, these authoritative sources did not deny the need for the measurement and control of variables, and much criticism by qualitative researchers of the concept of rigour has, instead, relied on the argument that there are fundamental philosophical differences between quantitative and qualitative approaches. It was often argued that quantitative research had failed to live up to its own conception of rigour, not just by laxity but because its methods are not appropriate, given the distinctive and complex nature of social phenomena. For example, from early in the twentieth century it was pointed out that the measurement scales used by quantitative social researchers rarely fully capture the concepts to which they relate (Blumer 1940; see Hammersley 1989a). Furthermore, it was argued that the very attempt to control variables often has effects on the people being studied that can lead to erroneous conclusions (Rosnow 1981). For instance, in the case of experiments it is uncertain whether what happens in the laboratory would also occur in the social circumstances to which the findings are supposed to apply. To take a very famous example: Did Milgram's (1974) subjects agree to inflict pain (so they thought) on their fellow subjects because of their assumptions about scientific experiments, so that they would not have been willing to do this in other situations (Miller 1986)? Similarly, it was pointed out that requiring survey interviewers to follow closely specified scripts tends to render their interactions with respondents artificial, and thereby may produce data that do not provide a sound basis for inferring people's opinions or attitudes as these operate under normal circumstances. Also noted, again in relation to survey research, was the not uncommon discrepancy between what people say and what they do (Deutscher 1973; Jerolmack and Khan 2014). The extent to which the production of quantitative data necessarily involves processes of interpretation, and potential misrepresentation, was emphasised

(Cicourel 1964; Phillips 1973). In light of such problems, an increasing number of social scientists advocated the use of qualitative methods in the second half of the twentieth century, and this has continued up to today. As a result, the fortunes of 'rigour' as a methodological concept suffered a decline, though it enjoyed a revival in the context of 'mixed methods' research.

Indeed, many qualitative researchers have rejected this concept completely, on the basis of radical epistemological, ontological, and/or axiological assumptions, these often implying rejection of the model of science in favour of inspiration drawn from the humanities and the arts (see Introduction).[4] Relativist and sceptical ideas were frequently involved here. If it is assumed that a research study can only offer one perspective on the world among many alternatives, with these being treated as each true in its own terms, then the concept of rigour must either be abandoned or totally transformed. Much the same is true if it is assumed that research creates the phenomena that it claims to represent, as claimed by some forms of social constructionism. Furthermore, if the aim of research is held to be bringing about practical improvement or wider social change, then, at the very least, rigour may be regarded as a low priority, except insofar as it is seen as likely to increase the persuasive force of the conclusions reached, and thereby the impact of the research.

As a result of these developments, many 'anti-positivist' approaches to qualitative research shifted attention away from countering threats to validity – indeed, the concept of truth was often rejected along with that of rigour (see Chapter 3). Instead, the emphasis often fell on political and ethical considerations, or on how to generate and develop new theoretical ideas or aesthetically pleasing fictions. This has not been true across the board, however; and there are those who have given attention to what is required if the likely validity of qualitative research conclusions is to be increased (for example, Mahoney 2001; Gerring 2007; Small 2009; Duneier 2011; Becker 2017). This has sometimes been prompted by criticism of particular studies. An example is the reaction to Alice Goffman's (2014) ethnographic investigation of an impoverished black neighbourhood in Philadelphia, a study that became very widely known outside the field of sociology, and was subjected to considerable scrutiny. One commentator challenged the validity of her account on the basis of a parallel with legal evidence-checking (Lubet 2018), thereby providing an interesting alternative to the notion of rigour associated with quantitative research, though one that has not been widely adopted.

Furthermore, in practice, most qualitative researchers have continued to be concerned with the quality of their work in ways that relate to a broad conception of rigour, as concerned with minimising the chances of reaching erroneous conclusions; sometimes broadly along the lines characteristic of historians. For example, most qualitative researchers are aware that they may be deceived by appearances, and also by their own predispositions and preferences; and they recognise that minimising these dangers requires carrying out necessary checks – for instance, of the validity of competing interpretations of the data. Also widely endorsed is the need to report research accurately, and not to exaggerate the likely validity of a study's findings. Of course, whether researchers are *sufficiently* aware of threats to validity, and engage in *enough* checking to minimise the risk of error, is another matter. And this is a question that can usefully be addressed to current quantitative as well as qualitative studies (see Laher 2016).

Rigour across qualitative and quantitative inquiry?

In the Introduction to this book, and elsewhere, I have argued that the same general methodological concepts apply to both quantitative and qualitative research; because they should have the same general goal of discovering true answers to factual research questions. At the same time, I believe it is counter-productive to apply a concept of rigour that is tailored to the use of a particular type of method across the board; and there was certainly a tendency to do this in the past, and perhaps still is today in some quarters. Thus, it is true that the strategies used in quantitative research to try to ensure rigour will often not be applicable in qualitative research; but, equally, we should note that, for example, random assignment to treatment groups is not applicable to most surveys, while random sampling of populations is rarely used in experimental research. It is important to recognise such differences, and to avoid treating some methods as necessarily deficient in rigour by comparison with others. The key consideration concerns what sort of rigour is required to answer the research questions being addressed.

Rather than there being a hierarchy of methods, or a single 'gold standard', most of the methods used by social scientists have both advantages and disadvantages as regards rigour; with these varying in their significance depending upon what is being investigated and the circumstances in which this is to be done. While many types of threat to validity can arise whatever method is used, how each can best be addressed, and indeed the extent to which they can be dealt with effectively, will vary according to the methods of data collection and analysis being employed. For example, systematic comparison of multiple empirical cases is not very common in qualitative research today, it can be very difficult to achieve, but it is an important means of checking causal interpretations. While reliance on thought experiments, or inference from what is taken to be a plausible theory, also have value, they are less effective.[5] The control exercised over competing explanatory hypotheses in a great deal of qualitative work is weaker than in much, though not all, quantitative research (just as the statistical control employed in survey research is weaker than experimental control). At the same time, qualitative research has greater capacity than most quantitative investigations to trace causal processes operating in particular cases. And there are methodological costs involved in both experimental and survey research: as already mentioned, there is the problem of the relationship between what is found under experimental conditions and what happens 'in the wild'. Similarly, investigation of cases through survey questionnaires or structured interviews usually allows only relatively superficial description. To reiterate, it is important to recognise the strengths and weaknesses of different methods rather than assuming some hierarchy.

It follows from my argument here that, while the same *criteria* of assessment apply in evaluating the findings of quantitative and qualitative studies (truth and relevance), there will necessarily be variation in the indicators that can be used to determine whether serious threats to validity have been minimised (see Hammersley 2022e). Dealing with these threats may, of course, require combining several methods of data collection and/or analysis, perhaps ones from different sides of the qualitative-quantitative divide; though such triangulation should not be seen as a simple solution (see Chapter 11). While it is important to draw a distinction between assessing the likely validity of research findings and evaluating the rigour with which a study has been carried out, the two are closely related: the second type of assessment serves as one basis for the first.

Assessing the rigour of any study involves, then, examining the extent to which the main threats to validity have been addressed. Some of the relevant questions that must be asked include:

1   *Conceptualisation issues*: Are the key terms in the research questions sufficiently clear to allow them to be answered in a relatively unequivocal fashion? Note that this is not a matter of whether concepts have been defined and operationalised at the beginning of a study but rather whether the senses given to them are sufficiently clear in the research report. In other words, conceptual clarification is often a goal towards which an investigation must move, rather than one that can be achieved at the start. Indeed, the research questions themselves may change significantly over the course of inquiry.
2   *Case selection issues*: Do the case or cases generated or selected for investigation provide a sound basis for drawing conclusions about competing answers to the research questions? One issue here concerns the sampling of cases. Where the aim is to generalise to a population: Are there good reasons to believe that the sample will be representative of that population in relevant respects? Where the aim is to produce an explanation, what is important is whether the cases provide the comparisons that are required for assessing the likely validity of competing theories; for example by allowing the control of confounding variables.
3   *Data issues*: Would the sort of data collected have allowed analysis of the kind required to answer the research questions? Does it provide sound evidence about the attitudes or behaviour that are the focus of inquiry? Does it allow for the identification of potential causal mechanisms?
4   *Analysis issues*: Are the analytic methods employed appropriate both for the research questions being addressed and for the sort of data being used? Relevant here are the dangers of imposing simplistic interpretations, or cherry-picking data to support an interpretation. Equally important is the question of whether all reasonable alternative hypotheses have been assessed.

In addition, there are at least two overarching questions that need to be asked:

Does it seem likely that the researcher was fully aware of the demands of rigour, and carried out the research in light of these?

Did the researcher (or funders or other stakeholders) have preconceptions, preferences, or interests that would favour one set of answers to the research questions rather than another? Note that a positive answer to this question does not indicate that bias was operating, only that there is a need to check whether this was the case.

While by no means exhaustive, these questions identify issues relating to rigour that all researchers, and anyone assessing particular studies, must consider. There will also be particular threats to validity that need to be taken into account that are made salient by the methods used, the questions addressed, and the contexts in which the research took place.

Conclusion

In this chapter I began by outlining the conception of rigour that came to be associated with quantitative social science in the twentieth century, and then examined the responses of qualitative researchers to this. I argued that while that conception is clearly not appropriate for all forms of social science, a more general notion of rigour – as involving care and thoroughness in dealing with threats to the validity of the findings – does have this broad relevance. I emphasised that there is no hierarchy of methods in terms of rigour, that particular methods of selecting or generating cases, producing data, and analysing it, have distinctive advantages and disadvantages. Finally, I outlined some threats to validity that apply to both quantitative and qualitative research, and the relevance of these to the process of assessing the likely validity of research findings on the basis of the rigour with which a study was carried out.

Notes

1 On the concept of threats to validity, see the early and highly influential discussion by Campbell and Stanley 1963.
2 In recent times, this has produced what is often referred to as the reproducibility crisis, see Ritchie 2020.
3 In my view, there are serious problems with the interpretation of these concepts, see Hammersley 1987, 1991.
4 Though it should be noted that the idea of scientific rigour has long had some influence within those disciplines too, especially in the study of history and of language. For the case of history, see the classic discussion provided by Langlois and Seignobos 1898.
5 While Grounded Theorising and Analytic Induction both depend upon comparative analysis, it is rare for these to involve the investigation of both necessary and jointly sufficient causes of outcomes. By contrast, this *is* a feature of Qualitative Comparative Analysis. See Cooper et al. 2012.

7 Data and evidence

What should count as data or evidence? Are they what a researcher goes out to collect, what is written up in data records, or what is presented or referred to in a final research report as supporting the conclusions reached? Can data capture the phenomena we want to understand? Are data *found* in the world or are they *constructed*? These questions address issues that underpin the whole research enterprise, and relate to significant disagreements among social scientists.[1] Yet, while in the methodological literature there is much discussion of *types of data or evidence* – experimental or survey responses, transcripts of social interaction, field-notes, documents, and so on – of *how they are generated* – through observation, participation, questionnaires, interviewing, and collection or elicitation of relevant documents (online or offline) – and of *how they should be analysed*, the issue of exactly what the terms 'data' and 'evidence' mean is usually taken for granted.

'Data' and 'evidence' are frequently used as synonyms, but in this chapter I draw a distinction between the two. This captures a tension between the assumption that what these terms refer to are givens, independent of the process of inquiry, and the idea that they are constructed by the researcher for the purposes of producing knowledge. While it is common to use the phrase 'data *collection*', as if data were objects lying around in the world waiting to be gathered up, etymologically a datum is a premiss on which an argument is based. Both these senses of the term are important. Empirical research must ultimately relate to what happens in the world independently of our investigations of it, otherwise it would offer only a fictional narrative. On the other hand, data are the building blocks by which empirical knowledge is produced; and, I will suggest, data are transformed into evidence through this process.[2]

Therefore, I will define 'data' as referring to what is closer to the pole of being simply given, while 'evidence' refers to what has been constructed out of data to address research questions. However, this is a dimension not a dichotomy: even data are selected by, and often actually produced through the work of, researchers; equally, evidence must retain reference to what is independent of the research process if it is to serve its function. There is an analogy here with an industrial production process, with raw materials (data) being transformed into more refined material (evidence) that eventually feeds into creating an end-product (research findings). Thus, in any investigation, some of the data

DOI: 10.4324/9781003350354-8

are gradually turned into evidence during the course of inquiry, but the starting point is not the purely given (even raw materials must be found and extracted), and evidence still retains external reference (final products contain something of what was in the raw materials).

This process of transformation is clearest in the case of unstructured data: these must be translated into categories relevant to the research questions being addressed, so that they can count for or against potential answers to those questions. By contrast, structured data are already assigned to research-relevant categories at the point of collection: what 'structure' means, in this context, is a set of categories, or a scale, that operationalises the key concepts built into the research questions. So, for instance, while the questions making up a questionnaire are not the same as the research questions of the study concerned, the terms in which they are framed will be relevant to those research questions. However, even though there is a sense in which structured data are evidence from the start, they will usually be transformed subsequently, for instance through the use of descriptive and inferential statistics (Bateson 1984).

As this illustrates, the extent of the difference between data and evidence varies across different kinds of research, this partly reflecting the distinction between hypothesis-testing and more 'inductive' approaches (see Chapter 8). Some of the unstructured types of data employed in qualitative inquiry are produced independently of the research process (for example, official reports or personal diaries produced before the research began), and even where they are generated by the researcher their relationship to a research topic is much more uncertain than is the case in quantitative inquiry, not least because the initial focus of qualitative investigations is usually much more broadly defined, and is open to development and change. Nevertheless, in both cases evidence is a product generated over the course of the research.[3]

Data are much more varied in function than is evidence. Evidence operates solely to support or to count against candidate answers to research questions. By contrast, data, as well as being a resource that may subsequently be turned into evidence, can provide background information about the phenomena being studied. In addition, it can be used to determine what questions may or may not be fruitful to address. It might suggest, for instance, that an assumption built into one or more of the initial research questions is false, leading to their reformulation or abandonment (though here it is serving what is close to an evidential function). It can also prompt new research questions that are worth investigating, as well as potential answers to research questions that had not previously been considered.

Data

As commonly used, the term 'data' refers to a heterogeneous collection of phenomena, such as: published statistics, and calculations based on these; ticks in boxes on a questionnaire or observational record, and frequencies, ratios or measurements derived from them; written documents (online and offline), or extracts from, or summaries of, these; images and/or sound recordings in various media (photographs, drawings, films, TV programmes, online video-clips, podcasts); observational or interview fieldnotes; audio- or video-recordings of events or interviews, along with transcriptions. Some of these (official statistics, questionnaire responses, images) are undoubtedly data in themselves, but others may perhaps be better thought of as *containing* data (fieldnotes, recordings, transcripts). This is one indication of the need for greater clarity about what the term means.

I suggest that there are several key components of the meaning of 'data': reference; givenness; relevance; stable persistence; and public availability. Some of these are relatively straightforward in character, but others are associated with challenging philosophical issues.

Reference

What I mean by 'reference' is that, in defining objects as data, we are not interested in them for themselves but rather treat them as signs that provide us with a basis for developing research questions and answering them. So, for instance, ticks in boxes on a questionnaire, or the words in an audio-transcript of an unstructured interview, are not usually of interest for their surface features but rather for what they are taken to represent: opinions or attitudes of respondents, say, or information that informants can supply that is germane to the research. Similarly, descriptions of observed behaviour provided in fieldnotes are of interest to the extent that they enable us to identify types of action that are pertinent to our research interests.

This points to the importance of recognising the distinction between data and the phenomena to which they are taken to refer. This may seem obvious, but it can easily be forgotten in the midst of data analysis. Moreover, the relationship between the two is not unproblematic. We can ask: Do data as representations capture everything (or even everything relevant) about the phenomena being represented? Are there phenomena important to us that are not representable via data, at least of the kinds that we have available? Or may it be that they cannot be represented through literal descriptions of the kind typically used as data in social research, but only via more allusive or poetic forms of description?[4] At one level, this comes down to the issue of whether every question is researchable, to which the answer is almost certainly 'no'. But the issue is deeper than this. Doubts about whether human social life can be truly represented by the sort of data employed by social scientists have most frequently been directed at quantitative inquiry, with some qualitative researchers claiming, for instance, that only data in which the voices of participants are captured in their own terms can offer authentic representations. But questions about whether phenomena have been authentically represented can be, and occasionally have been, directed at qualitative data too (Tyler 1986; MacLure 2011, 2020). There are also issues about what 'authentic representation' means, of course. These developments are one of the reasons why some qualitative researchers have turned to imaginative literature and art, and away from science, as the model for understanding human social life.[5]

At issue here, in part, is the function of research. It is certainly true that it cannot *reproduce* experience or reality 'as it is'. However, that is not its purpose: its task is to answer specific questions (see Chapter 2). And, while some questions will not be answerable, others will be – even if they do not extend to all those we would like answered. Furthermore, what is involved in social research is not fundamentally different from the efforts we all make in everyday life to answer questions about particular people and relationships, groups, institutions, social trends, etc. The sorts of data employed are also similar, for the most part, despite important refinements in social science methods. Observing and asking questions are ubiquitous means of gaining knowledge; questionnaires are used as administrative devices; audio-recordings are made 'for training purposes'; and so on. The aim of social research is not to discover 'the meaning of life' or 'the true nature of human being'; its task is more prosaic, closer to our everyday concerns, and therefore more straightforward – though still far from easy to achieve.

Givenness and relevance

These two further features defining 'data' were mentioned near the beginning of this chapter, and I noted there that they are in tension with one another. What I mean by 'givenness' is that the informational content of data is not entirely determined by the research process.[6] Some types of data approximate to being simply given, waiting to be collected and analysed, notably documentary material that was already available prior to the research: organisational records, official statistics or reports, personal diaries or online blogs produced in the past, and so forth. However, most of the data used by social scientists are at least partly generated by them, and perhaps co-constructed with research participants. Clearly, questions can clearly be raised, and have been, about whether what these offer is independent of the research process.

Even in the case of extant documents, we must recognise that they have usually been produced for some purpose and with some audience(s) in mind. Furthermore, it is the researcher who identifies them as data that are likely to be useful in a particular research project. And their contents will often be selectively appropriated, on the basis of judgements about what is and is not pertinent. But, as already noted, researchers play an even greater role in producing other sorts of data. And the rhetoric of 'data collection' or 'data gathering', with its implication that data lie around in the world waiting to be picked up, is especially problematic here. So, does this mean that there can be no sense in which data are simply 'given'? And, if that is the case, does this undercut the very possibility of there being evidence that could support or count against particular answers to research questions?

It is important to note that what is involved here is not a matter of either/ or. Data may be the result of a considerable amount of productive work on the part of researchers but still offer information that is 'given', in the sense that the content was not entirely determined by the research process. As already noted, the constructive role of the researcher is particularly conspicuous in the case of structured data, whether produced by experiments or surveys. The people being studied are put into situations where, to some degree at least, they have little option but to produce what will count as data for the study concerned. But, while subjects are constrained to respond in a relevant fashion, *which available option they choose can be independent of the researcher and the research procedure*; even if this is not always the case, as a result of reactivity, suggestibility, desire to please, and so on. A parallel here is that, in everyday life, we recognise that people do not always tell the truth, but this does not lead us to deny that they can *ever* tell the truth, or to believe that we can *never* rely on what they say as accurate. Indeed, we could not live like that. Similarly, there is no reason to dismiss structured data as simply a product of the research process rather than of the phenomena being investigated.

Considerable work on the part of the researcher is also involved in producing most kinds of qualitative data. Video-recording offers an instructive illustration. The data produced by this are sometimes taken to be closest to documenting reality directly. Yet, of course, many decisions go into producing a recording: the researcher decides the time and place to record; where to place the camera and any additional microphones; when to switch the camera and microphones on and off. There is also the work that the camera itself does: it will record only what is within focus, this varying somewhat according to the type of lens used. The sounds recorded will only be within certain frequencies and levels of loudness. Aside from the limitations implied in what has already been said, each of the objects within focus will usually only be visible from some angles, for example it may not be possible to see the faces of all the people 'in shot'. It should be clear from this that, even here, what is produced is not 'reality in all its fullness', if that phrase has any meaning.

At the same time, it is essential to recognise, once again, that, while the decisions of the researcher and the capacities of the audio-video recording equipment shape what is recorded, they do not *determine* its content. There is a clear distinction between a research recording of this kind and what is involved in making a movie, where there are actors following a script, in a specially designed set, under the control of a director or producer. Thus, what is available in a video-recording is 'given' as well as being constructed as relevant by the researcher. Of course, the ways in which such data have been produced must be taken into account in the analysis, insofar as this could lead to misleading inferences from these data. Similar points can be made about the process of *transcribing* audio and video data (see Hammersley 2010b).

In summary, data can be 'given' in the sense of their content being independent of the research process in significant respects, even though the researcher has played a major role in producing them. And it is only because of the researcher's contribution that data can have its third necessary characteristic: *relevance*.

Data are only data if they are judged to be potentially germane to a research topic – not everything counts as data. As already indicated, the difference from evidence is a matter of degree, and this is greatest in the case of qualitative inquiry. One reason for this is that here research questions are often only vaguely defined at the beginning, may be reformulated, and can even be fundamentally changed, or abandoned, over the course of an investigation. As a result, what is relevant can be uncertain and unstable: what was earlier regarded as relevant may no longer be, while what previously did not count as data may come to be regarded as important. Indeed, as noted earlier, data can play a significant role in shaping judgements about what are and are not fruitful research questions. So the process is reciprocal.

Where highly structured data are employed, the data are pre-designed to be relevant to answering some set of research questions, so that judgements about relevance are less uncertain than in the case of qualitative inquiry; though, for instance, it is common to include an 'Other' response category in questionnaires, on the basis that this may produce data that indicates errors in prior assumptions about what is relevant. Furthermore, even in quantitative research the focus of inquiry can sometimes change over its course. Returning to the issue of givenness: the structuring involved in both quantitative and qualitative research must *not* be designed to produce particular answers to the research questions, only to facilitate gaining true answers to those questions.

Stable persistence

A fourth component of the meaning of 'data' is that, unlike many of the phenomena that research data refer to – which are often (though by no means always) ephemeral in existential status, only continuing to exist in people's memories – data must persist in a stable and accessible fashion so as to be open to repeated examination. This feature is of obvious importance if data are eventually to serve as evidence in a research report for or against some answer to a research question. But data must also be open to repeated examination if they are to facilitate the development of fruitful research questions and the pursuit of answers to them.

It may be asked whether this feature necessarily implies distortion of the phenomena represented. For example, if we repeatedly listen to an audio-recording of an interview, or read a transcript of it, are we moving further and further away from the actual experience of the interviewer and interviewee, since this occurred in 'real time'? I suggest that whether this is a problem depends upon the purpose for which the data are to be used; and, for most purposes, repeated examination of the data will enhance understanding. There is a danger here, once again, of assuming that the aim of research is to capture experience or reality 'as it is', rather than to answer specific questions about it.

Publicly available

A final feature of data is that people other than the researcher can access it, at least in principle. This is clearly necessary in the case of data serving as evidence in research reports. While it is rare for all of the data used in an investigation to be presented, some of it, transformed into evidence, will usually need to be included, in one form or another. Furthermore, it is increasingly demanded that the data collected by projects are archived, and one of the functions this serves is for readers of research reports to check how data were transformed into evidence (Hammersley 1997). This feature of data rules out what Sanjek (1990) refers to as 'headnotes', in other words what is available to a researcher solely via memory. Of course, this is not to deny that memories inform the production of data – whether as a basis for informants' accounts, or as the source of a researcher's fieldnotes written up after the event. Furthermore, the analysis of data will almost always draw on background knowledge not directly contained in the data, perhaps including familiarity with the people and settings to which they relate. But the public availability of data is nevertheless essential.

A question arising here concerns whether the data are 'the same data' when accessed by people other than those directly involved in their production? This is an issue that has been central to discussions about secondary analysis, especially in the context of qualitative research (Mauthner et al. 1998; Moore 2006; Hammersley 2010a). Indeed, it has been suggested that, even when researchers revisit data that they themselves produced in the past, there may be a significant sense in which these have become different from how they were.

In response to this, it is tempting to draw a distinction between the data themselves and the meaning they are taken to have, with the first not changing even though the second may well do so. Indeed, the same data can be used as a basis for quite different inferences, depending upon the questions they are being used to answer (though the answers should not be contradictory). While this is not an entirely satisfactory argument, since data are never purely given in character, nevertheless what is at the data end of the spectrum is less likely to be open to reasonable doubt than what is at the evidence end of it. For example, it is true that transcripts of audio-recordings are constructions, in the sense that various decisions are made about how to represent textually what is heard on a recording (Hammersley 2010b), but, generally speaking, there will be less disagreement about what is heard and how to transcribe it than there is about inferences from what was recorded to conclusions about the beliefs and attitudes of the speaker, or about the validity of any statements he or she made. There is a scale of likely error involved here. So, for the most part, data can be treated as fixed in character even though they may be open to different interpretations; and despite the fact that, sometimes, the process of data production may need to be unpicked, for example by returning to an audio-recording to produce a new transcript.

Reference, givenness, relevance, stable persistence, and public availability are necessary and sufficient conditions for something to serve as data. In other words, data must have all of these features to a sufficient degree, and anything that has all these features can count as data. As we have seen, there are certainly questions that can be asked about some of these features, but those questions do not warrant any form of fundamental epistemological doubt about the viability of social research, or redefinition of its goal.

Evidence

Earlier, I noted how some data are turned into evidence during the process of research. And I defined 'evidence' as facts that support or count against the likely validity of an answer to a research question (on facts, see Chapter 4). Not all evidence comes from data: in doing empirical research we necessarily rely on what we take to be existing knowledge, both that produced by previous research and some derived from common human experience. However, evidence coming from data plays a crucial role.

What is important here is both the reliability of the data, in the straightforward sense of whether it can be relied upon (for example, that what is reported did happen, or was actually said), and the question of whether the inferences drawn from it about the validity of research conclusions are likely to be sound. Very often, in coming to conclusions about both these matters, it is essential to rely on *further* evidence (see Chapter 3). This may involve employing multiple sources, a strategy sometimes labelled triangulation – though that term has a range of meanings (see Chapter 11). Similarly, where an explanation is being sought for some event or outcome, evidence may need to be provided by both process tracing and comparative analysis (see Hammersley 2014a: chapter 1). It should be noted that the strength of the evidence for any proposition also depends upon the evidence available for *competing* knowledge claims. So, the issue is not just whether the evidence is convincing in its own terms but also whether it shows that the knowledge claim to which it relates is more likely to be true than alternatives.

What is involved here is not a matter of 'proven' versus 'not proven': evidence can vary in the strength of support it offers for a conclusion; there is an important distinction to be drawn between weaker and stronger evidence. Moreover, part of what is involved in assessing the strength of any evidence is to consider the likely implications for this of how it was produced. It is also important to stress the difference between there being *no* evidence, or only *weak* evidence, for a conclusion and there being *evidence that it is false*. It is not uncommon for the fact that there is no strong evidence for a conclusion to be taken to imply that it is false, whereas this only indicates that belief in it is unjustified (on the distinction between truth and justification, see Chapter 3). This not only applies to the answers to research questions being put forward by a researcher but also to alternative answers.

The five features I outlined earlier as essential characteristics of data are also necessary for anything to count as evidence. The difference concerns the feature of relevance: this becomes much more narrowly and clearly defined as data turn into evidence, as a result of processes of selection and refinement. This is obviously beneficial for the function that evidence is to serve, but, following on from the previous discussion, we could also ask whether something is lost in that process. The answer to this is surely 'yes'. But the key question is whether what is lost is important for the purposes of the research.

The most significant potential loss concerns whether what the evidence refers to remains independent of the research process. To conceptualise this, we can draw on a related but different analogy from that used in the previous section, this time a culinary one. We could say that ingredients (data) must be cooked, and in the process will change somewhat in character, even while retaining some of their original characteristics. But the phrase 'cooked data' points to a clear danger involved in turning data into evidence: that the aim may become simply building a case in support of a particular answer to a research question, rather than providing all the relevant evidence on the basis of which a sound judgement could be made about its likely validity. Furthermore, illegitimate 'cooking' of the data can arise not just from deliberate intent but also inadvertently. This is the problem of bias (see Chapter 5).

It is a required feature of research reports, then, that the premises on which their conclusions rely refer accurately to features of the world that exist independently of the process of inquiry. If this condition were impossible to meet, then such inquiry could only create fictions: the result would be no different from imaginative literature, albeit perhaps of rather poorer quality. While there are researchers who purport to adopt this position (for an early example, see Denzin 1997), few if any have drawn the obvious practical conclusion and renounced academic research in favour of trying to make a living as novelists or dramatists. While, as I noted earlier, there are difficult philosophical problems surrounding the idea of the independence of data, these do not mean that social research is impossible, any more than they rule out more mundane empirical inquiries.

At the same time, it is necessary to recognise that all evidence is fallible: to say that its content is independent of the research process does not imply that it is inherently true. Sometimes there is an assumption that evidence must appeal to something ultimate that is beyond all possible doubt, as in the case of a form of empiricism according to which the only true evidence is that which is imposed immediately on the senses, and is thereby beyond all question. A more common kind of foundationalism today appeals to a privileged research paradigm or method as determining validity with certainty, for example the experimental methodology employed in randomised controlled trials (RCTs). Yet no approach or method, not even this one, is infallible. All approaches and methods have advantages and disadvantages – they involve trade-offs among various threats to validity (Hammersley 2015b: see Chapter 6).

Furthermore, it should be noted that what counts as evidence, and what counts as *strong* evidence, depends upon what question(s) we are trying to answer. For instance, in the context of medicine, an RCT, or a systematic review of several trials, may be able to inform us quite conclusively about survival rates following some treatment, but will not tell us about survival rates for those categories of person that have been screened out of the trial, or (usually) about the long-term effects of treatment. Thus, even in that part of medicine where RCTs offer a great deal of very reliable knowledge, they often will not, and sometimes cannot, answer all the relevant questions we might want to answer. Much the same applies to any other means of producing evidence.

It might be thought that the conception of evidence I am putting forward here is more relevant to hypothesis-testing research than to more 'inductive' forms of qualitative inquiry. This is not the case. All research aims to answer research questions, however exploratory it is. Given that the answers offered will almost always be open to reasonable doubt (otherwise the research would have little news value), empirical evidence will usually be required if a convincing case is to be made about the likely validity of the answers provided. Given this, clarity about the nature of evidence is of crucial importance.

Conclusion

In this chapter I have examined the meanings of the terms 'data' and 'evidence', suggesting a significant distinction between the two; albeit one that is based on a dimension not a dichotomy. Researchers using these terms rarely pay much attention to what they mean, and yet their meanings relate to some fundamental philosophical difficulties that have been implicated in many of the debates about research methodology. I argued that we must look at both data and evidence as products, even as constructions, but that this does not undermine the independence that is necessary if they are to serve their functions. While many kinds of data are a direct product of researcher activity, they are not simply invented or created. There is a significant difference, for example, between a researcher making an audio-recording of a conversation and transcribing it, on the one hand, and a novelist making up a stretch of dialogue as part of a story, on the other. Similarly, there is a difference between getting respondents to fill in a questionnaire and recording their answers, on the one hand, and the researcher simply making up the results, on the other. The latter is research fraud.

Data, and the evidence that can be produced from it, are essential to empirical inquiry. So too is careful attention on the part of researchers to their production and interpretation.

Notes

1 For discussions of the nature of data that take a very different approach from mine, see *Cultural Studies ↔ Critical Methodologies* 13(4), 2013. The editors of this special issue state that it is 'dedicated to (un)knowing and (un)doing data' (Koro-Ljungberg and MacLure 2013:219–222). There is also a relatively trivial matter that perhaps should be mentioned here: whether 'data' is grammatically plural or singular. It is the plural of 'datum', a term that is rarely used today. However, as the Oxford English Dictionary points out, 'data' can be used as a mass or as a count noun, and therefore in both the singular and the plural. Since the count/mass distinction is often difficult to apply in the context of research, I suggest that this is indeed a trivial issue: no more ink should be spilt over it.

2 This relates to a longstanding philosophical problem, in Kantian terms about 'intuition', what is given in perception (see Holzhey 2010). Another formulation is Peirce's

distinction between firstness, secondness, and thirdness: between what is given before we apprehend it, what is made sense of in pragmatic terms, and understandings of it that are theoretical, in the sense that phenomena are understood in terms of a well-defined and explicit system of categories. On Peirce, see Hookway 1985.

3 Of course, quantitative researchers sometimes use secondary data, such as 'official statistics', and the gap between these and the evidence required to provide answers to research questions is often greater than in the case of survey research data.

4 See, for instance, arguments for 'poetic transcription': Glesne 1997.

5 This is by no means a new development, see, for example, Handler 1983.

6 As I noted earlier, there are deep philosophical problems involved here.

8 Deduction, induction, and abduction

It is common for quantitative research to be treated as 'deductive' (or 'hypothetico-deductive') in character while qualitative research is portrayed as 'inductive', or sometimes 'abductive'. Indeed, these are often treated as *defining features* of the two sorts of research. The primary contrast implied here is between developing concepts *from a prior theory* versus deriving them *out of a body of data*. Alternatively, we could say that the difference is between inquiry that begins with a theory or set of hypotheses, and research which is more exploratory in character, starting from interest in a particular type of action, setting, group of people, or general issue, or prompted by the occurrence of an event or the availability of a body of material that is believed to have significance for some topic.

Some caution needs to be exercised, however, regarding the meaning of the terms 'deduction' and 'induction', especially in treating them as referring to defining features of two kinds of research. The deductive/inductive contrast is complex, and by no means unproblematic. Furthermore, while it does pick out some differences in orientation between much quantitative and much qualitative inquiry, there is quantitative work that has an 'inductive' character (for example, the 'exploratory data analysis' of Tukey 1977; see also Baldamus 1976) as well as qualitative research that is 'deductive' in the sense of being strongly guided by some prior theory, or concerned with investigating a critical case in order to test a hypothesis.[1]

In order to clarify the meaning of these terms, it is necessary to explore some of their history, both in philosophy and social science.

Debate within the philosophy of science

There has been a long history of discussion about the nature of and justification for induction, and about whether science is fundamentally deductive or inductive in character. In the seventeenth century, much philosophical thinking centred on whether investigation of physical, and other, phenomena should follow the model laid down by Aristotle, this frequently being seen as deductive, or whether it should instead adopt a more inductive and empirical approach, this being championed, for instance, by Francis Bacon.

DOI: 10.4324/9781003350354-9

For Aristotle, and especially for much scholastic philosophy, conclusions were to be reached by means of logical deduction from premises that were taken as self-evident. An influential model for this was the geometrical proofs of Euclid, and this even influenced early attempts to understand human behaviour, notably in the work of Hobbes (but see Skinner 1996). By contrast, Bacon argued that we could only gain knowledge of empirical phenomena by observation and experimentation: by discovering regularities and testing these to determine whether they represented scientific laws (see Quinton 1980). He insisted that careful observation of multiple cases was required, including ones that were designed to check whether any patterns discovered held under all relevant conditions. The promotion of an inductive approach also involved rejection of speculative theorising, on the grounds that this led to interminable debates about matters for which no strong evidence was available. If a question is not open to inductive investigation, it was argued, it cannot be resolved scientifically, or perhaps even in any rational manner; and therefore, it should be left on one side. Moreover, theoretical assumptions were often seen as a source of bias, prejudging what ought to be a matter of discovery.[2]

This inductivist conception of science largely carried the day and was elaborated into a highly influential version by John Stuart Mill in the nineteenth century (see Mackie 1967; Scarre 2006). Here scientific inquiry was viewed as starting with the observation of many instances of some phenomenon, subject to systematic comparison, and looking out for regular patterns in order to identify common preceding, or succeeding, factors, with a view to identifying the necessary and jointly sufficient conditions that produce the phenomenon to be explained. Mill identified a number of 'canons', of which the most relevant here are the 'method of agreement' and the 'method of difference'.[3] The first involves investigating cases in which the outcome to be explained occurs, looking for factors that seem always to be present in these, despite differences in other respects. By contrast, the method of difference requires comparing cases where the outcome to be explained occurs with those where it does not, looking for factors that are present in the first type of case but not in the second. Later, there were attempts to develop an 'inductive logic' that would guarantee the validity of the conclusions of such inferences, in a parallel manner to deductive logic.[4]

However, more deductive conceptions of science never completely disappeared, and in the early twentieth century inductivism came under very strong challenge in the philosophy of science. Its most influential critic was Karl Popper (1959), who put forward a hypothetico-deductive conception of scientific method (see also Hempel 1965). He saw scientific inquiry as starting with the creative development of a potential explanation for some puzzling phenomenon, from which hypotheses were derived and then tested. He tended to caricature inductivist conceptions of science as assuming that scientific explanations could be developed mechanically by identifying recurrent patterns or correlations between some type of factor and some type of outcome. He argued that this is an inaccurate account of how natural scientists do their work, and that the idea of an inductive logic is fallacious.

This hypothetico-deductive conception of science involved drawing a sharp distinction between the context of discovery, the processes through which theoretical ideas are generated, and the context of justification, where they are tested. Only the latter was seen as open to rational investigation: for Popper it did not matter where theoretical ideas came from or how they were developed, the key requirement was that attempts were made to falsify them. Hypotheses produced through sustained empirical investigation of cases were no more likely to be true than those produced in other ways, for example through speculative theorising. But a single case could disprove a hypothesis. So, for Popper, the main task of scientists is to attempt to falsify theories by subjecting them to the strongest possible test. If a theory survives this, it can be treated as true, but always with the recognition that it could turn out to be false in the future because of new evidence (this is a philosophical position often referred to as fallibilism).

Thus, the hypothetico-deductive method involves the 'deduction' of a hypothesis from some theory; the operationalisation of the concepts making up this hypothesis so as to render it testable; and then empirical investigation specifically designed to test whether the hypothesis is true or false. From this point of view, an initial theory, formulated as coherently as possible, provides the basis for deciding what data to collect.

This broad change of viewpoint in the philosophy of science – from inductivist to hypothetico-deductive positions – was motivated by what came to be referred to as the problem of induction: the failure of attempts to provide a logical account of induction equivalent to that available for deduction; in other words, one which showed how induction could generate conclusions whose validity is absolutely certain. As we have seen, Popper, and others, denied that any such logic is possible, no doubt rightly. However, it should be noted that the hypothetico-deductive method itself does not provide a means of logically deducing conclusions from evidence in an infallible manner – even about the falsity of a theory (see Newton-Smith 1981).

Conflicting views within social science

Within the social sciences, too, there has been advocacy of both inductivist and hypothetico-deductive approaches, as well as debates about which is most appropriate. In the early twentieth century, promotion of the hypothetico-deductive method within the philosophy of science significantly affected the thinking of many social scientists, especially those employing quantitative methods, so that they often came to insist that the research process must always begin with careful refinement of a set of research questions into specific hypotheses that can be operationalised so as to make them testable. And this conception of research design has persisted in some quarters (see, for instance, de Vaus 2001).

However, many qualitative researchers reacted sharply against this model, often drawing on older nineteenth-century ideas about the nature of science; for instance, taking the research of Darwin as a model, or natural history more generally (for example, Lofland 1967). On this basis, they insisted that careful description and classification of phenomena is the essential foundation for any science, before any process of theory development and testing can begin.[5]

Another important influence in this direction was the tradition of hermeneutic philosophy that had developed and shaped work in the humanities and social sciences, particularly in Germany, and whose influence spread in the twentieth century (Palmer 1969; Bleicher 1980). Here there was an emphasis on the need to understand the cultural background of the social phenomena being investigated. This encouraged an exploratory approach because it emphasised that the researcher must learn the culture of the people whose beliefs and actions are to be understood. This philosophical influence transformed anthropology around the beginning of the twentieth century, a discipline that, in turn, shaped research in other areas, especially sociology, not least through promoting the concepts of 'culture' and 'ethnography'.

A number of specific qualitative approaches can be identified that are of a broadly inductive kind. Probably the earliest was 'analytic induction', developed by Znaniecki (1934) and Lindesmith (1947) as a conception of scientific method that challenged the growing influence of statistical method within US sociology. They argued that the latter was at odds with the methods used by natural scientists, and they sought to formulate a version of scientific method appropriate to social science. They insisted that the aim of any science is to discover universal laws, rather than *statistical* generalisations, and that this requires in-depth examination of particular cases, developing and testing hypotheses on the basis of this, and often revising initial conceptualisations of the phenomenon to be explained. Despite the fact that hypothesis-testing is a key part of analytic induction, the starting point is an examination of cases in which the phenomenon being investigated occurs, not an initial theory, and it therefore lives up to its name as inductive.[6]

A second inductive approach, one that has been even more influential among qualitative researchers, is grounded theorising. Glaser and Strauss (1967) argued that the most effective means of developing fruitful theoretical ideas is through exploratory investigation that is systematically directed towards developing explanations that take account of the complexities of the social world; in short, that are 'grounded' in these. They explicitly rejected what they labelled 'verificationism', the idea that research must start with a theoretical framework from which hypotheses can be derived for testing. Key examples of this at the time Glaser and Strauss were writing included Lipset et al.'s (1956) study of *Union Democracy*, which was concerned with Michels' 'iron law of oligarchy', and Blauner's (1964) attempt to test Marx's theory of alienation. Glaser and Strauss argue that theory 'grounded' in – that is, developed out of – close empirical study of the social world is more likely to be true than that which is produced by 'armchair theorists'. In this respect their position is in line with the spirit of other 'inductivist' forms of social research, and is more or less the opposite of Popper's view, and of the hypothetico-deductive account of science that is still characteristic of much writing about quantitative social science methodology today.[7]

A third inductive approach within social science, of more recent provenance, is Qualitative Comparative Analysis (QCA) (Ragin 1987, 2008). Here, hypothetical explanations are developed by examining the patterns of occurrence of factors within cases, rather than being derived from some prior theory – though the latter is used as a resource. In many respects this is a direct application of Mill's methods of agreement and difference. Like analytic induction, it was initially aimed at discovering universal patterns within a dataset, rather than statistical frequencies (though it was subsequently modified to document probabilistic relationships as well). It applies Boolean algebra to the task of discovering necessary and jointly sufficient conditions for the occurrence of some type of outcome. QCA developed from criticism of standard forms of quantitative analysis that are concerned with estimating the individual contributions that particular factors make to the likelihood of an outcome occurring. One problem with this latter kind of analysis is that it does not easily facilitate investigation of *combinations* of factors, or recognise the distinction between necessary and sufficient conditions. In other words, it does not take enough account of the complexity of causal processes in the social world.[8]

In recent times, a number of authors have advocated an 'abductive' approach to qualitative research (see Reichertz 2004). This term is sometimes used in ways that are close to making it a synonym for 'inductive' but at other times it is taken to represent an approach that lies somewhere between the inductive strategy characteristic of grounded theorising and research that starts from an initial theory (see Tavory and Timmermans 2014). The term 'abduction' was popularised by the scientist and philosopher Charles Sanders Peirce, a founder of American philosophical pragmatism. He saw the processes to which it referred as playing a key role in the creative development of theoretical explanations for observed phenomena. But he insisted that the ideas developed must be subjected to subsequent test before being accepted into the body of scientific knowledge.[9]

Aside from these specific, labelled approaches, a great deal of qualitative research, from ethnography (Hammersley and Atkinson 2019) to comparative historical analysis (Skocpol and Somers 1980), has tended to adopt an inductive approach. This is also true of what has been called the 'ontological turn' in anthropology (Holbraad and Pedersen 2017). This insists that phenomena must be investigated for what they reveal themselves to be; and that this requires the anthropologist to suspend the categories he or she would normally employ (even such general ones as culture, politics, and religion). It is argued that these are a source of likely distortion; and immersion in the experience of the people being studied is essential if they are to be overcome.

Another radically 'inductive' approach, albeit very different in character, is Conversation Analysis. This is usually data-driven, starting from the analysis of a particular set of data, or from some phenomenon of interest, rather than from pre-determined theoretical categories. It may also involve the analysis of multiple cases and a commitment to producing an analysis that makes sense of both standard and deviant patterns (see Hutchby and Wooffitt 1998: 94–95). For example, Schegloff (1968) collected and analysed a large number of openings of telephone conversations: his PhD thesis was entitled 'The First Five Seconds', which provides an indication of how much of each of these conversations he was examining. Discovering an exception to the standard pattern, he revised his account to treat the ringing telephone as the first move in telephone conversations, identifying this as a summons, which explains why it is usually the receiver of a call who speaks first, not the caller.

It is important to recognise, however, that what is involved in the use of terms like 'deduction', 'induction', and 'abduction' is not a simple dichotomy or trichotomy: there can be variation in the *degree* to which theoretical presuppositions control the initial stages of inquiry; and no research can start without presuppositions. Similarly, there can be variation in the extent to which effort is devoted to the generation and development of theoretical ideas versus the testing of hypotheses derived from such ideas. It is rarely the case that research labelled as 'inductive' is simply exploratory or developmental in character, involving no claims about the likely validity of its results; meanwhile, 'deductive' research usually involves developmental work, it is not *solely* concerned with testing.

Furthermore, even if we retain the distinction between hypothetico-deductive and inductive/abductive approaches, there is no reason to assume that only one of them is valid, or that one is superior to the other. Some commentators have recognised that each approach has advantages and disadvantages, these more or less mirroring one another. For instance, an inductive approach reduces the danger that the initial starting point is one that involves false presuppositions, since it allows the researcher to modify research questions during the course of inquiry to try to ensure that the presuppositions involved reflect the nature of the phenomena being investigated. This has particular significance in the case of social research because, to some degree at least, these presuppositions will relate to the beliefs and practices of the people being studied; and it is easy to make false assumptions about these on the basis of one's own experience and background culture. There is also a danger that overly simple assumptions will be made about the nature of social phenomena, whereas an inductive approach allows for complexities to be discovered.

By contrast, a hypothetico-deductive approach facilitates a much more focused inquiry, in which there is more chance that all of the data relevant to explanatory hypotheses will be collected. It also makes easier strategic decision-making about how to produce data relevant to key concepts. And, most obviously, it allows for the systematic testing of hypotheses – in Popper's terms, attempts at falsification – to a greater degree than more inductive investigation.

Deduction and induction as specific modes of argument

Rather than being used to refer to whole approaches, or competing conceptions of scientific method, the terms 'deduction' and 'induction' can also be employed to distinguish specific forms of argument or types of reasoning.

Indeed, this is the core sense of the distinction. Here 'deduction' is reasoning from a set of premises, for example those built into a theory, to conclusions that necessarily follow from those premises. Using an ancient example, it is reasoning from a general premiss ('all humans die'), plus a statement about some particular case ('Socrates is human'), to a further conclusion about that case ('Socrates is mortal'). Involved here is subsumption of a particular case under some law, rule, or principle. By contrast, 'induction' is reasoning from statements about some observed cases to statements about other, unobserved, cases, or – more usually – to a general claim about most or all cases of the same kind, or belonging to the same population.

The key difference between these two kinds of reasoning is that induction is ampliative – the conclusion reached is not already contained in the starting assumptions – whereas deduction can tell us no more than what is logically implied by the premises (for example that since mortality is a defining feature of being human, all humans die). Therefore, the truth of a conclusion reached by deduction, where this takes a valid logical form, depends solely upon how the terms in the premises were defined, as well as whether these premises are true. For instance, deductively, it would be the case that 'all swans are white' if white feathers were treated as a defining feature of the meaning of 'swan'; but, if this is not a defining feature, it may be possible to discover (by induction) that there are black swans.

It is important to note that if we treat 'induction' and 'deduction' in this way, as referring to forms of reasoning, they can be combined within a single process of analysis. Indeed, it could be argued that all analysis relies upon *both* types of argument. In fact, though, there are several kinds of inductive reasoning that can play a variety of roles in social science:

1   *Enumerative induction.* This involves generalisation from a sample, whose features have been studied, to a larger, finite population of cases many of which have not been investigated. This form of inference serves as a substitute for a complete enumeration or census; in other words, where a whole population not a sample of it is studied. Within the social sciences, most obviously, enumerative induction is fundamental to much social survey research.
2   *Hypothetical induction (also sometimes called 'abduction', 'retroduction', or 'inference to the best explanation').* Here, inference is from what is observed to what is taken to be the most likely explanation for the observed phenomenon, this often being developed into a general theoretical principle (usually attributing causality) that would apply to other cases. This is a central feature of analytic induction and of grounded theorising. For instance, Cressey (1950) sought to explain why some people in positions of financial trust embezzle funds. He developed and tested the idea that it is because they experience financial difficulties that they feel they cannot reveal to others, because they believe they can 'borrow' funds secretly, and because they have developed an excuse for doing this that they find persuasive.

3   *Probative or eliminative induction.* This involves reasoning from evidence collected for the purpose of testing a hypothesis or theory back to a conclusion about its validity. This is a form of reasoning that is essential to any hypothesis-testing, whether in quantitative or qualitative research (this reveals that viewing hypothesis-testing as 'deductive' rather than 'inductive' is misleading). Eliminative induction was a key element of the method adopted by Durkheim, for example, in his study of suicide (Schmaus 1994: chapter 5).

These forms of induction serve different functions within the process of inquiry; they are not competitors or substitutes for one another.[10]

Conclusion

The distinction between 'inductive' or 'abductive' and 'deductive' approaches is central to many discussions of social research methodology. However, as we have seen, the meaning of these terms can vary considerably, and conflicting attitudes have been adopted towards the approaches and forms of reasoning to which they refer. Moreover, this distinction does not map on to that between qualitative and quantitative forms of inquiry in the manner that is often assumed. What are involved here are complex variations in research strategy, not a simple dichotomy. The most specific sense of the distinction is between types of reasoning. And the several types of inductive inference, along with deductive forms of argument, are all frequently involved within the same study, whether 'qualitative' or 'quantitative'. They are not necessarily competitors, nor are they substitutes. The problem with arguments advocating either 'deductive' or 'inductive/abductive' approaches to social research is that they tend to neglect these complexities.

Notes

1 See, for instance, Burawoy 1998. For a classic example of hypothesis-testing via qualitative research, see Festinger et al. 1956.
2 For a more detailed discussion of the philosophical arguments around induction, see Henderson 2020. For background to the ideas of Bacon, see Gaukroger 2001. On the meaning of 'theory', see Chapter 12.
3 However, it is important to note that Mill denied that the canons of scientific inference he identified were appropriate in social science. Instead, here he proposed a deductive method in which conclusions were logically derived from empirical laws discovered inductively by other sciences, notably psychology. Most social scientists have ignored this element of his position.
4 Reichertz (2004:159–160) has pointed out that much the same idea developed in other quarters, notably among artificial intelligence researchers, under the heading of 'abduction'.
5 It is important to remember, however, that Darwin's research was framed within a set of developing theoretical ideas that were by no means simply 'derived from the data'.
6 On analytic induction, see Hammersley 1989b, Becker 1998, and Cooper et al. 2012.

7 On grounded theorising, see Dey 1999 and Bryant and Charmaz 2010. Reichertz 2009 has argued that grounded theorising involves abductive reasoning and qualitative induction.

8 Ragin (1987: chapter 3) argues that Mill's methods of agreement and difference cannot deal with assessing the role of combinations of factors. For a comparison of analytic induction and qualitative comparative analysis, see Cooper et al. 2012: chapter 5.

9 For discussion of Peirce's changing understanding of the concept, see Fann 1970.

10 For a useful discussion of different kinds of induction, see Rescher 1978.

9 Understanding and explanation

The task of social science is to understand or explain social phenomena. This may appear a truism, but built into this statement are some uncertainties that have generated quite diverse conceptions of what the task entails, and sometimes doubts about whether it is necessary or possible. One aspect of this is that the words 'understanding' (or, more usually, the German term *Verstehen*) and 'explanation' (German equivalent, *Erklären*) have sometimes been employed *not* as synonyms but as referring to quite different forms of knowledge and ways of producing it. This provided the basis for claims that the human sciences are distinct in character from the physical sciences in methodological terms; though there have been differences in view about what makes them different (von Wright 1971: chapter I; Hammersley 1989b: chapter 1).

Another axis of disagreement is that some commentators have insisted that, for the most part, we do not need social science to understand social phenomena (Hutchinson et al. 2008), while others have come close to denying the very possibility of understanding, at least in the case of people and situations different from those with which we are familiar (Holbraad and Pedersen 2017). Also implicated here is the question of whether understanding other people implies experiencing the world in exactly the same way as they do, or whether it is more indirect and abstract in character.

A third set of problems surrounds what the word 'explanation' should be taken to mean: does it involve logical inference from scientific theory to conclusions about what must have happened in some particular situation; is it the identification of a pattern of relationships among phenomena; or does it simply mean making sense of the unknown in terms of the known? All three of these interpretations can be found in the literature.

As this should make clear, the various meanings given to the terms 'understanding' and 'explanation' require clarification, especially since each can refer both to the intended product of social inquiry and to how this can be, or has been, achieved.

The history of *Verstehen*

The German word *Verstehen*, which can be roughly translated as 'understanding' or 'interpretation', has long been used to refer to what is widely taken to be an

DOI: 10.4324/9781003350354-10

essential capacity in studying human social life: grasping the meanings that have motivated and guided particular actions (Truzzi 1974; O'Hear 1996). As already indicated, this has sometimes been regarded as marking off the social from the natural sciences as their distinctive method. But this is far from an uncontentious claim. There are those who deny that *Verstehen* can play any legitimate role in scientific investigation, or who insist that it can only provide hypotheses to test (Abel 1948). Furthermore, while others have argued that this method is no less scientific than that of physical science, in the twentieth century there was an influential move towards rejecting the idea that *Verstehen* is a specialised *method* employed by social scientists. Instead, it was argued that it should be viewed as a universal human capacity, or one that is closer in character to philosophical understanding; and perhaps nearer to art than to science (Palmer 1969).

These arguments were associated with the development of historicism and hermeneutics in Germany in the nineteenth century: these related traditions of thought viewed people in the past as living in quite different experiential worlds from those of today (Berlin 1976; Hammersley 1989b: chapter 1). Hermeneutics was concerned with how, given this, we can come to understand those other worlds on the basis of the textual and other sorts of evidence available. While, initially, this concern developed in the context of philological, archaeological, and historical investigations, it also influenced social and economic thought in the nineteenth century as well as twentieth-century anthropology, notably through the work of Boas and Malinowski. And, subsequently, it had an impact on social science more generally, especially qualitative research in sociology and other fields. However, there has been continuing philosophical discussion about the nature and value of *Verstehen* (see, for instance, Winch 1958, 1964; Taylor 1964, 1971; Gadamer 2004)

Such discussion was concerned with exactly what *Verstehen* involves. In some of the early work of Dilthey, a key figure in nineteenth-century hermeneutics, it is portrayed as a psychological capacity for empathy, in which the social scientist draws on her or his own experience to imagine how the people being studied viewed the world, what they were thinking and feeling, and therefore why they did what they did. Sometimes it almost seemed to be suggested, as Max Weber noted, that one must become Caesar in order to understand Caesar. By contrast, later formulations emphasised the role of language, and presented *Verstehen* as closer to a cultural capacity to 'read the signs' in order to make sense of what other people believe, think, and do (Palmer 1969; Makkreel 1975; Ermarth 1978). Within anthropology both these interpretations can be found, even today.

The centrality of the method of participant observation to anthropology in much of the twentieth century reflected the assumption that it is necessary to learn other people's cultures before one can understand their behaviour, and this learning was conceived not just as cognitive but also as experiential. Indeed, sometimes it has been suggested that one must abandon one's existing mode of apprehending the world in order to gain access to that of those whose lives one is trying to understand (Jules-Rosette 1978). More recently, this idea has formed the core of what has been referred to as the 'ontological turn' in anthropology (Holbraad and Pedersen 2017). At the same time, through the influence of structuralism and post-structuralism, the idea that understanding involves reading cultural signs has also been influential (Clifford and Marcus 1986). And this view can be found today in the field of Cultural Studies and many other areas of social science.

The rationale for *Verstehen*

The rationale for *Verstehen* as applied to the study of contemporary social life, rather than the past, generally involves the following components:

1   A denial that social actions are an automatic product of causal factors of which actors are unaware. Instead, it is insisted that their character depends on the meanings actors give to the situations they face, to possible lines of action, and to their own identities. It is also pointed out that there is no direct correspondence between people's physical movements and what actions they are performing. Indeed, the same physical movement can have multiple meanings. For example, the rapid closing of one eye a couple of times could be a physical tic that is not under the control of the person concerned; a wink designed to indicate a shared secret or a joke; or someone practising winking (Ryle 1971; Geertz 1973). This gap between physical evidence and meaningful social activity suggests that a different approach is required in social inquiry from the method of physical science, where the physical behaviour of objects is observed and described with a view to discovering empirical patterns of co-occurrence and recurrence that reflect the operation of causal laws. And this argument about the distinctive nature of human action may also be taken to rule out accounts that seek to explain it in terms of the unmediated effects of psychological or social factors (Blumer 1969).

2   Equally important is the idea that human social life takes diverse cultural forms: past societies vary in culture from those same societies today; and contemporaneous societies also differ from one another in cultural terms. Furthermore, there is subcultural variation even *within* societies. This suggests that it is rarely sufficient to rely on one's existing knowledge and capabilities in seeking to understand others' behaviour, one must find a way to grasp what they feel and think; in other words, deploy *Verstehen* in some form or another.

3   At the same time, it is frequently argued that, despite cultural variation, there is an underlying shared human nature or set of capabilities that provide a basis for understanding people who belong to other cultures or subcultures. Without this shared basis, such understanding would be impossible.

These arguments can be interpreted in various ways, and have been subject to a long history of dispute. Indeed, they have been challenged from diverse directions.

The role of meanings

As regards the first point, it has been objected that much action appears to be automatic, rather than the product of conscious interpretation and deliberation. Furthermore, actors themselves often use causal language to account for their own behaviour and that of others. There is some truth in both sides of the argument here. What is required, I suggest, is to recognise that there is variation in human behaviour in this respect: from that which is habitual, in the sense that there is 'immediate recognition' of what is going on and what would be an appropriate response, to the other extreme of situations that are hard to make sense of, or where difficult choices have to be made, resulting in conscious deliberation. Whether or not we use the language of causation, we must take account of the full range of such variability.

Another issue concerns whether actors have immediate *and therefore accurate* understanding of their own behaviour, and are therefore capable of providing sound accounts of the processes involved. Both empathy and learning the culture, as strategies for gaining understanding, appear to rely on this assumption; even though, in practice, those who use them rarely accept participant understandings entirely at face value. By contrast, some critics of *Verstehen*, often influenced by positivism but also for example by Marxism, have denied that actors necessarily have accurate insight into why they do what they do; though this does not automatically lead to rejection of the role of *Verstehen* (see Uebel 2010, 2019). Thus, Abel (1948) argued that people's own understandings of their behaviour can offer hypotheses that must be tested to discover whether or not they truly represent the causal processes involved.

A related line of criticism has come from other directions: ordinary language philosophy and ethnomethodology (Hutchinson et al. 2008). Here it is argued that what people say about what they do should be treated not as a window into their thought processes or experiences but rather as a form of action in its own right: the accounts provided are always for particular purposes, in particular contexts, and for particular audiences. As a result, they do not tell us directly what people are feeling or thinking. These critics also resist the idea that human actions are, for the most part, guided by conscious sense-making. Rather, they claim that most sense-making takes place immediately: people simply see situations 'for what they are' and respond to these. However, these writers regard what is involved here as a matter of mutual intelligible action rather than as a causal process.

In my view, we certainly should not assume that people always have accurate understandings of their own behaviour, any more than that they will always be willing and able to provide true accounts of what they are doing and why. This assumption seems particularly questionable with behaviour that is close to the habitual end of the spectrum, though scepticism ought to be applied across the whole range. At the same time, people do often have access to evidence about their actions, and the reasons for these, that is not available to others. Given this, it is wise to take seriously what they say, rather than treating this as mere rationalisation or solely as a gloss provided for subsequent interactional purposes.[1] Similarly, participant observation is certainly an effective means of achieving more accurate understanding of people's behaviour, even though it should not be assumed that it is always the best method.

While it is true that people's explanations for their own behaviour should be treated as no more than hypotheses, albeit ones that must be taken into account, it is also important to recognise that the role of *Verstehen* goes beyond this. In checking the validity of hypotheses about what people are doing and why, the evidence we rely on itself depends upon sociocultural understanding. It is not possible to test our understanding of people's actions simply by recourse to description of their physical behaviour, the sounds they emit, and so on. Rather, we rely on our cultural capacity to understand what we see and hear. This is illustrated by the fact that, when we transcribe speech to produce data for analysis, we do not simply document the physical sounds made (for instance, in terms of pitch and loudness) but identify what words were spoken and what was being said. And in order to do this we must already know the language being used, or learn it. More than this, in order to produce an accurate transcription of what was said, we will often need to know something about the people speaking, the activities they were engaging in, and so on. This reflects the fact that language use is not simply a matter of encoding and decoding sounds by means of a semantic codebook but rather a practical cultural accomplishment. And researchers cannot avoid reliance on this.

We must also acknowledge the different forms of understanding involved in producing social science data. These include: understanding a message, for example the response to an interviewer's question; understanding an action directed towards a goal; and understanding an emotional reaction to some event, as observed by the researcher. While, in practice, these forms of understanding are frequently interrelated, they involve rather different processes. A further kind of understanding concerns rule-following behaviour, though this too is complex in character, since rules must be made sense of in contextually sensitive ways. And, of course, they may be violated in order to convey a message by allusion or as a basis for jokes.

Familiarity on the part of a researcher with the culture of the people being studied can be both facilitating and obstructive. It may allow us to work out what they are doing, and why, relatively accurately. But, equally, viewing their behaviour from an alien angle may prompt us into asking fruitful questions about it that familiarity tends to block. What this suggests is that *Verstehen* is essential, but that we should resist the temptation to assume that it is sufficient to generate or answer the sorts of question we address as social scientists. And this is where the idea of explanation comes in, which I will discuss later in this chapter.

Cultural diversity and common human nature

While few would deny that there is cultural variation between and within societies, different views have been taken about the extent and depth of the differences, and about their nature. Indeed, there is clearly some tension between the second and third components of the rationale for *Verstehen*. If cultural differences are very deep, then it may seem that cross-cultural understanding will be impossible. On the other hand, if emphasis is placed on what is common to all humans, then the need for *Verstehen* appears to recede. There are also questions about the nature of what humans, and even those belonging to 'the same' culture, share: substantive views of the world or values, on the one hand, or, on the other, ways of thinking and making sense of the world that facilitate but do not ensure mutual understanding? Furthermore, the idea that there are distinct cultures or subcultures has been questioned in favour of the assumption that what is shared and what differs forms part of much more complex, and overlapping, patterns (Hammersley 2019a: chapter 4).

As noted previously, there are those who have questioned whether the understanding produced by *Verstehen* can ever be an accurate representation of participant meanings. For instance, it may be argued that all accounts reflect the cultural background, personal qualities, presuppositions or preferences of the person doing the interpreting. This issue arises most strongly where the expressions or behaviour which are the focus of inquiry are those of people belonging to a very different culture from that of the researcher: Can we ever overcome our own cultural backgrounds? That we must always rely on existing cultural capabilities, as well as learning new ones, is certainly true. And it is also the case that we can never be absolutely certain that we have understood what is going on accurately. However, all scientific knowledge is fallible, and behind this argument about the impossibility of understanding other cultures lies an assumption that cultures are completely discrepant from one another, so that little or nothing is shared between the researcher and those whose behaviour he or she is trying to understand. Yet, this does not fit with what we know about cultural differences (Moody-Adams 1997; Hammersley 2019a). There may also be a second questionable assumption involved: that in order truly to understand someone's actions we must somehow become identical with them: once again, the idea that only Caesar could understand Caesar. But this is not required in our everyday understanding of one another, and it is not clear why it would be required for social science.

A more fundamental challenge to the possibility of understanding focuses on the nature of language: it may be suggested that it is a fallacy to assume that any linguistic account has a fixed meaning that can be retrieved as a univocal message. This argument obviously has implications for evidence coming from informants, leading to doubts about how interview data are normally used (see Hammersley 2008: chapter 5, 2017a). Often this results in denial that there are phenomena existing 'outside the discourse', and a shift of analytic focus towards investigating how phenomena are discursively constituted in what people say. However, this fundamental questioning of the possibility of understanding also challenges the capacity of the researcher to document the world, *including people's discursive practices*. On this account, do not research accounts themselves necessarily construct the phenomena they claim to document, including the discursive practices of other people? If so, this would appear to abolish any possibility of social research.

It is certainly true that language is never completely under the control of speakers or writers, there is always the potential for unintended implications and for misunderstanding. However, in most language-use people try to design their communications to make their message identifiable (as well as worthy of attention), and in receiving communications people attend to their design, and their contexts, in order to try to identify the intended messages. Of course, there are cases where communications are intended to deceive, and ones that intentionally make understanding elusive (much modernist poetry, for example), but these are parasitic practices (which is not to deny their value). It is important to insist, then, that communication can, and often does, help us to understand the world in which we live. To deny this is not just to undercut the possibility of social research but also of natural science and of the everyday forms of understanding on which we all rely.

We select forms or modes of communication to suit the purposes which they are to serve. It is true that there can be no use of language to document the empirical world that is *literal*, if what we mean by this is that it employs tokens, and combinations of these, whose meaning is entirely standard and unambiguous (in the manner that, arguably, mathematical notation is). But, as I have already indicated, it *is* possible to improve the chances of mutual understanding through the design of communications and through how one attends to them. Indeed, there is an obligation on the part of researchers to seek to understand the communications of informants as accurately as possible: the intended messages, the motives for these, and the contexts in which they occurred. Similarly, there is an obligation to try to convey the results of research in a manner that is as unambiguous and clear as possible for the target audience (see Chapter 13).

What is explanation?

Like 'understanding', the word 'explanation' carries several meanings. In one usage it is synonymous with 'explication', and refers to what is designed to facilitate understanding; as, for example, when someone says 'Please explain what you mean'. However, the main usage of the term, and the one that is most relevant to social science, concerns why something happened, why it has the features it does, what causes variation in some outcome, and so on. This is what is often referred to as causal explanation. I will focus on this, but even here there are different views about what is involved.[2]

One account in the philosophy of science, particularly influential in the past, presents explanations as drawing on universal laws, along with information about a particular situation, in order to explain why some event occurred in that situation. This is sometimes referred to as the covering law model, and was one basis for the contrast between explanation and understanding mentioned at the start of this chapter (see, also, Chapter 8). However, cogent questions have been raised about whether there can be laws of social life, and there are complexities even about the concept of laws in physics (see Cartwright 1983). A rival conception of explanation has insisted that it involves identifying causal mechanisms, with correlational claims about associations between variables being dismissed as insufficient (Bhaskar 2008; Maxwell 2012). But questions have been raised about whether what are involved in the social world are *mechanisms* or more fluid processes. Furthermore, there are multiple views about the nature of causality. Some have argued that the concept of causation necessarily involves the idea that intervention of a particular kind would bring about a predictable change (Woodward 2003). Another view, this time appealing to biology rather than physics, suggests that explanation requires finding a pattern of relationships among phenomena that explains their behaviour. An example is explaining the existence of various organs in the human body in terms of the functions they perform for one another, in such a way that they collectively enable continued life.

All these ideas about explanation and causality have had some influence within social science. And it seems to me that the differences among them, and between explanation and *Verstehen*, are less sharp than is sometimes suggested. For example, even if it is true that universal social laws are not available, we can identify institutionalised structures operating in the social world that, though only coming into being in particular locations and at particular times, nevertheless operate as causal forces producing regular patterns of outcome much of the time, and predictable variations in these. Different kinds of market relation would be one set of examples, family forms would be another. These will clearly be relevant to some social science explanations. Furthermore, whether we think of them as involving law-like patterns or causal mechanisms may not always matter much for the purposes of social investigation; though some have argued that it does (see Maxwell 2012).

However, the very idea of social science *explanation* has sometimes been rejected. Commenting on Hutchinson et al.'s (2008) book *There is No Such Thing as a Social Science*, Turner (2010:415) notes that for these authors: 'The craving for explanation is a disease to be therapeutically corrected, by showing that it arises from mistaken philosophical prejudices.' The authors' argument is that lay people can already explain their own behaviour, in the contexts in which it occurs, and that the general questions about such behaviour that social scientists address are often pointless. Instead, Hutchinson et al. suggest that the task of social science, if it has any at all, should be to *describe* processes of social interaction, and how these constitute the social world that we experience. In other words, the focus should be on *how* rather than *why*. While these authors make some important points about social science explanation, in my view their conclusions about the scope for social science are too pessimistic (see Hammersley 2017d).

It is important to emphasise the pragmatic character of explanations. One of the features of the covering law model of explanation that was rightly criticised is its implication that there is a single all-purpose, true explanation for any phenomenon: it is surely the case that explanations vary according to purpose and audience, and should do so (which is not to say that explanations that are true can be incompatible with one another). Explanations (like descriptions) are answers to questions, and in putting forward or assessing any explanation we need to be clear about the nature of the question being addressed, since this determines what would count as an adequate answer (explanation). An example was provided many years ago by the philosopher of history R. G. Collingwood (1940:302–303), when he pointed out that, while it may be true that a car came to a halt on a hill because the force of gravity was against it, this factor is not very relevant to the practical question of why the car stalled. More relevant would be the fact that a cable was loose so that the engine did not have the necessary power to get up the hill.

We need to ask what the implications of the pragmatic character of explanation are for social science (see Hammersley 2014a: chapter 2). While it is clear that what is relevant to the question of why a car has stalled on a hill is determined by what would enable us to get it going again, it is not clear that social science investigations are framed *directly* by practical questions of this kind, or should be. Nevertheless, particular fields of social inquiry are concerned with answering questions that are relevant to anyone with an interest in the topic concerned; and, indirectly at least, these do frequently relate to issues about what could be done about various practical problems. Perhaps this relatively weak framework can suffice.

A final question I will address here concerns the role of theory. As discussed in Chapter 12, that word has a wide range of meanings, so that what it refers to can play different roles in social science. But, as we have seen, one of its meanings concerns ideas about potential causal mechanisms or patterns of relationship whose value in explaining particular phenomena can be investigated on the basis of evidence about those phenomena. In these terms, especially, there is a close relationship between explanation and theory.

Conclusion

Understanding or explanation is normally regarded as the intended product of social inquiry. However, while these words are sometimes used as synonyms, they can also carry contrasting meanings. Indeed, the distinction between the two has often been used as a basis for differentiating the social from the physical sciences. Given that these words refer to the intended product of research, as well as to the means of achieving this, it is important that we have a clear sense of how they are to be interpreted in particular contexts. In this chapter, I looked first at the rationale for the notion of *Verstehen*, and at some of the debates surrounding it, and then at different interpretations of the concept of explanation. I suggested that many of the arguments on both sides of these disputes contain some truth but are frequently exaggerated. I concluded that there were no grounds for drawing a sharp distinction between understanding and explanation. Quite the reverse, in social science *Verstehen* is an essential element in the production of sound explanations. I also underlined the importance of recognising the fact that explanations are always answers to questions, and that in both producing and assessing them we need to be clear about what sort of question is involved and the implications of this for what would count as an answer.

Notes

1 I will leave on one side the question of whether causal language should be used to explain human behaviour. Much depends upon what meaning we give to the term 'causal' (Hammersley 2014a: chapter 1).
2 On the distinction between description and explanation, see Chapter 4.

10 Reflexivity

'Reflexivity' has come to be a widely used term, especially among qualitative researchers.[1] Sometimes it seems to be employed as little more than a magical incantation to ward off potential methodological criticism. But it has a diverse range of meanings (see Watson 1987; Czyzewski 1994; Lynch 2000; Breuer and Roth 2003; Babcock 2005; Davies 2008: chapter 1; Anderson and Sharrock 2015; Whitaker and Atkinson 2021: chapter 1). These must be recognised, along with the discrepant assumptions on which they rely. I begin by outlining different interpretations of the word, and then present what I believe to be the most appropriate interpretation in the context of research methodology.

A brief history

The term 'reflexive', and the abstract noun 'reflexivity', came into common use in the social research methodology literature during the 1970s and 1980s (Giddens 1976; Ruby 1982; Hammersley 1983; Hammersley and Atkinson 1983), and had already been employed earlier in discussions of sociological theory (see Gouldner 1970). However, the word 'reflexive' had been in more general use much longer. The Oxford English Dictionary (OED) includes among its main meanings:

> Of a mental action, process, etc.: turned or directed back upon the mind itself; involving intelligent self-awareness or self-examination; introspective.

One of the examples it provides is from 1653:

> Logick . . . giveth a reflexive knowledge to a man, that is, it makes a man not only know (directly) but makes him know that he knoweth a thing.

What is being referred to in this example is a process of epistemic control or guidance whereby the chances of producing knowledge, and avoiding error, are increased. This is an important strand of meaning in modern methodological usage, and one that I believe should be central. It is closely related to the

DOI: 10.4324/9781003350354-11

conception of objectivity that I proposed in Chapter 5. However, it is only one of many interpretations of 'reflexivity' that can be found in the literature.

There is another sense of the term 'reflexive' recorded in the OED that is also of some interest, captured in a theological example:

> Our love to God, which is an effect, or reflexive beame of Gods love to us.

What is referred to here is a reciprocal, constitutive process. An application of this sense of the term in social science is to be found in ethnomethodology (Lynch 2000; Watson 2005). Drawing on the idea of the hermeneutic circle (via Mannheim 1952: chapter 11) and Gestalt theory (as interpreted by Gurwitsch 1964; see Eisenmann and Lynch 2021), Garfinkel (1967) argues that all social phenomena have a reciprocal relationship with their contexts: each constitutes the other. What is involved here is a relational ontology, one that is opposed to the idea that there are separately existing types of object, each with its own fixed, durable, and universal substance. While it is not the only alternative to this sort of Aristotelian ontology, it carries quite radical implications for the practice of social research: for example, if all accounts – including those of researchers – have a mutually constitutive relationship with their contexts, what distinctive role can there be for social science? However, this sense of the term 'reflexivity' will not be my main focus here.[2]

Current meanings of 'reflexivity' within social science

If we look at the range of different senses that have been given to the term 'reflexivity' in social science (helpfully catalogued by Lynch 2000; see also Ashmore 1989: chapter 2 and Whitaker and Atkinson 2021: chapter 1), there seem to be two main dimensions underpinning them:

1   Whether the term refers to an empirical or ontological fact, on the one hand, or to a recommended virtue or form of activity, on the other.
2   Whether it is treated as a property of people (including researchers) and their practices, or whether it can be a feature of other objects, such as societies or texts.

Table 10.1 provides an overview of the main senses and their relationship to these two dimensions, along with a few examples.

The wide range of meanings given to the term 'reflexivity' should be clear from this table. While some are closely related to one another, others are incompatible; and it is not uncommon for one sense of the term to be promoted in explicit opposition to others (see, for instance, Lynch 2000; Whitaker and Atkinson 2021). Indeed, I will be doing this in the remainder of the chapter: outlining what I take to be the most fruitful senses of the term when thinking about social research methodology, and rejecting others on the basis of the methodological position outlined in the Introduction and in other chapters.

Table 10.1 A systematic presentation of the main meanings of 'reflexivity'

	Reflexivity as fact	Reflexivity as virtue
Reflexivity as a property of persons (including researchers) or practices	*Human beings reflect* on themselves, their thoughts and actions, and thereby change their behaviour (for instance, G. H. Mead 1934). *Researchers and research practices* are necessarily part of the social world they study (for example, Hammersley and Atkinson 1983). *Features of the researcher, or of research practice, construct,* or constitute, the phenomena investigated (for example, Whitaker and Atkinson 2021).	*Introspective investigation* of one's thoughts, feelings, assumptions, etc with a view to correcting or modifying these. The model here is sometimes Descartes. *Philosophical critique,* in the Kantian sense: investigating the constitution of experience, and the limits to knowledge of the world and of ourselves. *The application of sociological analysis* to the practice of sociology itself (for example, Gouldner 1970 and Bourdieu 1990). *In the course of inquiry researchers should monitor* how they and the research process may introduce threats to the validity of research findings (Hammersley and Atkinson 1983) or close off fruitful analytic possibilities (Whitaker and Atkinson 2021) *Explicit attention to the role of the researcher,* and of social research generally, in macro-economic, social, and political relations, for example being party to neo-imperialism (Marcus and Fischer 1986). *Explicit presentation of the researcher's standpoint* – biography, background assumptions, and beliefs – and how these have shaped the research process and its products (for instance, Richardson 2000).
Reflexivity as a feature of objects (including societies and texts)	*The reciprocal constitution of phenomena* and contexts (Garfinkel and ethnomethodology). *A self-monitoring and self-guiding system.* One application of this is the notion of reflexive modernisation (Beck et al. 1994).	*Research texts should reveal* how the representations they offer were constructed. *Reflexive research texts actively subvert* any tendency to be read as authoritatively factual, instead highlighting alternative constructions (for example, Woolgar 1988; Ashmore 1989).

Three forms of researcher reflexivity

Drawing on earlier discussions (Hammersley 1983; Hammersley and Atkinson 2019: chapter 1), I propose three, closely related, forms of researcher reflexivity. I will call the first *existential reflexivity*. This refers to the fact that researchers are themselves participants in the social life they investigate, rather than being separate from and independent of it. The important implications of this are: that researchers may influence the phenomena they investigate; and that they are subject to similar sorts of social forces, processes, and tensions as the people they study. Researchers necessarily rely on various assumptions inherited from background culture, disciplinary tradition, social location, and so on, that may affect how they carry out an investigation; and, in the course of data collection, they may affect the behaviour of the people being studied, and thus the data produced. Existential reflexivity points to the fact that it is not possible to step outside the social world in order to study it, in the manner assumed by what I referred to in Chapter 5 as 'objectivism'.

Thus, the findings produced by any inquiry will be affected by social processes in various ways. However, this does not mean that those findings are unavoidably erroneous or that they are fictions – to draw either of these conclusions is to adopt the objectivist assumption that true understanding can only be produced if the research process is insulated from all psychological and social factors. That assumption is confuted by the fact that such insulation is impossible yet knowledge of the world has been gained, not just in the natural and social sciences but in the course of practical activities as well.[3]

Practical reflexivity, the second form I will discuss, is a normative requirement that follows on from the fact of existential reflexivity: this requires that researchers monitor themselves and the research process in order to identify significant threats to the validity or fruitfulness of their conclusions, and that they act so as to minimise or discount these. I suggest that such practical reflexivity is an essential virtue on the part of researchers: it is part of researcher integrity (see Chapter 13). What is involved here is a pragmatic matter of making reasonable judgements about the likelihood and likely severity of potential threats to sound conclusions, and finding ways to deal with them; as well as identifying possibly fruitful lines of analysis that could be overlooked because of prior assumptions and decisions.[4]

The third form of reflexivity – *reporting reflexivity* – is concerned with facilitating the assessment of research reports by readers: it requires that sufficient information be provided about the researcher and the research process for them to understand how the findings were produced, what threats to validity and to the fruitfulness of conclusions could have been involved, and how well these were countered. It is perhaps necessary to emphasise the word 'sufficient' here: what is required is the provision of neither too little nor too much of this background information. The aim is not to render the research process 'transparent' in some absolute sense, since that is never possible and attempting it is undesirable.[5]

Discussion

As already indicated, these three forms of reflexivity imply a conception of research practice that serves as an alternative to what I have referred to elsewhere in this book as 'objectivism' (see Chapter 5): the idea that threats to validity can only be avoided if the research process approximates to the form of standardised procedures that are unaffected by whoever carries them out. At the same time, the overall conception of reflexivity I am putting forward is not in conflict with objectivity as a guiding principle for research, as defined in that earlier chapter. Furthermore, like objectivism, both practical and reporting reflexivity are aimed at countering threats to validity, and thereby maximising the chances that the answers produced to research questions will be true.

In this respect what I have proposed is at odds with several other influential conceptions of reflexivity in social science methodology. These typically rely on the idea that the research process *constitutes* or *constructs* the phenomena investigated, and verge on or explicitly adopt some form of epistemological relativism or scepticism. Some commentators treat all research accounts as matters of personal expression that reflect the sensibilities or beliefs of the individual researcher, or the categories of a particular academic discipline or culture, so that what research produces can only be one account amongst many possible ones, with no distinctive claim to epistemic validity. Sometimes, there is appeal here to the idea of a unique personal truth, or one that is representative of some social category, that can come from an individual's reflection on her or his own experience (what Ploder and Stadlbauer 2016 refer to as 'strong reflexivity').[6] Radical conceptions of reflexivity are also sometimes linked to forms of scepticism which require that any knowledge claim put forward must be simultaneously subverted if it is not to mislead (Woolgar 1988; Ashmore 1989). For several of these alternative conceptions of reflexivity, the main task is to make explicit the standpoint from which a research account has been produced, this being essential if readers are to understand and respond to it; and any evaluation of it must be in ethical, political, or aesthetic, not epistemic, terms. This is the other side of challenges to the concept of objectivity (see Chapter 5).

As I argued in Chapter 3, these forms of relativism and scepticism are unsustainable even in their own terms when applied consistently, and to apply them selectively is unjustifiable in academic terms. It is, of course, necessary to be aware that in carrying out research we select what is relevant to answering particular questions, and ignore what is not; and that the categories we use for making sense of phenomena are also derived from those questions. Similarly, we rely on disciplinary assumptions about what would, and would not, count as relevant in descriptions and explanations. And the methods we use involve assumptions about the phenomena being investigated and what would serve as data for understanding them. The key question is whether these various assumptions necessarily distort our understanding so as to introduce error into research findings, and whether it is impossible to identify and correct any error.

Here, it is crucial to distinguish, on the one hand, between the *philosophical* arguments about the extent to which, and ways in which, prior categories constitute our experience of the world – as represented, for instance, in the philosophies of Kant or Hegel – and, on the other, the *methodological* question of whether particular assumptions and decisions introduce error, or fail to counter some source of error, and whether they obstruct fruitful interpretations of the phenomena being investigated. The first issue is not relevant to the process of researcher reflexivity in my view – we can leave it to the philosophers – whereas the second certainly is.[7]

The most important point is that there is no incompatibility between *existential reflexivity* and at least some kind of rationalist epistemology and realist ontology; by which I mean the assumption that knowledge is possible about phenomena that exist and have characteristics that are independent of the research process. Moreover, there are good reasons for retaining a commitment to this assumption: without it the very enterprise of research, as a distinctive activity, becomes impossible – it would be assimilated to politics, commerce, ethics, imaginative literature, performance art, or some combination of these (see Chapter 2).

So, the fact that researchers are subject to the same forces and influences as other people does not undercut their capacity to produce knowledge about the world, any more than lay people are themselves cut off from such knowledge by these forces and influences. It also does not rule out the possibility that researchers may be able to pursue particular kinds of knowledge in ways that are likely to be relatively more successful than lay inquiries. All positions in the social world have advantages and disadvantages in this respect, while none guarantee sound knowledge. Researchers have access to more time and resources than most people to investigate questions about which there is disagreement, or that currently have no convincing answers. They can also learn from the efforts of fellow researchers and the experience of diverse groups. While biases may operate on research decisions, it is possible to detect and remedy these, at least to some degree. Research is a self-correcting process, even though not a perfect one. The fact that all knowledge, and all methodological assessment, is fallible does not mean that we can know nothing, that all knowledge claims are simply expressions of who we are. This would only be true if 'knowledge' were to be defined as 'beliefs whose validity is certain beyond all possible doubt'; and there is no good reason for adopting such a definition, given that it would make all practical activity impossible if we really believed it.

From this perspective, *practical* reflexivity provides the basis for operating in a manner that approximates to objectivity.[8] It entails careful reflection on ontological, epistemological and axiological assumptions and what is being done in the course of inquiry, *with a view to detecting how error could arise*. Of course, exactly what this demands at any particular point in a study is by no means straightforward. We can imagine both excessive and insufficient practical reflexivity. The former would involve, for instance, a level of scepticism that undermines the very possibility of empirical inquiry: little progress will be made if *too many* assumptions and decisions are subjected to too much explication and assessment. Meanwhile, *insufficient* reflexivity involves taking for granted starting assumptions that are open to reasonable doubt, overestimating the reliability of evidence and of inferences from it, opting simply for what seem the most obvious or appealing conclusions without considering alternatives, and so on. What level of practical reflexivity is required is always a matter of judgement, but that does not mean that this is 'arbitrary' or merely 'subjective'.

There are also important issues surrounding the third form of reflexivity, concerned with reporting information about the researcher and the research process for readers. Here, again, a middle way is required between two extremes. Some discussions of reflexivity in research reports imply that it is desirable, and possible, for the research process to be fully explicated, so that there is complete 'transparency'. One example of this is the idea that researchers must produce an 'audit trail', documenting all the various steps through which the research proceeded, how and why particular decisions were made, what were the consequences, and so on (Schwandt and Halpern 1988; Lincoln and Guba 1985; Erlandson et al. 1993; Bowen 2009). However, taken literally, this ideal is impossible to realise – the idea of the fully reflexive researcher, in this sense, is a myth; nor is seeking to achieve it desirable, since (potentially at least) it produces extremely lengthy reflexive accounts that readers will have little incentive to read. What *reporting reflexivity* requires, instead, is that readers are given *sufficient* background information about the research process for them to understand what was done and why, in broad terms, so that they can make an assessment of the likely validity of the findings (for discussion of this process of assessment, see Chapter 3; Hammersley 2022e). *Reporting reflexivity* is crucial because it serves as an essential part of the selection process whereby particular knowledge claims come to be included in or excluded from disciplinary bodies of knowledge (Kaufmann 1944).

Sufficiency is likely to vary somewhat according to the audience(s) being addressed. If the target audience is fellow researchers working in the same field, judgement about this may be relatively straightforward; though it should be noted that, if there are conflicting approaches in that field, their differing requirements will need to be taken into account. Where lay audiences are being addressed a significant dilemma often arises: on the one hand, many such audiences will have little interest in methodology but, on the other hand, they will also have little background knowledge about the kind of research approaches and techniques employed. In other words, there may be a conflict between what they want and what they need if they are to be able to make a sound assessment of the likely validity of the findings. Worse still, because of the central role that skilled judgement plays in the research process, it may not be possible to provide the information they require in a manner that will be accessible to them *even if they are motivated to learn about it*. This raises issues about the level of trust required of audiences for research (whether fellow researchers or lay audiences), what can reasonably be trusted, and what cannot.

After all, even aside from deliberate falsification of evidence, we are aware that everyone, including researchers, has unconscious biases that may interfere with the conclusions they reach. Furthermore, no researcher is perfect: he or she may overlook significant potential threats to validity in how an inquiry was carried out. The best that can be done, however, is try to supply readers with sufficient information to assess whether findings were significantly affected by such biases and threats. And judgements about what is sufficient may need to be revised in light of readers' responses to research reports. A dialogical process is involved.

Conclusion

There are multiple meanings of the term 'reflexivity', and they are complex and open to conflicting interpretations. So this term must be used with care; and how it is being used will usually need to be made explicit. I outlined the various meanings it has been given before going on to present what I believe is the most appropriate interpretation in the context of social research. I suggested that it has three forms: existential reflexivity, practical reflexivity, and reporting reflexivity.

In existential terms, reflexivity necessarily operates: we are all part of the social world, researchers included; and this carries important implications for how research findings must be assessed. However, what normative conclusions follow from this is a matter of dispute. Here I have tried to show that a form of *practical reflexivity* – involving self-monitoring of assumptions and decision-making during the course of inquiry – is compatible with objectivity; indeed, that it performs an essential function in increasing the chances that accurate and fruitful research conclusions will be produced. Finally, *reporting reflexivity* – the presentation of sufficient information about the research process for readers – is necessary if research results are to be assessed effectively, both within research communities and beyond. In the case of both practical and reporting reflexivity, judgements have to be made about how much reflexivity is required: what needs to be given attention, and what can be taken for granted (until further notice).

Notes

1 A distinction is sometimes drawn between the meanings of 'reflexive' and 'reflective', but both these terms have multiple meanings, some of them overlapping.

2 For assessments of this line of argument in the context of ethnomethodology and science studies, see Hammersley 2018 and 2022b. For approaches that draw extreme conclusions about social inquiry from this notion of reflexivity, see Pollner 1978 and Raffel and Sandywell 2016.

3 If one denies, or wishes to suspend, the assumption that we already have knowledge of the world, then a form of scepticism is being adopted that undercuts, or puts on hold, all practical engagement with the world, not just social research.

4 There is a link here with Schön's (1983) notion of the reflective practitioner, in effect practical reflexivity requires that researchers operate as reflective practitioners.

5 There is no inherent limit to what could be included in a reflexive account, as regards personal background, situational information, cultural history, or epistemological and ontological assumptions. Potentially, any such account could have the character of *Tristram Shandy*!

6 For an unusual version of this that draws on new materialisms, see Serra Undurraga 2020.

7 For a contrasting view, see Whitaker and Atkinson 2021 and my commentary on this: Hammersley 2022d.

8 As I have defined it in this book, 'objectivity' relates to bias as a threat to validity, whereas practical reflexivity is concerned with all threats to validity, and with barriers to discovering fruitful ways of answering research questions.

11 Triangulation

'Triangulation' is a term that is widely used, particularly among qualitative researchers. Often, it is simply taken to mean employment of more than one type or source of data, but the original methodological sense of the term goes beyond this. Furthermore, some alternative interpretations of its meaning have been developed (Ellingson 2009, 2011; Denzin 2012; Flick 2019). While it has generally been assumed that triangulation is beneficial, its value has some-times been questioned (Silverman 1985:21; Fielding and Fielding 1986:33; Flick 1992; McPhee 1992). Blaikie (1991:131) even proposed a moratorium on using the concept of triangulation in social research. In this chapter, I will outline the main meanings this term has been given, and consider the value of these.

Triangulation as validation

The original meaning of 'triangulation' within social science methodology referred to checking the validity of inferences from a single source of evidence by recourse to one or more further sources of strategically different types.[1] This might involve combining different methods, such as using an online question-naire to check conclusions reached via face-to-face interviews. But, equally, it could entail, for instance, comparing accounts of the same event or phenom-enon coming from witnesses occupying different social positions.

The idea behind this first concept of triangulation is that, by drawing data from additional sources that have very different potential threats to validity built into them, it is possible to assess whatever error there was in the original source. For example, in the case of face-to-face interviews, it is often suspected that there may be a tendency for people to give socially desirable rather than honest responses, and data from anonymous online questionnaires could be used to check whether this had been a source of bias in the interviews. If the evidence from one or more contrasting sources confirms the original analytic conclu-sions, then those conclusions can reasonably be held with more confidence than before; though there needs to be some check that all the sources of data were not in fact biased in the same direction. If there is a discrepancy among evidence from different sources, then this requires interpretation in terms of the

DOI: 10.4324/9781003350354-12

threats to validity likely to be involved in each type of data, and the direction of error that these would tend to produce. At the very least, a discrepancy may indicate the need for further investigation involving other sources of evidence, chosen to assess the effects of specific threats to validity. The strategy involved here is quite closely specified in terms of its goal – checking the validity of inferences from data – and in terms of the means for doing this – comparing data sources carrying distinctive threats to validity.

One starting point for the triangulation metaphor lies in navigation. For instance, sailors take bearings on two landmarks in order to locate their position: on a map, the lines represented by the two bearings, plus one between the landmarks, form a triangle, and the position of the observer is at the point where the two bearing lines cross one another. In short, location can be calculated by means of geometry. A similar method is employed in surveying, though the aim there is not to discover location but to document the physical relations amongst various points on a site.[2]

The original context for a metaphor does not, of course, correspond in all respects to the target context, and differences may render the metaphor misleading. Erzberger and Kelle (2003:461–462) argue that the logic of methodological triangulation in social research is significantly different from that underpinning triangulation in navigation and surveying (see also Blaikie 1991:118–119). In the case of navigation, the second measurement does not provide verification or validation of the first, but rather is a necessary complement required to identify one's location. By contrast, in methodological triangulation what is being investigated is the validity of the first source of evidence. In other words, whereas in navigation a single bearing can tell us that we are on a line in a particular direction from the landmark but not where we are located on that line, in social research a single source of evidence purports to tell us whether a knowledge claim is true: we engage in triangulation in order to *check* that answer, not to gain further information in order to *produce* an answer. A second difference is that in navigational triangulation, assuming that the landmarks have been correctly identified and that the bearings have been taken correctly, the validity of the result is relatively certain. In short, triangulation in navigation is not a device for detecting and discounting error; indeed, any error in identifying the landmarks or calculating the bearings will vitiate the triangulation process. By contrast, as I have already indicated, the outcome of methodological triangulation requires considerable interpretation, and it is concerned with detecting error.

Different kinds of methodological triangulation aimed at assessing the validity of inferences have been identified. So, there can be triangulation among evidence from two or more methods, say interviews versus observation, or online versus face-to-face questionnaires. Equally, as noted earlier, there could be triangulation between different informants, where information about the same events can be compared. Another form of triangulation would involve comparing the results produced by interviewers or observers with different social characteristics: a great deal of methodological research has been concerned

with the effects of the gender or race of an interviewer on the answers of inter-
viewees. This is sometimes referred to as 'investigator triangulation'. Another
version of this is illustrated by Smith and Geoffrey's (1968) classic study of a
classroom, in which data from an observer and from the teacher himself were
combined. It has also been suggested that, in the process of analysis, there can
be triangulation between different theoretical approaches. For instance, there
have even been attempts to triangulate grounded theory, feminist theory, and
critical theory (Kushner and Morrow 2003) or 'feminist intersectionality, critical, and symbolic interaction perspectives' (Pitre and Kushner 2015; see also
Perlesz and Lindsay 2003; Ribbens McCarthy et al. 2003).[3] However, while
theoretical triangulation has occasionally been presented as concerned with
checking the validity of inferences, often it has diverged into other conceptions
of the purpose of triangulation, of the kinds discussed in the next sections.

It is clear, then, that the meaning of the term 'triangulation' was transformed
in moving from navigation to social science. However, such transformations
are always involved in the use of metaphor, to one degree or another. The key
question is whether the transformation has rendered the metaphor useless and
misleading, or whether it is illuminating. Certainly, this original methodological concept of triangulation has been subject to considerable criticism and
many, especially among qualitative researchers, have adopted alternative interpretations of the term, or abandoned it altogether. However, as I will explain
later, I believe it should be retained.

Indefinite triangulation

A second interpretation of 'triangulation' arose in the work of Aaron Cicourel
and his colleagues: what he calls 'indefinite triangulation' requires collecting
accounts of the same event from several people, at one or more times, with
a view to documenting how these accounts were 'assembled from different
physical, temporal, and biographically provided perspectives'. Referring to the
research of his team on school classrooms, Cicourel reports that: 'Comparing the teacher's account of the lesson before and after it was presented, and
comparing the teacher's version with those of the children, produced different
accounts of the "same" scene' (Cicourel et al. 1974:4). The use of scare quotes
around the word 'same' here indicates that for Cicourel what is involved is not
an attempt to identify the truth about the scene witnessed, and therefore to
assess the accounts produced by different participants in terms of how well they
represent what went on. Rather, the approach adopted is closer to the sociology of knowledge: the interest is in the varying accounts produced, and in *how*
these have been constructed.[4]

Here, then, 'triangulation' is treated as a device for exploring differences in
perspectives and in how accounts of social phenomena are produced, rather
than for checking the validity of inferences about the phenomena to which
the accounts refer. Another version that bears some similarities is the approach
taken by Elliott and Adelman (1976) in the context of educational evaluation.

They saw triangulation as a means by which participants in a situation could be helped to develop their understanding of it, through being informed about the perspectives of others.

Triangulation as seeking complementary information

A third interpretation of 'triangulation' has been outlined by Erzberger and Kelle, amongst others, and is perhaps today the most common meaning of the term in routine use by researchers. These authors treat the use of different methods as analogous to observing a physical object from different angles, this yielding 'a fuller and more complete picture'. And they add a further metaphor to clarify what they have in mind, that of the jigsaw puzzle: this supplies 'a full image' when the pieces are put together (Erzberger and Kelle 2003:461).[5]

It is obviously true that information from different sources can be complementary, and that this is an important resource for researchers. However, it seems to me that the jigsaw analogy is misleading, since it implies that the task of research is to produce a reproduction of the phenomena being investigated. In my view, it is better to think of research as providing answers to particular questions about those phenomena. Different questions will produce different 'pictures'; though the visual metaphor is perhaps best avoided, too.

Using triangulation to produce complementary data and using it to serve validation are not incompatible, of course. Indeed, further information about a phenomenon could lead us to change the way we originally categorised it, on the grounds that it no longer looks like an X but appears to be a Y. Here, while the purpose for which the new data were collected was not validation, what has resulted is a correction of the initial interpretation that is analogous to what may occur in triangulation for validation. Triangulation to produce complementary data also has some affinities with the second kind of triangulation I discussed, that found in the work of Cicourel and his colleagues, but as I noted the latter suspend the assumption that the different accounts relate to the same phenomena. This connects with the next interpretation of 'triangulation' I will discuss.

Triangulation as epistemological dialogue or juxtaposition

Flick (1992, 2004, 2019) has put forward a formulation that may, at first sight, seem to be an example of the third type of triangulation, concerned with seeking complementary information. However, it introduces a new element (see also Fielding and Fielding 1986). He argues that different methods are frequently regarded as not simply providing varying kinds of information about the same object, but rather as constructing the world in different ways. This reflects the growing influence of constructionism, one version of which treats social phenomena as constituted through discursive practice (see the Introduction and the Glossary). If we apply this idea to the research process itself, we may be led to conclude that different methods construct the social world in conflicting ways, so that combining them will not lead either to validation or to added information about the same phenomenon, but rather to the presentation of diverse perspectives or multiple realities.

One response to this might be to argue that triangulation can facilitate dialogue between the epistemological positions built into different research methods, perhaps with a view to resolving or transcending their differences. We could call this dialogical triangulation.[6] A more radical position would be that data produced by methods having different epistemological assumptions can, at best, only be juxtaposed. Along these lines, Denzin and Lincoln adopted Richardson's argument that the model should be a crystal not a triangle. They write:

> Like crystals, Eisenstein's montage, the jazz solo, or the pieces in a quilt, the mixed genre text 'combines symmetry and substance with an infinite variety of shapes, substances, transmutations. . . . Crystals grow, change, alter . . . Crystals are prisms that reflect externalities and refract within themselves, creating different colors, patterns, arrays, casting off in different directions' (Richardson 2000:934).
>
> (Denzin and Lincoln 2011:5)[7]

This position, based on metaphors from both nature and art, perhaps reflects a refusal to choose among epistemological paradigms, or to let the reader do this easily. Instead, the goal is to put, and to keep, methods and epistemologies both in tension and in question; and to throw doubt on the idea that one or other approach is correct, or that the differences between them can be overcome. We might call this 'postmodernist triangulation'.[8]

Discussion

It should be clear that, in most methodological discussions of triangulation, what is involved goes beyond simply using more than one source of data. At the very least, there must be careful attention to how the evidence from one source relates to that from others, given the distinctive character of each. We also noted that there can be variation in what is being combined. There is a considerable difference between using data from more than one witness to an event, on the one hand, and seeking to combine different theoretical perspectives, on the other. And, in the case of methods, we may wish to distinguish within-method from between-method triangulation (Denzin 1989: chapter 10): using data from interviews with people who have different social backgrounds, or who play different social roles, would be an example of within-method triangulation, while combining data from an expert panel, focus groups, observation and interviews would be a case of between-method triangulation (for an example, see Nind and Lewthwaite 2020). However, this distinction requires a clear understanding of what the term 'method' refers to, and as we saw in Chapter 1 this is by no means agreed.

The notion of theoretical triangulation raises a key issue that underlies some of the variation in views about the purpose of triangulation that I have documented. Much depends upon what is meant by the term 'theory' here of course (see Chapter 12), but it is certainly true that some types of theory are likely to differ in the ontological and epistemological assumptions they involve. And, as we have seen, some commentators have suggested that this is also true of methods or methodologies, so that combining them may be problematic for the same reason. At the very least, what all this suggests is that in using triangulation we must be clear about what is being combined, in what way, and for what purpose.

Perhaps the most fundamental issue differentiating the first and third conceptions of triangulation from some of the others is the question of whether we can assume that there is a single reality to which the sources of information being triangulated relate, or whether we must treat them as producing different 'realities'. The notion of triangulation as juxtaposition, in particular, denies that there is a single reality. Instead, some form of relativism or scepticism is being adopted, of the kind that is associated with radical constructionism. So, here, different methods are clearly treated as involving conflicting ontological or epistemological assumptions.

A number of writers assert this. For example, Blaikie (1991) identifies empiricism, interpretivism, and realism as fundamentally different philosophical orientations that underpin various social research methods. And he ascribes 'ignorance or misunderstanding' to those who fail to 'recognise' the ontological and epistemological differences built into methods, and who thereby perpetuate 'confused' claims (Blaikie 1991:126 and 128; see also Massey 1999:183). However, neither he nor others effectively establish that conflicting epistemological and ontological assumptions are *necessarily* built into, or uniquely attached to, the use of specific methods. For example, interview data can be used for a range of purposes – to gain information from informants about events or situations, to document their perspectives or attitudes, or to examine how they discursively construct particular types of phenomena through what they say. Each of these ways of using interviews involves rather different (though not necessarily conflicting) epistemological and ontological assumptions; but this suggests that interviews as a method are compatible with diverse philosophical assumptions. Much the same is true of a method like participant observation: this may be employed on the grounds that it gives access to the lived experience of participants, or it may be focused on the formal properties of the processes of social interaction observed (see Atkinson 2015).

We should also note that the assumptions associated with how methods are used are not attached to a small number of internally coherent and clearly differentiated approaches, but rather are associated with labels (such as 'empiricism', 'interpretivism', 'realism', and 'postmodernism') whose meaning is diffuse, covering a wide range of partially overlapping sets of ideas about the nature of social phenomena and how they can best be understood (see the Glossary).

Thus, even if it were true that particular methods involved conflicting epistemological and ontological assumptions, it is not at all clear that they would then 'belong' uniquely to one or other of these approaches. The relationship between approaches and methods is looser than is often assumed; though this is not to deny that there are some fundamental discrepancies in assumption to be found within social science (see Halfpenny 1997; see Introduction).

We can explore this issue further by examining conflicts among some of the radical methodological approaches that stand opposed to sort of position I am advocating in this book. Take, first of all, what Pérez Huber (2009a, 2009b) describes as 'a Chicana feminist epistemology (CFE)' that 'validates the lived experiences' of the women she studied, using their 'testimonio' (personal testimony) (Pérez Huber 2009b:378). We can compare this with a constructionist approach that rejects the idea that interview accounts can provide information about people's experience, focusing instead on how experience is constituted discursively in and through the provision of such accounts (see, for instance, Potter and Hepburn 2005). The differences involved here seem to be both epistemological and ontological. In epistemological terms, Pérez Huber does not simply claim that the testimonio represent the experience of the women, she also assumes that this experience reflects facts about their lives – for example about the impact of racism. In other words, while there is often an ambiguity built into the meaning of 'experience', she seems to assume a correspondence between experience as 'what-was-perceived-and-felt' and as 'what-actually-happened'. By contrast, a constructionist approach suspends any relationship between accounts and phenomena to which they purport to refer, even when this is the personal experience of informants. From this constructionist point of view, interview data are to be examined solely for what they reveal about how reality is constituted in and through informants' accounts.

There is also an ontological difference involved here, in that Pérez Huber assumes the existence of a wider society in which her informants live that has structural features independent both of them and of the research process, these determining their experiences (for example, structural racism). By contrast, radical constructionism assumes that the world exists only as constituted in and through the accounts that people produce – the idea that there are external factors which determine the nature of those accounts is rejected.[9]

There are certainly deep divisions here: one could not consistently combine Pérez Huber's Chicana feminist epistemology with discursive constructionism.[10] But this conflict is at the level of these general methodological approaches, not at that of methods: the data to be found in testimonios could be analysed for the discursive practices employed, rather than treating it as providing evidence about informants' experiences of the world, or the nature of that world.[11] In short, triangulation of methods in the manner of the first and third conceptions is certainly possible, even if triangulation of methodological *approaches* with conflicting epistemological or ontological assumptions is not.

Aside from all this, though, we might also want to question whether conflict in ontological and epistemological assumptions is *necessarily* a barrier to triangulation. This depends upon what attitude we adopt towards those assumptions. If we treat them as absolute commitments, in other words as foundational and therefore beyond question, then they are certainly a major obstacle. But if we view them in a more instrumental fashion there may be much to be said for comparing what results are produced by applying different theoretical or methodological perspectives to the same data (for examples of this, see Perlesz and Lindsay 2003; Ribbens McCarthy et al. 2003). Of course, this instrumental approach relies on the assumption that, even if we do not know the nature of the phenomena we are investigating or how best to understand them, they do have a specific nature which we may be able to conceptualise. In broad terms, it assumes a realist ontology and rationalist epistemology, as against the sort of relativism or scepticism that seems to underpin the notion of triangulation as juxtaposition, and some other accounts of triangulation too.

Conclusion

Much discussion of the concept of triangulation illustrates how practical research strategies can become caught up in the philosophical debates that now plague social inquiry. Checking other sources of information – for the purposes of testing the validity of one's initial interpretation or to provide complementary information – is a routinely used practice in everyday life; and one that was incorporated into scholarly work in history and the human sciences long before the triangulation metaphor was deployed.[12] Yet, as I have outlined, that concept is now subject to sharp philosophical disagreement. I suspect that the stimulus for this has been, in part, the fact that 'triangulation' was introduced into the methodological literature by Donald Campbell in a way that reconceptualised this practical strategy as a validation *technique*.

While Campbell's (1974) own position was fallibilist, there has long been a tendency within much of the methodological literature to reduce the research process to the application of techniques or the following of rules. This is seen as providing for procedural objectivity by ruling out personal idiosyncrasies and thereby (it is assumed) greatly increasing the chances that research findings will be valid (see Chapter 5). In this context, triangulation comes to be treated as a feature of research design that can be included in checklists designed to evaluate the quality of studies. Indeed, as Seale points out, this became quite common (Seale 1999:56). To some degree, the criticisms of triangulation for validation are a negative reaction to this, arising from insistence on the interpretative judgement necessarily involved in the research process.

Yet, as we have seen, the criticisms often go well beyond challenging an overly technical orientation, to result in rejecting the idea that there is a single reality that it is the aim of social research to understand. Embedded in what I referred to as the juxtaposing strategy of triangulation, for instance, is the notion that there are multiple realities or forms of life, and that research is necessarily implicated in one or other of these, able at best only to draw attention to their incommensurability. While this line of argument highlights some difficult philosophical problems, I am not convinced that these problems have much significance for the practice of social research. Indeed, it seems to me that, in deciding to engage in research of any kind, one necessarily assumes that there is a single reality and that aspects of it can be known. Those assumptions are constitutive of the very nature of inquiry, of any kind (see Chapter 2). It is difficult to see what other distinctive goal inquiry could have than the production of knowledge, and in everyday usage 'knowledge' implies true understanding of something, where truth is independent of perspective (see Chapter 3). While we must certainly recognise that there are variations among people and groups in what is taken to be true, we need not and should not reduce 'truth' to 'what is believed to be true'.

If the aim of research is to produce knowledge of the social world, and specifically of the kind that most social scientists have traditionally pursued, then the most fruitful interpretations of 'triangulation' are the first and third ones that I identified. Moreover, as already noted, these interpretations are complementary rather than in competition. In other words, using data of different types can help us both to determine what interpretations of phenomena are more and less likely to be true *and* provide us with complementary information that illuminates different aspects of what we are studying. This is not to suggest that such triangulation is a simple matter of 'checking validity', the complexities involved must be recognised. Nevertheless, triangulation of these kinds can be of great value and also helps us to recognise the limits to what any particular type of data can supply.

Notes

1 The first methodological use of the term seems to have been in Campbell and Fiske's (1959:101) discussion of convergent and divergent validation of measurement instruments, but it was later elaborated in Webb et al. 1966. It was introduced into discussion of qualitative method by Denzin (1970). For useful brief accounts of triangulation, see Bryman 2004 and Flick 2019. See also Bryman's discussion of this concept in the context of the relationship between quantitative and qualitative method: Bryman 1988:131–134. Seale (1999: chapter 5) provides a useful discussion of epistemological criticisms of triangulation.

2 For a discussion of the analogy with surveying, see Blaikie 1991:118.

3 For an interesting discussion of the issue of theoretical triangulation in a particular field, that of accounting research, see Hoque et al. 2013, 2015, and Modell 2015.

4 There are similarities and differences between this and van Drie and Dekker's (2013) use of theoretical triangulation in classroom research.

5 Curiously, despite resort to a different metaphor, this third sense of 'triangulation' matches the source of the original metaphor better than did the first sense. Here, the different types of data being combined are complementary albeit in a somewhat different way from the two bearings in navigation. For another version of this notion of complementarity, drawing on the metaphor of a mosaic, see Becker 1970.

6 Something like this seems to be implied in Whitaker and Atkinson's (2021) account of reflexivity; see also Hammersley 2022d.

7 Denzin (1970:298–299) had earlier used the analogy of a kaleidoscope: 'this is not to imply that reality has the shifting qualities of the colored prism, but that it too is an object that moves and that will not permit one interpretation to be stamped upon it'.

8 For interesting discussions of the relationship between postmodernism and the use of multiple methods, see Fielding 2009a, 2009b; Healy 2009; and Pascale 2009.

9 There are parallels here with ethnomethodology, on which see Hammersley 2019, 2022b. This was an important influence on Cicourel's indefinite triangulation.

10 In fact, there is some ambivalence about the position being adopted by Pérez Huber. At one point she says that her 'role is not to determine what is truth in the testimonios, these women have shared with me', but she immediately goes on to say that her aim is to 'understand their realities within a larger context of structural and systematic inequality' (Pérez Huber 2009a:649).

11 For an excellent example of this approach, applied to Sylvia Fraser's autobiographical account of childhood sexual abuse, see Davies 1995. Pérez Huber (2009b:386) criticises the 'appropriation of testimonio by "non-critical" academics', but she does not provide any cogent justification for ruling this out.

12 For example, writing in 1898, Langlois and Seignobos declare:

> It is a principle common to all sciences of observation not to base a scientific conclusion on a single observation; the fact must have been corroborated by several independent observations before it is affirmed categorically. History, with its imperfect modes of acquiring information, has less right than any other science to claim exemption from this principle. An historical statement is, in the most favourable case, but an indifferently made observation, and needs other observations to corroborate it. It is by combining observations that every science is built up: a scientific fact is a centre on which several different observations converge. Each observation is subject to chances of error which cannot be entirely eliminated; but if several observations agree, this can hardly be in virtue of common error: the more probable explanation of the agreement is that the observers have all seen the same reality and have all described it correctly. Errors are personal and tend to diverge; it is the correct observations that agree.
>
> (Langlois and Seignobos 1913:196)

Seale (1999:55) also notes that, within sociology, the idea of comparing data from different sources was common in the writings of Becker and others before it was explicitly labelled 'triangulation' by Denzin.

12 Theory

While the importance of theory is widely accepted, some have questioned its value (see, for example, Winch 1958; Thomas 1997, 2007; Oakley 2000:310; Carr 2006; and Hutchinson et al. 2008: chapter 3 and *passim*). But underlying much discussion of this topic, and not always recognised, is the problem that the word 'theory' has a range of very different meanings (Abend 2008). In this chapter I will attempt to clarify these, and in the course of doing so I will mention conflicting attitudes that have been taken towards each type of theory, and the problems associated with it.

There are at least seven meanings that can be given to the term 'theory', often deriving from different contrasts. I will discuss each of these in turn.

Theory versus practice

Here the word refers to ideas about how a particular type of activity *ought to be* carried out, and about its value. It is usually assumed that actual practice deviates from this, perhaps quite sharply, and so theory may be used as a standard by which practice can be evaluated. Thus, on this interpretation, theory is normative in character (Lobkowicz 1967). Examples of this sort of theory would include some versions of educational theory (Hirst 1983) and political theory (Vincent 2007). It might also be suggested that methodology is a form of theory in this sense (see Chapter 1).

A variety of attitudes can be taken towards the role of theory of this kind. Some regard it as having the capacity to *transform* practice. A positive version treats it as providing a coherent underlying set of principles for understanding the world that must guide action. Sources of such theory would include, for instance, Catholicism or Marxism (see, for example, Althusser 1971). Alternatively, this kind of theory may be seen as playing a primarily negative role: subverting conventional wisdom, and perhaps thereby the current socio-political regime, so as to make way for something different (see Ball 1995).[1] However, there are less dramatic conceptions of normative theory which treat it as offering more modest guidance, these recognising that it will need to be moderated in light of experience and of information about the situation in which action is taking place. At the other end of the spectrum, theory of this kind may be

DOI: 10.4324/9781003350354-13

viewed as an irrelevance or obstruction, because it assumes idealised conditions that never hold: 'It's OK in theory, but it'll never work in practice'. In these terms, a contrast may be drawn between espoused theories (these being the sort of normative theory I am discussing here) and 'theories-in-action' (the assumptions that practitioners *actually* make in doing their work) (Argyris and Schön 1974). Kaplan's (1964: chapter 1) distinction between 'reconstructed logic' and 'logic-in-use' in the field of methodology is another example. Here the emphasis is usually on the primacy of practice over theory.

Theory versus fact

Sometimes it is said that a particular statement is 'only a theory', implying that it is not well-established knowledge but hypothetical in status. On this interpretation, theories are about the world as it is (rather than being normative) but they are speculative: their validity is uncertain. Alternatively, they may not be intended to be true but, rather, to serve as 'useful fictions' (see Vaihinger 1925). The contrast here is with one sense of the term 'fact', as referring to a true statement about a particular state of affairs (see Chapter 4).

There are a number of issues for debate around this sense of the term. One concerns the ontological status of the entities to which theories refer. As already noted, there is the question of whether these entities, and the relations amongst them that the theory proposes, are meant to represent how the world is or are simply intended to be useful devices that allow us to account for or predict what will happen in the world (van Fraassen 1980). Questions may even be raised about whether there is, in fact, any knowledge that is *not* fictional in this sense; and, if there is, about exactly how its empirical validity is to be established, what criteria should be employed for assessing candidate claims, and so on. For example, some qualitative researchers question whether there can be any facts about the social world, on the grounds that this makes the false assumption that independent phenomena exist, these having determinate characteristics beyond all interpretations of them (see Chapters 3 and 4). From this point of view, there is a sense in which all accounts of the world are necessarily theoretical fictions. Other social scientists insist, however, that the task of research is to produce theories that capture what is really going on in particular types of situation. This is true both of hypothetico-deductive approaches to explanation and of more inductive strategies, such as Grounded Theory (see Chapter 8).

Theory as abstraction as against concrete particulars

Here 'theory' is taken to refer either to *all* concepts or categories, by contrast with individual phenomena themselves and our experience of them; *or* it may be taken to refer to relatively abstract categories as against more concrete ones. The distinctive feature of theory here is that it operates at a level of abstraction that is higher than immediate experience, commonsense knowledge, and perhaps even low-level empirical generalisations. Given this character, it employs categories that gather together many phenomena that are usually treated as quite different in character, while sometimes treating as different what are generally regarded as the same.

In one version, what is involved is a distinction between an observation language, designed perhaps to capture sense-data relating to particular phenomena experienced at particular moments in time, and a theoretical language that is intended, at the very least, to identify stable features of particular types of objects, and the relations amongst them (see Nagel 1979:350–351). In more realist versions, theory is concerned with identifying the essential characteristics of types of phenomena, or the causal mechanisms that generate them; here the contrast is with commonsense categories that do not identify these effectively, or even obscure them. Some views see science as producing ever more abstract conceptualisations of the world, these designed to grasp the fundamental laws that operate behind appearances. This assumption is central to some positivist views of science but also to other approaches, for instance Marx's revolutionary science of society.

In more mundane ways, many qualitative researchers distinguish between formal/generic and substantive/topical concepts, as well as between those that are introduced by the analyst and those that are employed by the people they are studying (Glaser and Strauss 1967; Lofland 1971). They also often argue that a central task of social science is the development of typologies that identify general patterns in human social life (see McKinney 1966). Given that it is difficult to see how phenomena could ever be cognitively grasped *in themselves*, without recourse to categories of some kind, the key issue must be *degree* of abstraction. Yet not only are there questions about exactly what this involves, but also about the value of abstract theory. The sociological theory of Parsons, for example, was widely criticised for excessive abstraction (Mills 1959; Merton 1968), and much the same charge has been directed at more recent theories, for instance those of Bernstein, Giddens, and others (see, for example, Cherkaoui 1977:561; and Sharrock 2010:106–109).

Nevertheless, it does often seem necessary to distinguish between categories operating at different levels of abstraction, even if the aim of inquiry is to identify features or relations at the level of middle-range theory, rather than the highly abstract level occupied by theories such as those of Parsons or Luhmann, or for that matter Althusser or Bourdieu.

Theory by contrast with description

Here theories tell us 'what causes what', and such explanatory theories are sometimes treated as the main product of science. By contrast, descriptions simply tell us what exists, or existed, in a particular time/place location, what features some set of existing objects have, and so on (see Chapter 4). In these terms, theories are about not just what exists or what happened but *why* it exists or happened. While explanatory theories may be quite specific, offering an explanation for a particular event or type of event (in other words, they may operate at a relatively low level of abstraction), they are generally held to imply a universal or quite general pattern or process, by virtue of the fact that they rely upon counterfactual conditions: if we say that event A caused event B, we are implying that if A had not occurred then B would not have happened, other things being equal. And this is usually taken to imply a general relationship between events of type A and events of type B, one that always or usually occurs under given conditions, or 'other things being equal'.

There has been much discussion about whether causality operates in the social world, and if so what character it has, along with the implications of this for the nature and role of theory (MacIver 1942; Ragin 1987; McKim and Turner 1997; Warshay and Warshay 2005; Hammersley 2008, 2014a: chapter 1; Maxwell 2012). There are also some commentators who see theories as descriptive, in the sense that they describe generative mechanisms that operate in the world (see, for instance, Bhaskar 2008), as well as those who reject theory *in favour of* description (Hutchinson et al. 2008). However, in my view both these positions are misleading. The first obscures an essential distinction between an account which simply tells us what exists from one which informs us about why it exists. Much the same is true of the second, where it is insisted that the focus should be on how things occur, rather than on why. In my terms, answers to how questions, like those to why questions, are explanatory rather than descriptive in status. Of course, it is true that sometimes, in elliptical terms, a descriptive statement may serve an explanatory function: if I complain about the cold and someone says 'the window is open', that descriptive statement is being used to point to an explanation. However, the underlying distinction between descriptive and explanatory functions remains.

Theory as concerned with macro-level structures and processes, as against accounts of local events and practices

The issue here is what we might refer to as the socio-geographical spread or scale of the phenomena that an account refers to, with the term 'theory' being restricted to accounts that have a broad rather than a local focus. The main source of this conception of theory within the social sciences is, probably, Marxism, with its argument that we can only understand specific events in terms of the social totality (see Jay 1977). Other 'critical' approaches have also adopted this approach, even when focusing upon gender or ethnic inequalities rather than on class oppression as the key feature of the wider society. In fact, most contemporary social theory operates at the macro level.[2]

Numerous issues arise about this conception of theory. One concerns the nature of the totality, knowledge of which is required in order to understand local phenomena. This is sometimes interpreted as a particular national society; sometimes as the structure of a specific type of social formation, such as capitalism, that transcends national boundaries; sometimes as the 'world system'; sometimes as the whole process of socio-historical development that Marx,

Durkheim, Weber, Elias, Giddens, Castells, or whoever has identified as characteristic of the West or of the world more generally.

There are also questions about how we can acquire knowledge of such totalities. After all, if this is built up from investigation of local social phenomena, there may be problems of circularity if that knowledge is then used to explain those phenomena. Moreover, there are longstanding questions about the viability of, or need for, macro theories (Martin and Dennis 2010). And, of course, post-structuralists have not only challenged all claims to knowledge of totalities but also argued that it was precisely the pretence to such knowledge that generated the forms of political oppression that were carried out in the name of Marxism during the twentieth century (Dews 2007).

While the distinction between macro and micro may be a useful one, it is best framed in its own terms, rather than being implicated in the definition of 'theory'. Thus, there can be both macro and micro theories in most of the other senses of the term I am discussing here.

Theory as an explanatory language rather than consisting of a single explanatory principle

There is sometimes a refusal to apply the term 'theory' to a single explanatory principle – for example, one which states that phenomena of type A tend to cause phenomena of type B (under given conditions) – on the grounds that any true theory must be a *set* of principles that tell us about the whole range of behaviour of related types of phenomena, or of all social phenomena. This is the sense of the term employed, for instance, by Parsons and Luhmann. The demand is that any theory should be much more informative than a statement about a single causal regularity. In these terms, theories are sometimes directed at capturing the basic principles of particular causal systems, these being regarded as hidden from ordinary forms of perception and cognition. The models for this sort of theory are usually to be found in natural science, for instance the kinetic theory of gases or perhaps even evolutionary biology; though an example from within the human sciences might be Lévi-Strauss's use of structural linguistics as a model (see Jenkins 1979).

As with the fourth type of theory, there are issues here about whether such causal systems operate within the social world, largely because of doubts about the nature of social causation; and, if they do, about how we can gain knowledge of them. Moreover, there is a fuzzy line between this category and the next, of which there are plenty of social scientific examples.

Theory as an approach or 'paradigm'

What is distinctive about this final interpretation is that theories are here treated as involving whole philosophies, in the sense of distinctive sets of ontological, epistemological, and perhaps also axiological, assumptions. This type of theory often combines features from the others: such theories may carry normative, practical implications (as with sense 1); they usually operate at a relatively abstract level (sense 3); they certainly claim to provide, or at least to facilitate, explanations not just descriptions (sense 4); and they are not singular explanatory principles but offer a language for talking about social phenomena (sense 6). The concept of 'paradigm' often employed to refer to such theories derives from Thomas Kuhn's historical account of the natural sciences, where it refers to a well-defined framework of assumptions, incommensurable with other such frameworks, these being embodied in what are treated as exemplary studies (Kuhn 1970). However, social scientists reinterpreted this term in ways that moved it away from the sense that Kuhn had given it (see Introduction).

In fact, Kuhn argued that social science is pre-paradigmatic, and raised doubts about whether it would ever escape this state (Kuhn 2000). He portrayed natural sciences as each dominated by a single paradigm most of the time, whereas many paradigms persist in parallel within social sciences. Furthermore, Kuhn is often misrepresented as arguing that paradigms are impositions on our experience of the world that reconstitute it in ways that are essentially arbitrary. This was not his view, since he retained a concept of scientific progress.[3] An effect of this misreading of Kuhn is a tendency for social science paradigms to become close in character to ideologies, often operating as sets of blinkers, with the task of research becoming simply to 'demonstrate' the validity of the assumptions on which they are founded: what can be referred to as paradigmitis (Hammersley 1984). Another set of problems arises from the fact that particular social science paradigms are rarely well-defined; and most of them subsequently fragment into competing versions, so that there is a built-in process of proliferation. At the same time, their adherents tend to assume too strong a relationship between fundamental philosophical assumptions, on the one hand, and ways of investigating specific phenomena and the conclusions reached, on the other (see Halfpenny 1997; see Chapter 1).

In many ways, the original model for theory as an approach or paradigm in the social sciences is Marxism, which provides a set of concepts – notably, 'social class', 'class struggle', 'ideology', 'commodification', and 'overproduction crises' – that, it is claimed, constitutes a comprehensive framework for understanding human social life, or at least the development of modern western societies, their past and future. However, the second half of the twentieth century witnessed not only the decomposition of Marxism but also the emergence of a very large number of self-declared 'new paradigms', of various kinds and located in diverse fields.

Conclusion

The interpretations of 'theory' I have discussed are clearly very different from one another; so that, at the very least, it is necessary to make clear which of them is intended when the term is used. Aside from this, though, the legitimacy of some of them is open to question in the context of social research. For instance, in my view social science cannot produce normative theory

(Hammersley 2014a, 2017c). Similarly, the idea of theories as paradigms is troublesome, especially when different approaches are treated as 'incommensurable', and therefore as impossible to evaluate comparatively (see Hammersley 2019c). In Chapter 11 I argued that some of the discrepant assumptions underpinning different 'paradigms' can be evaluated in instrumental terms, assessing their relative value in producing worthwhile knowledge. At the same time, there are epistemological, ontological, and (especially) axiological assumptions that cannot be dealt with in this way, because they are incompatible with assumptions that define the very nature of social research (see Chapter 2).

In my view, the most useful sense of the term 'theory' is that referring to general accounts of 'what type of phenomenon tends to cause what other type of phenomenon, or variation in this'. Theories of this kind are necessarily involved in explanations, and I believe that explanations are the most distinctive product of social science. Indeed, most social research puts forward explanations and offers evidence in support of them. There is an important, and difficult, question about whether social theories of this kind can be tested. Many commentators would insist that they can be, but I am not so sure (Hammersley 2014a: chapter 2).

Notes

1 There are other, even less determinate, characterisations that fall into this category. For instance, Miller (2007:6) writes: 'What we call theory is a series of ongoing debates about meaning, texts, knowledge, and subjectivity that extend from the Platonic dialogues, through Aristotle to Cicero, Seneca, Augustine, Aquinas, Dante, and so on to the present'.
2 This was not always so, a key example being the work of Simmel on the effects of group size or on secret societies (Wolff 1950).
3 For useful discussions of Kuhn's work, see Bird 2000, Sharrock and Read 2002.

13 Researcher integrity

The term 'researcher integrity' (or sometimes 'research integrity') has come to be widely used in recent years, especially in official documents relating to the governance of scientific research (see Banks 2015, 2018; but see also Macfarlane 2009). These draw attention to aspects of the role obligations of researchers that have not always received the attention they deserve: those relating to the actual task of producing knowledge, as compared with the (equally important) ethical issues that focus primarily on the treatment of research participants. It is these epistemic issues I will be concerned with here.[1]

Such epistemic integrity is closely related to objectivity (Chapter 5), rigour (Chapter 6), and reflexivity (Chapter 10), and requires that a researcher strives to make sound judgements regarding how any piece of research can best be pursued so as to maximise the chances of discovering true answers to research questions. I will examine what this requires in each of the main aspects of the research process: formulating and developing research questions; using the existing literature; selecting cases for investigation; collecting and analysing data; writing research reports; and engaging with critics.

Selecting and developing research questions

Whether initial research questions are relatively vague and open-ended in character or take the form of specific hypotheses, they must be evaluated for their likely fruitfulness. One criterion here is whether answers to them would be relevant to perennial practical concerns or at least to matters of general human interest. There is frequently pressure for them to address what are taken to be the most pressing contemporary issues, but not only may this be too strict a requirement (leading other important issues to be neglected), it is often in conflict with a second evaluation criterion: that investigation of research questions must be sufficiently feasible to allow a reasonable chance of reaching convincing conclusions. What this implies, first of all, is that they must be capable of being answered by means of empirical research. This is far from true of many of the 'big questions' to which we would like answers, most of which have value components (see Rule 1978). Furthermore, even questions that could be addressed in principle will often not be answerable in

DOI: 10.4324/9781003350354-14

practice given the resources available to a particular project at the particular time.

Therefore, as regards research questions, integrity requires that researchers tackle questions that have broad relevance and importance, but also only ones that are open to effective investigation. Furthermore, it demands that researchers are honest about the limits to what can be achieved. Above all, it proscribes producing research reports that pretend to have answered questions that the research did not tackle effectively, and perhaps could not have tackled. This may seem obvious, but it is a requirement that is frequently breached.

Use of the existing literature

A researcher has an obligation adequately to search for relevant literature, and to provide sufficient information to readers about how this was done. Of course, searches can never be absolutely exhaustive. One reason for this is that time and other resources are scarce, and those that are allocated to searching the literature are not available for other activities, including reading and reviewing what is found. More fundamentally, there are often no built-in limits to what could count as relevant literature. Indeed, it would be better to think of relevant research *literatures*, since there are often several – relating to different aspects of the research questions, as well as to the methods to be used for investigating them. Moreover, in each case, what could be relevant extends indefinitely, at least potentially, so that some judgement has to be made about cut-off points. Nevertheless, if researchers do not search effectively for relevant literature, there is a danger that they will go over much the same ground as others without learning from the past. This is, I suggest, a quite common occurrence in many fields.

We should also note that what is relevant literature for a project may well change as research questions develop, and as methodological strategies are adapted to deal with emerging conditions and the developing process of inquiry. There is a need, then, to recognise the changing needs of a project as regards the literature, and to carry out new searches as appropriate, as well as re-reading what was found previously. It is thus rarely possible to write the final version of a literature review, to be incorporated in the research report, before one has collected, or even analysed, the data.

There are also obligations regarding how relevant previous studies are presented in research reports. There may be a temptation here to downplay or even to misrepresent their contribution, in order to clear the way for one's own study. This is perhaps especially likely when studies are used as illustrations of the inadequacies of previous investigations, or as exemplifying a misguided approach. Unfortunately, it is not uncommon for previous work to be caricatured in this process, which is not to deny that it may well have major failings. Integrity requires that the literature is shown appropriate respect, in other words sufficient effort must be made to grasp what previous authors have done; the evidence and methods they have used; and the reasons for the choices they made in carrying out their work.

However, while the literature must be respected, this does not, of course, mean that it should not be critically assessed, especially in the case of key studies directly relevant to one's work; and this assessment must be made explicit. There is an obligation to engage in such criticism, and this can focus on a number of features: the concepts used – how well-formulated they are, how appropriate, and how well they are applied; the formulation of research questions; the selection of cases for investigation; the types of data employed and how these are presented in the report; and the likely validity of the findings and conclusions.

Selecting cases for investigation

It is an obvious requirement that the cases selected for study must be appropriate for the research questions being investigated. However, cases can serve different functions. Is the aim to study what is *typical* of some category, or representative of some population? Or is the aim comparative analysis of some sort? In which case, decisions need to be made about whether differences between the cases are being minimised or maximised, as well as about which differences are thought to be relevant. Of course, a case may be selected initially as an instance of something interesting and/or important, with a view to providing a description and explanation of its unique features. But in most research, including almost all qualitative inquiry, more general claims will come to be made explicitly or implicitly, and when this happens the rationale for generalisation (empirical or theoretical) needs to be considered, and stated. There is a whole host of issues around the selection of cases, then, that researchers must take into account if they are to do their research well.

Thus, where the aim is generalisation to some finite population the nature of this population must be made clear, and the grounds for assuming that the case(s) studied are representative examined. Similarly, where the goal is to identify some conditional causal relationship among categories of phenomena, the nature of that relationship and the evidence for concluding that it operates must be carefully considered. Neither kind of generalisation is unproblematic in the context of social science (Gomm et al. 2000; Cooper et al. 2012; Hammersley 2014a), and achieving either with a high level of likely validity is challenging. It is important that there is honesty about what is being attempted and about the degree of success likely to be achieved or actually achieved.

The other side of this issue is that, given that it is not possible to represent any case exhaustively, there must be clarity about which aspects of cases are to be represented and why. Of course, in the early stages of research what is relevant may not be clear to the researcher: it is unavoidable, indeed often desirable, to operate on the basis of 'hunch', relying on one's best judgement about what will be fruitful, and erring on the side of inclusion rather than exclusion. But, as the research goes on, the rationale for what is being focused on and what ignored in studying particular cases (along with why study of these cases is appropriate) needs to be made as explicit as possible, and evaluated. Crucial here, of course, is the link back to research questions.

A couple of ancillary points should also be mentioned. One is that while sampling based on statistical theory can be an extremely useful technique, it does not, in itself, facilitate the task of selecting cases for comparative analysis. Nor is it always feasible or necessary even when the concern is with what is typical or representative of a population. Its use is certainly not mandatory for research integrity. What *is* mandatory is attention to how well whatever sampling strategy is adopted serves the purposes of the research, both in principle and in practice (for example when 'non-response' or 'attrition' is taken into account). It also needs to be remembered that if research questions change over the course of an inquiry it may be necessary for the sampling strategy to be modified: the strategy must serve the research questions that are eventually addressed in the research report, not those that were initially formulated.

Data collection or production

A first question that needs to be addressed under this heading is whether, in fact, new data are required. There should be at least some consideration given to whether the necessary data are already publicly available or can be accessed in an archive. There is now a considerable amount of archived research material, especially quantitative but also qualitative; and it is often argued that this is under-utilised. While, very often, these data will not be sufficient to address the research questions of a new study, they can sometimes be a worthwhile supplement to new data.

Given that what type of question is being addressed can make a significant difference to what (if any) new data need to be collected, careful attention must be given to this relationship, throughout the research process. For example, if the aim is to produce a *description* of some phenomenon, what is necessary will be different from where the aim is to *explain* the occurrence or nature of that phenomenon (on the distinction between descriptions and explanations see Chapter 4). Producing explanations still requires descriptions (of cases in which what is to be explained occurs or is absent, or differs sharply, and perhaps also of those in which various potential explanatory factors are present or absent, or are present to some degree), though here the descriptions will need to be tailored to the explanatory task. And explanation also requires some sort of comparative analysis, even if this amounts to a thought experiment rather than a systematic comparison of actually existing cases of different kinds. Careful consideration needs to be given to what are the most productive comparisons, and what conclusions can be drawn from these; with some assessment of this being provided in research reports. Furthermore, there can be change in the requirements of description and explanation, as the research questions are clarified and the research process becomes more progressively focused. All this reinforces a point made earlier: that integrity requires that we be as clear as possible at each stage of the research about our goal, and about the requirements of achieving it, making adjustments to the research design as appropriate.

Another important element of integrity is that the researcher must consider the full range of methods that could be used to obtain data relevant to answering the research questions. There may be a tendency for researchers to choose from a relatively narrow range. For example, an initial decision could be made to adopt a quantitative or qualitative approach without the value of 'mixing methods' being considered. Similarly, it has been claimed that many qualitative researchers opt immediately for interviews. It is important to remember not only that there are several other sources of social data available (observation, documentary material online and offline), but also that interviews (like other methods) can be carried out in a variety of ways: the number of participants may vary (on both sides), as can where the interviews are carried out (for example on whose territory), the projected length, whether a single interview is to be employed or repeated interviews, the sorts of question to be asked (not just whether these are strongly or weakly structured but also what form they take – such as invitations to reflect, requests for detailed description, challenges to claims that have been made, etc.), whether prompts of various kinds are to be used (photographs, video-extracts, magazines, etc.), and so on. Given that there is an array of methods that social researchers can employ, and internal diversity in the use of particular methods, careful (and continual) attention must be given to the manner in which data are being collected. There is an obligation to reflect on the assumptions built into whatever approach is employed.

A further point is that in using any methods there is a need to deploy these in ways that reflect an understanding of what has been learned about them in the past by other researchers. This means that some familiarity with the methodological literature is required, but also reflection upon the method and how it would be best to use it in one's own project (see Chapter 1). Often this is a matter of balancing different potential features of a method. For example, an essential element of interviewing is to listen very carefully to what informants say. This is obvious, but it can easily be forgotten, especially if one is preoccupied with what question to ask next. It is particularly important in relatively unstructured interviews, where the next question one asks should usually be based upon what the informant has just said (rather than following a prearranged sequence of pre-formulated questions). Here, any tendency to force what people say into one's own prior framework must be resisted. At the same time, people do not always tell, or know, the truth, nor do they always produce responses that are authentic in other respects (they may say what they assume the researcher wishes to hear, or what would show them in the best light). Nor is what they say always relevant to the research, though care must be exercised before treating it as irrelevant. Therefore, it is sometimes necessary to challenge what people say, to stimulate them to reflect on what they have said, to test out the implications of what they seem to be meaning, or to steer them back to what is relevant to the research. This is not incompatible with listening to people carefully, with a view to understanding the logic and validity of what they are saying. However, in the context of the interview, and in that of analysis, there may well be a tension between these two concerns. Integrity requires that an appropriate balance is struck, as far as possible. Of course, once again, what this means in any particular case is a matter of judgement and may well be a contestable matter.

Similar issues arise with other methods than interviewing. For example, in the case of observation, what form should this take (structured or unstructured), should audio- or video-recording be used, where and when are observations to be carried out, and so on. Difficult decisions are involved, and there must be continual reflection on the advantages and disadvantages of particular strategies (see Chapter 10).

Data production is a challenging task, not least because it involves decision-making in conditions of considerable uncertainty. It is almost impossible to avoid what, in hindsight, seem like mistakes. However, these rarely undercut the whole value of a study; and what may have been a mistake in one respect can have beneficial consequences in others.

Data analysis

What is required here can be described fairly simply: development of the most appropriate mode of analysis for answering the research questions, as currently constituted, in light of the nature of the data available. However, even more than data production, analysis is by no means simply a matter of choice from a range of well-defined options. The most obvious axis of variation is quantitative versus qualitative analysis: between an approach in which data are structured so as to provide counts, rankings, and/or measurements, and one that assigns data to various categories or themes that are not mutually exclusive or exhaustive, and may be significantly reformulated in the analytic process. In the first approach, a clearly defined set of categories, or scale, is developed within which each relevant data item can be assigned to its place, with the category system or scale being exhaustive of the relevant data. In the second approach, the data are assigned to categories in a way that is flexible and multiple, these categories often serving as sensitising concepts that are refined or modified so as better to serve the development of descriptive or explanatory ideas.

However, there is a range of strategies under these two broad headings, as well as some overlap; plus room for combining very different strategies within the same study. If the data have been structured in a way that allows counts, rankings, or measurements, there is still considerable scope for variation in mode of analysis, from the use of relatively simple descriptive statistics (percentage differences, rates, indexes, averages and measures of variation, and so on) to much more sophisticated techniques that can be very demanding in the requirements they place upon the data. These techniques can vary, too, according to whether they are aggregate-based or case-focused (see Byrne and Ragin 2009).[2] Similarly, if the data have been structured in a looser way to facilitate the development of 'thick descriptions' or explanatory theories, there are various possibilities regarding how this is to be done, from those characteristic of grounded theorising to those associated with narrative or discourse analysis.

Choice amongst ways of analysing the data, as well as the particular substantive categories or scales developed, must show due care and diligence, avoiding overly superficial analysis, but also eschewing the use of complex techniques that make excessive demands on the data available or speculative forms of analysis that overinterpret the data.

A key aspect too, as with data production, is to be aware of the risk of bias, guard against it, and check whether it has been in operation. As explained in Chapter 5, researcher bias can occur in a variety of ways: it may stem from external pressures, including from funders, the people being studied or gatekeepers, but also from sources related to the researcher, such as her or his political or practical commitments, presuppositions, and preferences, as well as a desire to find answers to 'big questions' or even just to produce a coherent story. None of these features is problematic in itself, indeed they can be productive for the research, but they may also lead to error; and therefore must be closely monitored.

Reporting the research

A first requirement here is that the research questions eventually addressed (which as noted earlier will almost always be somewhat different from those identified at the start) are presented clearly, *and distinguished from the assumptions that have underpinned the research*. This may seem self-evident, but it is not uncommon to find research reports that do not clearly present the specific research questions being addressed, or which give the impression that rather grander ones have been tackled than is actually the case, and/or that conflate findings with what appear to have been guiding assumptions of the research.

Also required is that sufficient information is provided about how the research was carried out (see Chapter 10). In some fields, notably psychology, what may be demanded is sufficient information for the research process to be *replicated*. But the more basic requirement is sufficient information for readers to understand what was done and why, and for them to be able to assess the likely validity of the findings by taking account of potential threats to validity. Furthermore, too much information about how the research was carried out, or about the researcher, can be almost as bad as giving insufficient information. This is because it clutters up and obscures the necessary information supplied, or it may deprive other parts of the report of sufficient space. However, just what level and kinds of information are necessary, and how this should be presented, cannot be determined *precisely* in general terms – reasonable judgements are required. And it may turn out that further information needs to be presented in response to requests and criticisms from audiences.[3]

It is also important that sufficient *evidence* is provided in research reports. Here, again, it may be difficult to determine what is required. But the *basic* requirement is that sufficient evidence is supplied to allow readers to assess the likely validity of the findings. Most empirical research reports include only summaries and/or small samples of the data, and very often this will be all that is necessary. Once again, though, researchers must be prepared (where possible and ethical) to offer more evidence should this be needed by audiences. It may be possible to archive all the data for this purpose.

A further requirement is that the findings are presented consistently as neither more *nor less* likely to be true than is reasonable. Knowing what likely validity to assign to conclusions is not easy, and is never a precise matter, but here too sound judgements can be made – and unreasonable ones are usually easily identifiable by the researcher, if not always by readers. It might be thought that researchers would never put forward their findings as *less* likely to be true than they actually are, but this sometimes occurs in parts of a research report where they are anticipating criticism; for example, the research may be presented as only exploratory, whereas elsewhere the findings are treated as conclusive. Qualitative researchers, in particular, sometimes oscillate between emphasising the tentative character of their research findings and presenting these confidently as true, even if they are hesitant to use that word.

In line with a point made earlier about research questions, integrity also demands that the 'findings' offered must not be of a type that empirical research cannot validate on its own. In particular, they should not be practical evaluations and prescriptions. Such value conclusions can only be legitimate if put forward in conditional terms, in other words as dependent upon the adoption of a specified set of value judgements. However, it is not uncommon for them to be presented as if they derived directly from the research evidence; and, often, the value assumptions involved are not made explicit, even less provided with any justification, despite the fact that they are likely to be contentious in at least some quarters.

Overall, it should be clear from my discussion that, in order to maintain integrity, researchers must continually assess the judgements they have made and reflect on their character and consequences, as well as on their implications for future decisions. At the core of this assessment are judgements of the validity and worth of what they are producing, as well as of the effectiveness (alongside ethicality and prudence) of what they have done. And some of these reflections may need to be included in research reports (see Chapter 10).

Engaging with critics

In my view, the academic research process does not end with publication: the dialectic of communal assessment is an essential element of it (Hammersley 2011b: chapter 7).[4] Any knowledge claims produced by a single study must be assessed by the relevant research community. And, for this to be done effectively, the researcher must engage with colleagues, not least with those who may be sharply critical of the study. Of course, the researcher will have already participated in this dialectic in producing a literature review, but this engagement must continue after the research report has been published. In the course of discussions in the research community, issues and arguments may surface that did not emerge for the researcher in the course of carrying out the investigation, as well as ones that did but need further attention. What is required in such discussion is that researchers seek to understand any criticisms properly, and to respond to them in a way that contributes to the collective task of building knowledge. In particular, criticisms must not be immediately dismissed as the product of ignorance, incompetence, malice, or political commitment. Of course, not all criticism of research will be accurate, judicious or well-intentioned, but the researcher's starting assumption must be that it is – even if this judgement is revised later. It perhaps ought to be said that discussion within research communities by no means always meets these requirements.[5]

Conclusion

In this chapter I have focused on aspects of researcher integrity that relate to epistemic issues, discussing how these arise in different aspects of the research process: in relation to selecting and formulating research questions; using the literature; selecting cases for investigation; producing and analysing data; presenting findings; and engaging with critics. Generally speaking, these aspects of research integrity have been given less attention than those that come under the heading of research ethics, but they represent important obligations that apply to anyone engaging in academic social research.

It should be clear from the discussion in this chapter that a wide range of considerations must be taken into account, and difficult decisions made at key points. Furthermore, there will often be quite severe limits on what it is possible for researchers to do. Research cannot be carried out in a way that is perfect in all respects. All that can be expected of researchers is that they do it as well as they can; and are honest about the problems and failings, as well as about what has been achieved.

Notes

1 For a discussion of research ethics, see Hammersley and Traianou 2012.
2 There are also more specific issues, for example about how far to go in data reduction, where there may be a trade-off between delicacy in representing variation and ensuring that categories have a sufficient number of cases in them for statistical or some other form of analysis.
3 It perhaps should be underlined here that what information is necessary may vary according to the audience being addressed.
4 There are further aspects of integrity associated with playing the role of a reviewer for journals, publishers, and funding bodies; editing journals; evaluating colleagues in appointment and promotion committees; and so on. In relation to editing journals and refereeing articles, there are questions not just about detecting fraud, or about what is and is not worth publishing, but also about the danger of publication bias arising from the failure to publish statistically non-significant, inconclusive, or negative findings.
5 It is not easy to find clearly displayed examples of the sort of dialectical engagement I am recommending here. One from outside of social science, but dealing with a topic that is not completely unconnected with some of the issues discussed in this book, is provided by the efforts of Burnyeat and others to understand the views of ancient sceptics: see Burnyeat and Frede 1998.

References

Abel, A. (1948) 'The operation called verstehen', *American Journal of Sociology*, 54, 3, pp. 211–218.

Abend, G. (2008) 'The meaning of "theory"', *Sociological Theory*, 26, 2, pp. 173–199.

Allen, B. (1993) *Truth in Philosophy*. Cambridge, MA, Harvard University Press.

Almeder, R. (1980) *The Philosophy of Charles S. Peirce*. Oxford, Blackwell.

Althusser, L. (1971) *Lenin and Philosophy and Other Essays*. Cambridge, MA, MIT Press.

Anderson, R. J. and Sharrock, W. W. (2015) *'Radical reflexivity'*, unpublished paper. Available at: sharrockandanderson.co.uk.

Argyris, C. and Schön, D. (1974) *Theory in Practice: Increasing Professional Effectiveness*. San Francisco, CA, Jossey-Bass.

Ashmore, M. (1989) *The Reflexive Thesis: Wrighting Sociology of Scientific Knowledge*. Chicago, IL, University of Chicago Press.

Atkinson, P. (2015) *For Ethnography*. London, SAGE.

Babcock, B. A. (2005) 'Reflexivity', in Jones, L. (ed.) *Encyclopedia of Religion*, 2nd ed., vol. 11. Detroit, MI, Macmillan Reference USA, pp. 7647–7651. Available at: https://link.gale.com/apps/doc/CX3424502606/GVRL?u=tou&sid=bookmark-GVRL&xid=16417f0f [accessed 18 January 2022].

Baldamus, W. (1976) *The Structure of Sociological Inference*. London, Martin Robertson.

Ball, S. J. (1995) 'Intellectuals or technicians? The urgent role of theory in educational studies', *British Journal of Educational Studies*, 43, 3, pp. 255–271.

Banks, S. (2015) 'From research integrity to researcher integrity: issues of conduct, competence and commitment', paper given at Academy of Social Sciences seminar on Virtue Ethics in the Practice and Review of Social Research, London, May. Available at: www.acss.org.uk/wp-content/uploads/2015/03/Banks-From-research-integrity-to-researcher-integrity-AcSS-BSA-Virtue-ethics-1st-May-2015.pdf.

Banks, S. (2018) 'Cultivating researcher integrity: virtue based approaches to research ethics', in Emmerich, N. (ed.) *Virtue Ethics in the Conduct and Governance of Social Science Research*. Bingley, Emerald. (This is a revised version of Banks 2015).

Bar On, B.-A. (1993) 'Marginality and epistemic privilege', in Alcoff, L. and Potter, E. (eds.) *Feminist Epistemologies*. New York, Routledge.

Barone, T. E. (1992) 'On the demise of subjectivity in educational inquiry', *Curriculum Inquiry*, 22, pp. 25–38.

Barone, T. E. and Eisner, E. (2011) *Arts-Based Research*. Thousand Oaks, CA, SAGE.

Bateson, N. (1984) *Data Construction in Surveys*. London, Allen and Unwin.

Beck, U., Giddens, A. and Lash, S. (1994) *Reflexive Modernization: Politics, Tradition and Aesthetics in the Modern Social Order*. Stanford, CA, Stanford University Press.

Becker, H. S. (1963) *Outsiders*. New York, Free Press.

Becker, H. S. (1970) 'Life history and the scientific mosaic', in *Sociological Work*. Chicago, IL, Aldine.

Becker, H. S. (1998) *Tricks of the Trade*. Chicago, IL, University of Chicago Press.

Becker, H. S. (2017) *Evidence*. Chicago, IL, University of Chicago Press.

Benjamin, A. (1999) 'Contract and covenant in Curaçao: reciprocal relations in scholarly research', in King, N. M. P., Henderson, G. E. and Stein, J. (eds.) *Beyond Regulations: Ethics in Human Subjects Research*. Chapel Hill, NC, University of North Carolina Press, pp. 49–66.

Berlin, I. (1976) *Vico and Herder*. Oxford, Oxford University Press.

Bhaskar, R. (2008) *A Realist Theory of Science*, 3rd edition. London, Routledge.

Bird, A. (2000) *Thomas Kuhn*. Princeton, NJ, Princeton University Press.

Bishop, R. (1998) 'Freeing ourselves from neocolonial domination in research: a Maori approach to creating knowledge', *International Journal of Qualitative Studies in Education*, 11, 2, pp. 199–219.

Blackburn, S. (2005) *Truth; A Guide for the Perplexed*. London, Penguin.

Blackburn, S. (2017) *Truth*. London, Profile Books.

Blaikie, N. W. H. (1991) 'A critique of the use of triangulation in social research', *Quality and Quantity*, 25, 2, pp. 115–136.

Blauner, R. (1964) *Alienation and Freedom*. Chicago, IL, University of Chicago Press.

Bleicher, J. (1980) *Contemporary Hermeneutics*. London, Routledge and Kegan Paul.

Blumer, H. (1940) 'The problem of the concept in social psychology', *American Journal of Sociology*, 45, pp. 707–719.

Blumer, H. (1969) *Symbolic Interactionism*. Englewood Cliffs, NJ, Prentice-Hall.

Bohlin, I. (2016) 'Conceptualising epistemological barriers to the synthesis of educational research: a challenge to science and technology studies', in Elmgren, I. M., Folke-Fichtelius, M., Hallsén, S., Román, H. and Wermke, W. (eds.) *Att ta utbildningens komplexitet på allvar – En vänskrift till Eva Forsberg*. Uppsala, Uppsala Universitet.

Bourdieu, P. (1990) *In Other Words: Essays Towards a Reflexive Sociology*. Stanford, CA, Stanford University Press.

Bowen, G. A. (2009) 'Supporting a grounded theory with an audit trail: an illustration', *International Journal of Social Research Methodology*, 12, 4, pp. 305–316.

Breuer, F. and Roth, W. -M. (2003) 'Subjectivity and reflexivity in the social sciences: epistemic windows and methodical consequences', *Forum Qualitative Sozialforschung/Forum: Qualitative Social Research*, 4, 2, Art. 25. http://nbn-resolving.de/urn:nbn:de:0114-fqs0302258.

Bridgman, P. W. (1955) *Reflections of a Physicist*. New York, Philosophical Library.

Bruun, H. H. (2007) *Science, Values and Politics in Max Weber's Methodology*, 2nd edition. Aldershot, Ashgate (1st edition: Copenhagen, Munksgaard, 1972).

Bryant, A. and Charmaz, K. (eds.) (2010) *The Sage Handbook of Grounded Theory*. Thousand Oaks, CA, SAGE.

Bryant, C. G. A. (1985) *Positivism in Social Theory and Research*. London, Macmillan.

Bryman, A. (1988) *Quantity and Quality in Social Research*. London, Allen and Unwin.

Bryman, A. (1994) 'The Mead/Freeman controversy: some implications for qualitative researchers', in Burgess, R. G. (ed.) *Studies in Qualitative Methodology*, Vol. 4. Greenwich, CT, JAI Press.

Bryman, A. (2004) 'Triangulation', in Lewis-Beck, M., Bryman, A. and Liao, T. F. (eds.) *Encyclopedia of Social Science Research Methods*. Thousand Oaks, CA, SAGE.

Bryman, A. (2016) *Social Research Methods*, 5th edition. Oxford, Oxford University Press.

Burawoy, M. (1998) 'The extended case method', *Sociological Theory*, 16, pp. 4–34.

Burnyeat, M. and Frede, D. (1998) *The Original Sceptics*. Indianapolis, IN, Hackett.

Buscha, F. and Sturgis, P. (2018) 'Declining social mobility? Evidence from five linked censuses in England and Wales 1971–2011', *British Journal of Sociology*, 69, 1, pp. 154–182.

Byrne, D. and Ragin, C. (eds.) (2009) *The Sage Handbook of Case-Based Methods*. London, SAGE.

Cahnmann-Taylor, M. and Siegesmund, R. (eds.) (2017) *Arts-Based Research in Education*, 2nd edition. New York, Routledge.

Campbell, D. T. (1974) 'Evolutionary epistemology', in Schilpp, P. A. (ed.) *The Philosophy of Karl Popper*, Book 1. La Salle, IL, Open Court, pp. 413–463.

Campbell, D. T. and Fiske, D. W. (1959) 'Convergent and discriminant validation by the multitrait-multimethod matrix', *Psychological Bulletin*, 56, 2, pp. 81–105.

Campbell, D. T. and Stanley, J. C. (1963) *Experimental and Quasi-experimental Designs for Research*. Chicago, IL, Rand-McNally.

Campbell, R. (2011) *The Concept of Truth*. Basingstoke, Palgrave Macmillan.

Carr, W. (2006) 'Education without theory', *British Journal of Educational Studies*, 54, 2, pp. 136–159.

Cartwright, N. (1983) *How the Laws of Physics Lie*. Oxford, Oxford University Press.

Chalmers, J. (2017) 'The transformation of academic knowledges: understanding the relationship between decolonising and indigenous research methodologies', *Socialist Studies / Études Socialistes*, 12, 1, pp. 97–116.

Chamberlain, K. (2000) 'Methodolatry and qualitative health research', *Journal of Health Psychology*, 5, 3, pp. 285–296.

Cherkaoui, M. (1977) 'Bernstein and Durkheim: two theories of change in educational systems', *Harvard Educational Review*, 4, 47, pp. 556–564.

Cicourel, A. V. (1964) *Method and Measurement in Sociology*. New York, Free Press.

Cicourel, A. V., Jennings, K. H., Jennings, S. H., Leiter, K. C. W., MacKay, R., Mehan, H. and Roth, D. H. (1974) *Language Use and School Performance*. New York, Academic Press.

Clarke, T., Foster, L., Sloan, L. and Bryman, A. (2021) *Bryman's Social Research Methods*, 6th edition. Oxford, Oxford University Press.

Clifford, J. and Marcus, G. (eds.) (1986) *Writing Culture: The Poetics and Politics of Ethnography*. Berkeley, CA, University of California Press.

Collingwood, R. G. (1940) *An Essay in Metaphysics*. Oxford, Oxford University Press.

Coole, D. and Frost, S. (eds.) (2010) *New Materialisms: Ontology, Agency and Politics*. Durham, NC, Duke University Press.

Cooper, B., Glaesser, J., Gomm, R. and Hammersley, M. (2012) *Challenging the Qualitative-Quantitative Divide*. London, Continuum/Bloomsbury.

Cressey, D. (1950) 'The criminal violation of financial trust', *American Sociological Review*, 15, pp. 738–743.

Czyzewski, M. (1994) 'Reflexivity of actors versus reflexivity of accounts', *Theory, Culture and Society*, 11, 4, pp. 161–168.

Davies, C. A. (2008) *Reflexive Ethnography*. London, Routledge.

Davies, M. L. (1995) *Childhood Sexual Abuse and the Construction of Identity: Healing Sylvia*. London, Taylor and Francis.

Denzin, N. K. (1970) *The Research Act: A Theoretical Introduction to Sociological Methods*. Englewood Cliffs, NJ, Prentice Hall.

Denzin, N. K. (1989) *The Research Act*, 3rd edition. Englewood Cliffs, NJ, Prentice Hall.

Denzin, N. K. (1997) *Interpretive Ethnography: Ethnographic Practices for the 21st Century*. Thousand Oaks, CA, SAGE.

Denzin, N. K. (2012) 'Triangulation 2.0', *Journal of Mixed Methods Research*, 6, pp. 80–88.

Denzin, N. K. and Lincoln, Y. S. (eds.) (2011) *The Sage Handbook of Qualitative Research*, 4th edition. Thousand Oaks, CA, SAGE.

Denzin, N. K. and Lincoln, Y. S. (eds.) (2018) *The Sage Handbook of Qualitative Research*, 5th edition. Thousand Oaks, CA, SAGE.

Deutscher, I. (1973) *What We Say/What We Do: Sentiments and Acts*. Glenview IL, Scott Foresman.

De Vaus, D. (2001) *Research Design in Social Science*. London, SAGE.

Dewey, J. (1938) *Logic: The Theory of Inquiry*. New York, Henry Holt.

Dews, P. (2007) *Logics of Disintegration: Poststructuralist Thought and the Claims for Critical Theory*. London, Verso.

Dey, I. (1999) *Grounding Grounded Theory*. San Diego, CA, Academic Press.

Duneier, M. (2000) 'Race and peeing on Sixth Avenue', in Twine, F. W. and Warren, J. W. (eds.) *Racing Research, Researching Race*. New York, New York University Press.

Duneier, M. (2011) 'How not to lie with ethnography', *Sociological Methodology*, 41, pp. 1–11.

Dunne, J. (1993) *Back to the Rough Ground: 'Phronesis' and 'Techne' in Modern Philosophy and in Aristotle*. Notre Dame, IND, University of Notre Dame Press.

Eisenmann, C. and Lynch, M. (2021) 'Introduction to Harold Garfinkel's ethnomethodological "misreading" of Aron Gurwitsch on the phenomenal field', *Human Studies*, 44, pp. 1–17.

Eisner, E. (1992) 'Objectivity in educational research', *Curriculum Inquiry*, 22, 1, pp. 9–15.

Ellingson, L. L. (2009) *Engaging Crystallization in Qualitative Research*, Thousand Oaks, CA, SAGE.

Ellingson, L. L. (2011) 'Analysis and representation across the continuum', in Denzin, N. K. and Lincoln, Y. S. (eds.) *Handbook of Qualitative Research*, 4th edition. Thousand Oaks, CA, SAGE, pp. 595–610.

Elliott, J. and Adelman, C. (1976) 'Innovation at the classroom level: a case study of the Ford Teaching Project', unit 28 of the Open University course *Curriculum Design and Development*. Milton Keynes, Open University Press.

Ember, M. (1985) 'Evidence and science in ethnography: reflections on the Freeman-Mead controversy', *American Anthropologist*, 87, pp. 906–910.

Emke, I. (1996) 'Methodology and methodolatry: creativity and the impoverishment of the imagination in sociology', *The Canadian Journal of Sociology/Cahiers Canadiens de Sociologie*, 21, 1, pp. 77–90.

Erlandson, D., Harris, E., Skipper, B. and Allen, S. (1993) *Doing Naturalistic Inquiry: A Guide to Methods*. Newbury Park, CA, SAGE.

Ermarth, M. (1978) *Wilhelm Dilthey: The Critique of Historical Reason*. Chicago, IL, University of Chicago Press.

Erzberger, C. and Kelle, U. (2003) 'Making inferences in mixed methods: the rules of integration', in Tashakkori, A. and Teddlie, C. (eds.) *Handbook of Mixed Methods in Social and Behavioral Research*. Thousand Oaks, CA, SAGE.

Fairclough, N. (2003) *Analysing Discourse: Textual Analysis for Social Research*. London, Routledge and Kegan Paul.

Fann, K. (1970) *Peirce's Theory of Abduction*. The Hague, Martinus Nijhoff.

Festinger, L., Riecken, H. and Schachter, S. (1956) *When Prophecy Fails*. Minneapolis, MN, University of Minnesota Press.

Feyerabend, P. (1975) *Against Method*. London, Verso.

Fielding, N. G. (2009a) 'Going out on a limb: postmodernism and multiple method research', *Current Sociology*, 57, 3, pp. 427–447.

Fielding, N. G. (2009b) 'Of bridges and limbs: a response to Pascale and Healy', *Current Sociology*, 57, 3, pp. 462–465.

Fielding, N. G. and Fielding, J. (1986) *Linking Data*. London, SAGE.

Fitzgerald, R. (2019) 'The data and methodology of Harvey Sacks: lessons from the archive', *Journal of Pragmatics*, 143, pp. 205–214.

Flax, J. (1983) 'Political philosophy and the patriarchal unconscious: a psychoanalytic perspective on epistemology and metaphysics' in Harding, S. and Hintikka, M. B. (eds.) (1983) *Discovering Reality: Feminist Perspectives on Epistemology, Metaphysics, Methodology and Philosophy of Science*. Dordrecht, Reidel.

Flick, U. (1992) 'Triangulation revisited: strategy of validation or alternative?', *Journal for the Theory of Social Behaviour*, 22, 2, pp. 175–197.

Flick, U. (2004) 'Triangulation in qualitative research', in Flick, U., von Kardoff, E. and Steinke, I. (eds.) *A Companion to Qualitative Research*. London, SAGE.

Flick, U. (2019) 'Triangulation', in Atkinson, P., Delamont, S., Cernat, A., Sakshaug, J. W. and Williams, R. A. (eds.) *SAGE Research Methods Foundations*. Available at: https://www-doi-org.libezproxy.open.ac.uk/10.4135/9781526421036826100.

Foster, P., Gomm, R. and Hammersley, M. (1996) *Constructing Educational Inequality: An Assessment of Research on School Processes*. London, Falmer.

Freeman, D. (1983) *Margaret Mead and Samoa: The Making and Unmaking of an Anthropological Myth*. Cambridge, MA, Harvard University Press.

Freeman, D. (1998) *The Fateful Hoaxing of Margaret Mead: A Historical Analysis of Her Samoan Research*. Boulder, CO, Westview Press.

Gadamer, H. -G. (2001) *Gadamer in Conversation: Reflections and Commentary* (Ed. and Trans. R. E. Palmer). New Haven, CT, Yale University Press.

Gadamer, H. -G. (2004) *Truth and Method*. London, Continuum. (First published in German in 1960).

Gage, N. L. (1989) 'The paradigm wars and their aftermath a "historical" sketch of research on teaching since 1989', *Educational Researcher*, 18, 7, pp. 4–10.

Galdas, P. (2017) 'Revisiting bias in qualitative research: reflections on its relationship with funding and impact', *International Journal of Qualitative Methods*, 16, pp. 1–2. https://doi.org/10.1177/1609406917748992.

Garfinkel, H. (1967) *Studies in Ethnomethodology*. Englewood Cliffs, NJ, Prentice Hall.

Gaukroger, S. (2001) *Francis Bacon and the Transformation of Early-Modern Philosophy*. Cambridge, Cambridge University Press.

Geertz, C. (1973) 'On thick description', in *The Interpretation of Cultures*. New York, Basic Books.

Geertz, C. (1980) 'Blurred genres: the refiguration of social thought', *The American Scholar*, 49, 2, pp. 165–179.

Gerring, J. (2007) *Case Study Research*. Cambridge, Cambridge University Press.

Giddens, A. (1976) *New Rules of Sociological Method*. London, Hutchinson.

Giorgi, A. (2010) 'Phenomenological psychology: a brief history and its challenges', *Journal of Phenomenological Psychology*, 41, 2, pp. 145–179.

Gitlin, A. D., Siegel, M. and Boru, K. (1989) 'The politics of method: from Leftist ethnography to educative research', *International Journal of Qualitative Studies in Education*, 2, 3, pp. 237–253.

Glanzberg, M. (2021) 'Truth', *The Stanford Encyclopedia of Philosophy* (Summer 2021 Edition), Edward N. Zalta (ed.). Available at: https://plato.stanford.edu/archives/sum2021/entries/truth/

Glaser, B. and Strauss, A. (1967) *The Discovery of Grounded Theory*. Chicago, IL, Aldine.

Glesne, C. (1997) 'That rare feeling: re-presenting research through poetic transcription', *Qualitative Inquiry*, 3, 2, pp. 202–221.

Goffman, A. (2014) *On the Run: Fugitive Life in an American City*. Chicago, IL, University of Chicago Press.

Gomm, R. (2022) 'SATs, sets and allegations of bias: the allocation of 11-year-old students to mathematics sets in some English schools in 2015: a response to Connolly et al., 2019', *British Educational Research Journal*. https://doi.org/10.1002/berj.3790.

Gomm, R., Hammersley, M. and Foster, P. (eds.) (2000) *Case Study Method*. London, SAGE.

Gouldner, A. V. (1965) *Enter Plato: Classical Greece and the Origins of Social Theory*. New York, Basic Books.

Gouldner, A. V. (1970) *The Coming Crisis of Western Sociology*. New York, Basic Books.

Guba, E. (ed.) (1990) *The Paradigm Dialog*. Newbury Park, CA, SAGE.

Guba, E. (1992) 'Relativism', *Curriculum Inquiry*, 22, 1, pp. 17–23.

Gurwitsch, A. (1964) *The Field of Consciousness*. Pittsburgh, PA, Duquesne University Press.

Haack, S. (2003) *Defending Science – Within Reason*. Amherst, NY, Prometheus Books.

Haack, S. (2019) 'Post "post-truth": Are we there yet?', *Theoria*, 85, pp. 258–275.

Halfpenny, P. (1982) *Positivism and Sociology*. London, Allen and Unwin.

Halfpenny, P. (1997) 'The relation between quantitative and qualitative research', *Bulletin of Sociological Methodology/Bulletin de Méthodologie Sociologique*, 57, 1, pp. 49–64. (For a response, see response-to-halfpenny-on-the-relation-between-quantitative-and-qualitative-research.doc (live.com))

Hammersley, M. (1983) 'Reflexivity and naturalism in ethnography', in Hammersley, M. (ed.) *The Ethnography of Schooling*. Driffield, Nafferton Books.

Hammersley, M. (1984) 'The paradigmatic mentality: a diagnosis', in Barton, L. and Walker, S. (eds.) *Social Crisis and Educational Research*. London, Croom Helm, pp. 230–255.

Hammersley, M. (1987) 'Some Notes on the Terms "Validity" and "Reliability"', *British Educational Research Journal*, 13, 1, pp. 73–81.

Hammersley, M. (1989a) 'The problem of the concept: Herbert Bumer and the relation between concepts and data', *Journal of Contemporary Ethnography*, 18, 2, pp. 133–159.

Hammersley, M. (1989b) *The Dilemma of Qualitative Method*. London, Routledge and Kegan Paul.

Hammersley, M. (1991) 'A note on Campbell's distinction between internal and external validity', *Quality and Quantity*, 25, 4, pp. 381–387.

Hammersley, M. (1995) *The Politics of Social Research*. London, SAGE.

Hammersley, M. (1997) 'Qualitative data archiving: some reflections on its prospects and problems', *Sociology*, 31, pp. 131–142.

Hammersley, M. (1998) 'Get real! A defence of realism', in Hodkinson, P. (ed.) *The Nature of Educational Research: Realism, Relativism, or Post-Modernism?*. Crewe, Crewe School of Education, Manchester Metropolitan University. (Reprinted in Piper, H. and Stronach, I. (eds.) *Educational Research: Difference and Diversity*. Aldershot, Ashgate, 2004).

Hammersley, M. (2000) *Taking Sides in Social Research: Essays on Partisanship and Bias*. London, Routledge.

Hammersley, M. (2002) *Educational Research, Policymaking and Practice*. London, Paul Chapman/SAGE.

Hammersley, M. (2008) *Questioning Qualitative Inquiry*. London, SAGE.

Hammersley, M. (2010a) 'Can we re-use qualitative data via secondary analysis? Notes on some terminological and substantive issues', *Sociological Research Online*, 15, 1. Available at: www.socresonline.org.uk/15/1/5.html.

Hammersley, M. (2010b) 'Reproducing or constructing? Some questions about transcription in social research', *Qualitative Research*, 10, 5, pp. 553–569.

Hammersley, M. (2011a) 'Objectivity: a reconceptualisation', in Williams, M. and Vogt, W. P. (eds.) *The Sage Handbook of Innovation in Social Research Methods*. London, SAGE. (Revised version published in Hammersley 2011b).

Hammersley, M. (2011b) *Methodology Who Needs It?*. London, SAGE.

Hammersley, M. (2014a) *The Limits of Social Science*. London, SAGE.

Hammersley, M. (2014b) 'The perils of "impact" for academic social science', *Contemporary Social Science*, 9, 3, pp. 345–355.

Hammersley, M. (2015a) 'Research ethics and the concept of children's rights', *Children and Society*, 29, 6, pp. 569–582.

Hammersley, M. (2015b) 'Against "gold standards" in research: on the problem of assessment criteria', paper given at 'Was heißt hier eigentlich "Evidenz"?', Frühjahrstagung 2015 des AK Methoden in der Evaluation Gesellschaft für Evaluation (DeGEval), Fakultät für Sozialwissenschaften, Hochschule für Technik und Wirtschaft des Saarlandes, Saarbrücken, May. Available at: https://martynhammersley.files.wordpress.com/2013/06/hammersley_saarbrucken.pdf

Hammersley, M. (2016) 'An ideological dispute: accusations of Marxist bias in the sociology of education during the 1970s', *Contemporary British History*, 30, 2, pp. 242–259.

Hammersley, M. (2017a) 'Interview data: a qualified defence against the radical critique', *Qualitative Research*, 17, 2, pp. 173–186.

Hammersley, M. (2017b) 'Childhood studies: a sustainable paradigm?', *Childhood*, 24, 1, pp. 113–127.

Hammersley, M. (2017c) 'On the role of values in social research: Weber vindicated?', *Sociological Research Online*, 22, 1, pp. 130–141. Available at: www.socresonline.org.uk/22/1/7.html.

Hammersley, M. (2017d) 'Is there any such thing as social science evidence? On a Winchian critique', *Ethnographic Studies*, 14. Available at: https://zenodo.org/record/823047

Hammersley, M. (2018) *The Radicalism of Ethnomethodology*. Manchester, Manchester University Press.

Hammersley, M. (2019a) *The Concept of Culture*. Cham, Palgrave Macmillan.

Hammersley, M. (2019b) 'Exploring the distinctive ontological attitude of ethnomethodology via suicide, death, and money', *Journal of Classical Sociology*, 19, 2, pp. 185–204.

Hammersley, M. (2019c) 'Understanding a dispute about ethnomethodology: Watson and Sharrock's response to Atkinson's "critical review"', *Forum Qualitative Sozialforschung/Forum: Qualitative Social Research*, 20, 1. https://doi.org/10.17169/fqs-20.1.3048.

Hammersley, M. (2020) *Troubling Sociological Concepts: An Interrogation*. Cham, Palgrave Macmillan.

Hammersley, M. (2022a) 'Sociology as a profession in a post-truth world', in Leroux, R., Martin, T. and Turner, S. (eds.) *Where Is Sociology Going? Ideology or Objective Social Science*. London, Routledge.

Hammersley, M. (2022b) 'Is "representation" a folk term? Some thoughts on a theme in science studies', *Philosophy of Social Sciences*, 52, 3, pp. 132–149.

Hammersley, M. (2022c) 'Max Weber, science, and the problem of value relativism: the challenge of conservative criticism', *Journal of Classical Sociology*, forthcoming.

Hammersley, M. (2022d) 'Whitaker and Atkinson on reflexivity', unpublished manuscript. Available at: https://martynhammersley.files.wordpress.com/2022/10/review-of-whitaker-and-atkinson-on-reflexivity.pdf

Hammersley, M. (2022e) 'Are there assessment criteria for qualitative findings? A challenge facing mixed methods research', *Forum Qualitative Sozialforschung/Forum: Qualitative Social Research*, forthcoming.

Hammersley, M. and Atkinson, P. (1983) *Ethnography: Principles in Practice*, 1st edition. London, Tavistock.

Hammersley, M. and Atkinson, P. (2019) *Ethnography: Principles in Practice*, 4th edition. London, Routledge.

Hammersley, M. and Traianou, A. (2012) *Ethics in Qualitative Research*. London, SAGE.

Handler, R. (1983) 'The dainty and the hungry man: Literature and anthropology in the work of Edward Sapir', in Stocking, G. W. (ed.) *Observers Observed: Essays on Ethnographic Fieldwork*. Madison, WI, University of Wisconsin Press.

Haraway, D. (1997) *Modest Witness@Second Millennium.FemaleMan© Meets OncoMouse™: Feminism and Technoscience*. New York, Routledge.

Harding, S. (1993) 'After the neutrality ideal: science, politics and "strong objectivity"', *Social Research*, 59, 3, pp. 568–587.

Harding, S. (1995) ' "Strong objectivity": a response to the new objectivity question', *Synthese*, 104, pp. 331–349.

Harding, S. (ed.) (2004) *The Feminist Standpoint Theory Reader*. London, Routledge.

Hartsock, N. (1983) 'The feminist standpoint', in Harding, S. and Hintikka, M. B. (eds.) *Discovering Reality: Feminist Perspectives on Epistemology, Metaphysics, Methodology and Philosophy of Science*. Dordrecht, Reidel.

Hartsock, N. (1987) 'The feminist standpoint: developing the ground for a specifically feminist historical materialism', in Harding, S. (ed.) *Feminism and Methodology: Social Science Issues*. Bloomington, IN, Indiana University Press.

Healy, P. (2009) 'The view from further out: a response to Fielding's "going out on a limb: postmodernism and multiple method research', *Current Sociology*, 57, 3, pp. 455–461.

Heller, E. (1961) 'Goethe and the idea of scientific truth', in *The Disinherited Mind*. Harmondsworth, Penguin.

Hempel, C. (1965) *Aspects of Scientific Explanation*. New York, Free Press.

Henderson, L. (2020) 'The problem of induction', *The Stanford Encyclopedia of Philosophy* (Spring 2020 Edition), Edward N. Zalta (ed.). Available at: https://plato.stanford.edu/archives/spr2020/entries/induction-problem/.

Heywood, P. (2017) 'The ontological turn', in Stein, F., Lazar, S., Candea, M., Diemberger, H., Robbins, J., Sanchez, A. and Stasch R. (eds.) *The Cambridge Encyclopedia of Anthropology*. Cambridge, University of Cambridge. Available at: www.anthroencyclopedia.com/entry/ontological-turn.

Hirst, P. H. (1983) 'Educational theory', in Hirst, P. H. (ed.) *Educational Theory and Its Foundation Disciplines*. London, Routledge and Kegan Paul.

Holbraad, M. (2009) 'Ontography and alterity: defining anthropological truth', *Social Analysis*, 53, 2, pp. 80–93.

Holbraad, M. and Pedersen, M. A. (2017) *The Ontological Turn: An Anthropological Exposition*. Cambridge, Cambridge University Press.

Holzhey, H. (2010) 'Neo-Kantianism and phenomenology: the problem of intuition', in Makkreel, R. and Luft, S. (eds.) *Neo-Kantianism in Contemporary Philosophy*. Bloomington, IN, Indiana University Press.

Hookway, C. (1985) *Peirce*. London, Routledge and Kegan Paul.

Hoque, Z., Covaleski, M. and Gooneratne, T. (2013) 'Theoretical triangulation and pluralism in research methods in organizational and accounting research', *Accounting, Auditing & Accountability Journal*, 26, 7, pp. 1170–1198.

Hoque, Z., Covaleski, M. and Gooneratne, T. (2015) 'A response to "Theoretical triangulation and pluralism in accounting research: a critical realist critique"', *Accounting, Auditing & Accountability Journal*, 28, 7, pp. 1151–1159.

Hoyningen-Huene, P. (1993) *Reconstructing Scientific Revolutions: Thomas S. Kuhn's Philosophy of Science*. Chicago, IL, University of Chicago Press.

Hutchby, I. and Wooffitt, R. (1998) *Conversation Analysis: Principles, Practices and Applications*, Cambridge, Polity Press.

Hutchinson, P., Read, R. and Sharrock, W. (2008) *There is No Such Thing as a Social Science*, Aldershot, Ashgate.

Janesick, V. J. (1994) 'The dance of qualitative research design: metaphor, methodolatry, and meaning', in Denzin, N. K. and Lincoln, Y. S. (eds.) *Handbook of Qualitative Research*, Thousand Oaks, CA, SAGE, pp. 209–219.

Jay, M. (1977) 'The concept of totality in the work of Lukacs and Adorno', in Avineri, S. (ed.) *Varieties of Marxism*. London, Springer.

Jenkins, A. (1979) *The Social Theory of Claude Lévi-Strauss*. London, Macmillan.

Jensen, C. B. (2017) 'New ontologies? Reflections on some recent "turns" in STS, anthropology and philosophy', *Social Anthropology/Anthropologie Sociale*, 25, 4, pp. 525–545.

Jerolmack, C. and Khan, S. (2014) 'Talk is cheap: ethnography and the attitudinal fallacy', *Sociological Methods and Research*, 43, 2, pp. 178–209.

Jules-Rosette, B. (1978) 'Toward a theory of ethnography', *Sociological Symposium*, 24, pp. 81–98.

Kaplan, A. (1964) *The Conduct of Inquiry*. San Francisco, CA, Chandler Publishing Company.

Karjalainen, H. and Levell, P. (2022) 'Inflation hits 9% with poorest households facing even higher rates', *Institute for Fiscal Studies*, 18 May. Available at: https://ifs.org.uk/news/inflation-hits-9-poorest-households-facing-even-higher-rates#:~:text=Heidi%20Karjalainen%2C%20a%20Research%20Economist,even%20higher%20rate%20of%20inflation

Kaufmann, F. (1944) *Methodology of the Social Sciences*. New York, Oxford University Press.

Kellett, M. (2005) 'Children as active researchers: a new research paradigm for the 21st century?' *ESRC*. Available at: http://oro.open.ac.uk/7539/1/MethodsReviewPaperNCRM-003.pdf [accessed 25 July 2022].

Koro-Ljungberg, M. and MacLure, M. (2013) 'Provocations, re-un-visions, death, and other possibilities of "data"', *Cultural Studies ↔ Critical Methodologies*, 13, 4, pp. 219–222.

Kuhn, T. S. (1962) *The Structure of Scientific Revolutions*. Chicago, IL, University of Chicago Press. (2nd edition: 1970).

Kuhn, T. S. (2000) *The Road Since Structure*. Chicago, IL, University of Chicago Press.

Kushner, K. and Morrow, R. (2003) 'Grounded theory, feminist theory, critical theory: toward theoretical triangulation', *Advances in Nursing Science*, 26, 1, pp. 30–43.

Laher, S. (2016) 'Ostinato rigore: establishing methodological rigour in quantitative research', *South African Journal of Psychology*, 46, 3, pp. 316–327.

Lakatos, I. and Feyerabend, P. (1999) *For and Against Method* (Edited. M. Motterlini). Chicago, IL, University of Chicago Press.

Langlois, C. V. and Seignobos, C. (1898) *Introduction to the Study of History*, English translation. London, Duckworth, 1913.

Lather, P. (1986) 'Issues of validity in openly ideological research', *Interchange*, 17, 4, pp. 63–84.

Lather, P. (1993) 'Fertile obsession: validity after poststructuralism', *Sociological Quarterly*, 34, 4, pp. 673–693.

Lather, P. (2007) *Getting Lost: Feminist Efforts Toward a Double(d) Science*. Albany, NY, State University of New York Press.

Lather, P. and St. Pierre, E. (2013) 'Post-qualitative research', *International Journal of Qualitative Studies in Education*, 26, 6, pp. 629–633.

Law, J. (2004) *After Method: Mess in Social Science Research*. London, Routledge.

Law, J., Ruppert, E. and Savage, M. (2011) *The Double Social Life of Methods* (CRESC working paper series no: 95), March. Milton Keynes, The Open University.

Lazarsfeld, P. F. and Rosenberg, M. (eds.) (1955) *The Language of Social Research*. Glencoe, IL, Free Press.

Lear, J. (1988) *Aristotle: The Desire to Understand*. Cambridge, Cambridge University Press.

Leavy, P. (ed.) (2015) *Method Meets Art*, 2nd edition. New York, Guilford Press.

Leavy, P. (ed.) (2018) *Handbook of Arts-based Research*. New York, Guilford Press.

Lincoln, Y. S. and Guba, E. G. (1985) *Naturalistic Inquiry*. Beverly Hills, CA, SAGE.

Lindesmith, A. (1947) *Opiate Addiction*. Bloomington, IN, Principia Press.

Lipset, S. M., Trow, M. and Coleman, J. (1956) *Union Democracy*. New York, Free Press.

Lobkowicz, N. (1967) *Theory and Practice: History of a Concept from Aristotle to Marx*. Notre Dame, IN, University of Notre Dame Press.

Lofland, J. (1967) 'Notes on naturalism', *Kansas Journal of Sociology*, 3, 2, pp. 45–61.

Lofland, J. (1971) *Analysing Social Settings*. Belmont, CA, Wadsworth.

Losee, J. (2001) *A Historical Introduction to the Philosophy of Science*, 4th edition. Oxford, Oxford University Press.

Lubet, S. (2018) *Interrogating Ethnography: Why Evidence Matters*. New York, Oxford University Press.

Luckmann, T. (ed.) (1978) *Phenomenology and Sociology*. Harmondsworth, Penguin.

Lundy, C. (2013) 'From structuralism to poststructuralism', in Dillet, B., MacKenzie, I. and Porter, R. (eds.) *The Edinburgh Companion to Poststructuralism*. Edinburgh, Edinburgh University Press.

Lynch, M. (2000) 'Against reflexivity as an academic virtue and source of privileged knowledge', *Theory, Culture and Society*, 17, 3, pp. 26–54.

MacDonald, I. (2020) 'Did Peirce misrepresent Descartes? Reinvestigating and defending Peirce's case', *Transactions of the Charles S. Peirce Society*, 56, 1, pp. 1–18.

Macfarlane, B. (2009) *Researching with Integrity: The Ethics of Academic Enquiry*. London, Routledge.

MacIver, R. M. (1942) *Social Causation*. Boston, MA, Ginn and Co.

Mackie, J. L. (1967) 'Mill's methods of induction', in Edwards, P. (ed.) *The Encyclopedia of Philosophy*, Vol 4. New York, Macmillan.

MacLure, M. (2011) 'Qualitative research: where are the ruins?', *Qualitative Inquiry*, 17, 10, pp. 997–1005.

MacLure, M. (2020) 'Inquiry as divination', *Qualitative Inquiry*, 27, 5, pp. 502–511.

MacLure, M. (2022) 'Resistance, desistance: bad girls of post-qualitative inquiry', *International Journal of Qualitative Studies in Education*, forthcoming.

Mahoney, J. (2001) 'Beyond correlational analysis: recent innovations in theory and method', *Sociological Forum*, 16, 3, pp. 575–593.

Makkreel, R. (1975) *Wilhelm Dilthey: Philosopher of the Human Studies*. Princeton, NJ, Princeton University Press.

Mannheim, K. (1952) *Essays in the Sociology of Knowledge*. London, Routledge and Kegan Paul.

Marcus, G. and Fischer, M. (1986) *Anthropology as Cultural Critique*. Chicago, IL, University of Chicago Press.

Martin, P. J. and Dennis, A. (eds.) (2010) *Human Agents and Social Structures*. Manchester, Manchester University Press.

Massey, A. (1999) 'Methodological triangulation, or how to get lost without being found out', in Walford, G. and Massey, A. (eds.) *Explorations in Methodology* (*Studies in Educational Ethnography, Vol. 2*). Bingley, Emerald, pp. 183–197.

Mattern, S. (2013) 'Methodolatry and the art of measure', *Places Journal*. https://doi.org/10.22269/131105 [accessed 3 July 2022].

Mauthner, N. S., Parry, O. and Backett-Milburn, K. (1998) 'The data are out there, or are they? Implications for archiving and revisiting qualitative data', *Sociology*, 32, 4, pp. 733–745.

Maxwell, J. A. (2012) *A Realist Approach for Qualitative Research*. Thousand Oaks, CA, SAGE.

McCain, K. (2014) 'The problem of the criterion', *Internet Encyclopedia of Philosophy*. Available at: https://iep.utm.edu/problem-of-the-criterion/

McKim, V. and Turner, S. P. (eds.) (1997) *Causality in Crisis? Statistical Methods & Search for Causal Knowledge in Social Sciences*. Notre Dame, IN, University of Notre Dame Press.

McKinney, J. C. (1966) *Constructive Typology and Social Theory*. New York, Appleton-Century-Crofts.

McPhee, G. (1992) 'Triangulation in research: two confusions', *Educational Research*, 34, 3, pp. 215–219.

McSweeney, B. (2022a) 'Fooling ourselves and others: confirmation bias and the trustworthiness of qualitative research – part 1 the threat', *Journal of Organizational Change Management*, 34, 5, pp. 1063–1075.

McSweeney, B. (2022b) 'Fooling ourselves and others: confirmation bias and the trustworthiness of qualitative research – part 2 cross-examining the dismissals', *Journal of Organizational Change Management*, 34, 5, pp. 841–859.

Mead, G. H. (1934) *Mind, Self, and Society*. Chicago, IL, University of Chicago Press.

Mead, M. (1928) *Coming of Age in Samoa*. New York, Morrow.

Merton, R. K. (1968) *Social Theory and Social Structure*. New York, Free Press.

Milgram, S. (1974) *Obedience to Authority*. New York, Harper and Row.

Miller, A. G. (1986) *The Obedience Experiments: A Case Study of Controversy in Social Science*. New York, Praeger.

Miller, P. A. (2007) *Postmodern Spiritual Practices: The Construction of the Subject and the Reception of Plato in Lacan, Derrida and Foucault*. Columbus, OH, Ohio State University Press.

Mills, C. W. (1959) *The Sociological Imagination*. New York, Oxford University Press.

Modell, S. (2015) 'Theoretical triangulation and pluralism in accounting research: a critical realist critique', *Accounting, Auditing & Accountability Journal*, 28, 7, pp. 1138–1150.

Moody-Adams, M. (1997) *Fieldwork in Familiar Places: Morality, Culture and Philosophy*. Cambridge, MA, Harvard University Press.

Moore, N. (2006) 'The contexts of context: broadening perspectives in the (re)use of qualitative data', *Methodological Innovations Online*, 1, 2. Available at: https://journals.sagepub.com/doi/pdf/10.4256/mio.2006.0009

Morse, J. M. (2015) 'Critical analysis of strategies for determining rigor in qualitative inquiry', *Qualitative Health Research*, 25, 9, pp. 1212–1222.

Mulligan, K. and Correia, F. (2021) 'Facts', *The Stanford Encyclopedia of Philosophy* (Winter 2021 Edition), Edward N. Zalta (ed.). Available at: https://plato.stanford.edu/archives/win2021/entries/facts/

Nagel, E. (1979) *The Structure of Science*. Indianapolis, IN, Hackett.

Newton-Smith, W. H. (1981) *The Rationality of Science*. London, Routledge.

Nietzsche, F. (1967) *The Will to Power* (Trans. W. Kaufmann and R. J. Hollingdale). New York, Random House.

Nind, M. and Lewthwaite, S. (2020) 'A conceptual-empirical typology of social science research methods pedagogy', *Research Papers in Education*, 35, 4, pp. 467–487.

Oakley, A. (2000) *Experiments in Knowing: Gender and Method in the Social Sciences*. Cambridge, Polity Press.

O'Hear, A. (ed.) (1996) *Verstehen and Human Understanding*. Cambridge, Cambridge University Press.

Palmer, R. E. (1969) *Hermeneutics*. Evanston, IL, Northwestern University Press.

Pascale, C. -M. (2009) 'Emerging landscapes in social research: comments on Nigel Field-ing, postmodern thought and social research', *Current Sociology*, 57, 3, pp. 448–454.

Peirce, C. S. (1877) 'The fixation of belief', *Popular Science Monthly*, 12, pp. 1–15. (Reprinted in Peirce, C. S. (Ed.) *Collected Papers*, Vol. 5 and 6. Cambridge, MA, Harvard University Press, 1934, pp. 223–233).

Pérez Huber, L. (2009a) 'Disrupting apartheid of knowledge: *testimonio* as methodology in Latina/o critical race research in education', *International Journal of Qualitative Studies in Education*, 22, 6, pp. 639–654.

Pérez Huber, L. (2009b) '*Testimonio* as LatCrit methodology in education', in Dela-mont, S. (ed.) *Handbook of Qualitative Research in Education*. Cheltenham, Edward Elgar, pp. 377–390.

Perlesz, A. and Lindsay, J. (2003) 'Methodological triangulation in researching families: making sense of dissonant data', *International Journal of Social Research Methodology*, 6, 1, pp. 25–40.

Phillips, D. (1973) *Abandoning Method*. San Francisco, CA, Jossey-Bass.

Phillips, D. C. and Burbules, N. C. (2000) *Postpositivism and Educational Research*, Lanham, MD, Rowman & Littlefield.

Pitre, N. and Kushner, K. (2015) 'Theoretical Triangulation as an Extension of Feminist Intersectionality in Qualitative Family Research', *Journal of Family Theory & Review*, 7, pp. 284–298.

Ploder, A. and Stadlbauer, J. (2016) 'Strong reflexivity and its critics: responses to autoeth-nography in the German-speaking cultural and social sciences', *Qualitative Inquiry*, 22, 9, pp. 753–765.

Polanyi, M. (1958) *Personal Knowledge*. Chicago, IL, University of Chicago Press.

Pollner, M. (1974) 'Sociological and common-sense models of the labelling process', in Turner, R. (ed.) *Ethnomethodology*. Harmondsworth, Penguin.

Pollner, M. (1978) 'Constitutive and mundane versions of labelling theory', *Human Studies*, 1, 3, pp. 269–288.

Poovey, M. (1998) *A History of the Modern Fact*. Chicago, IL, University of Chicago Press.

Popkin, R. H. (1979) *The History of Scepticism: From Erasmus to Spinoza*, Berkeley, CA, University of California Press.

Popper, K. (1959) *The Logic of Scientific Discovery*. London, Hutchinson.

Porter, S. and O'Halloran, P. (2009) 'The postmodernist war on evidence-based practice', *International Journal of Nursing Studies*, 46, pp. 740–748.

Potter, J. and Hepburn, A. (2005) 'Qualitative interviews in psychology: problems and pos-sibilities', *Qualitative Research in Psychology*, 2, 4, pp. 281–307.

Quinton, A. (1980) *Bacon*. Oxford, Oxford University Press.

Raffel, S. and Sandywell, B. (eds.) (2016) *The Reflexive Initiative: On the Grounds and Prospects of Analytic Theorizing*. London, Routledge.

Ragin, C. (1987) *The Comparative Method: Moving Beyond Qualitative and Quantitative Strate-gies*. Berkeley, CA, University of California Press.

Ragin, C. (2008) *Redesigning Social Inquiry*. Chicago, University of Chicago Press.

Reichertz, J. (2004) 'Abduction, deduction and induction in qualitative research', in Flick, U., von Kardoff, E. and Steinke, I. (eds.) *A Companion to Qualitative Research*. London, SAGE.

Reichertz, J. (2009) 'Abduction: the logic of discovery of grounded theory' [39 paragraphs], *Forum Qualitative Sozialforschung/Forum: Qualitative Social Research*, 11, 1, Art. 13. Avail-able at: http://nbn-resolving.de/urn:nbn:de:0114-fqs1001135

Rescher, N. (1978) *Peirce's Philosophy of Science*. South Bend, IN, University of Notre Dame Press.

Rescher, N. (1997) *Objectivity: The Obligations of Impersonal Reason*. Notre Dame, IN, University of Notre Dame Press.

Ribbens McCarthy, J., Holland, J. and Gillies, V. (2003) 'Multiple perspectives on the "family" lives of young people: methodological and theoretical issues in case research', *International Journal of Social Research Methodology*, 6, 1, pp. 1–23.

Richardson, L. (2000) 'Evaluating ethnography', *Qualitative Inquiry*, 6, 2, pp. 253–255.

Riordan, S. and Jopling, M. (2021) 'The £350 billion home-schooling question', *BERA Blog*, 25 February. Available at: https://www.bera.ac.uk/blog/the-350-billion-home-schooling-question

Ritchie, S. (2020) *Science Fictions: Exposing Fraud, Bias, Negligence and Hype in Science*. London, Bodley Head.

Rolfe, G. (2006) 'Validity, trustworthiness and rigour: quality and the idea of qualitative research', *Journal of Advanced Nursing*, 53, 3, pp. 304–310.

Rosenthal, R. (1976) *Expectation Effects in Behavioral Research*. New York, Wiley.

Rosenthal, R. and Rosnow, R. (eds.) (1969) *Artifact in Behavioral Research*, New York, Academic Press.

Rosnow, R. (1981) *Paradigms in Transition*. New York, Oxford University Press.

Roulston, K. and Shelton, S. A. (2015) 'Reconceptualizing bias in teaching qualitative research methods', *Qualitative Inquiry*, 21, 4, pp. 332–342.

Ruby, J. (ed.) (1982) *A Crack in the Mirror: Reflexive Perspectives in Anthropology*. Philadelphia, PA, University of Pennsylvania Press.

Rule, J. B. (1978) *Insight and Social Betterment*. New York, Oxford University Press.

Ryle, G. (1949) *The Concept of Mind*. London, Hutchinson.

Ryle, G. (1971) 'Thinking and reflecting', in Ryle, G. (ed.) *Collected Papers*, Vol. 2. London, Hutchinson.

Sandelowski, M. (1993) 'Rigor or rigor mortis: the problem of rigor in qualitative research revisited', *Advances in Nursing Science*, 16, 2, pp. 1–8.

Sanjek, R. (ed.) (1990) *Fieldnotes: The Makings of Anthropology*. Ithaca, NY, Cornell University Press.

Santos, B. D. S. (2014) *Epistemologies of the South: Justice against Epistemicide*, London, Routledge.

Scarre, G. (2006) 'Mill on induction and scientific method', in Skorupski, J. (ed.) *Cambridge Companion to Mill*. Cambridge, Cambridge University Press.

Schegloff, E. A. (1968) 'Sequencing in conversational openings', *American Anthropologist*, 70, pp. 1075–1095.

Schmaus, W. (1994) *Durkheim's Philosophy of Science and the Sociology of Knowledge*. Chicago, IL, University of Chicago Press.

Schön, D. (1983) *The Reflective Practitioner: How Professionals Think in Action*. New York, Basic Books.

Schwandt, T. and Halpern, E. (1988) *Linking Auditing and Metaevaluation*. Newbury Park, CA, SAGE.

Seale, C. (1999) *The Quality of Qualitative Research*. London, SAGE.

Serra Undurraga, J. K. A. (2020) 'Reflexivities as affective ways of relating that produce', *Qualitative Inquiry*, 26, 7, pp. 920–930.

Sharrock, W. (2010) 'The production and reproduction of social order: is structuration a solution?', in Martin, P. J. and Dennis, A. (eds.) *Human Agents and Social Structures*. Manchester, Manchester University Press.

Sharrock, W. and Read, R. (2002) *Kuhn: Philosopher of Scientific Revolution*. Cambridge, Polity.

Silverman, D. (1975) *Reading Castaneda: A Prologue to the Social Sciences*. London, Routledge and Kegan Paul.

Silverman, D. (1985) *Qualitative Methodology and Sociology*. Aldershot, Gower.

Skinner, Q. (1996) *Reason and Rhetoric in the Philosophy of Hobbes*. Cambridge, Cambridge University Press.

Skocpol, T. and Somers, M. (1980) 'The uses of comparative history in macrosocial inquiry', *Comparative Studies in Society and History*, 22, 2, pp. 174–197.

Small, M. (2009) ' "How many cases do I need?" On science and the logic of case selection in field-based research', *Ethnography*, 10, 1, pp. 5–38.

Smith, J. K. (1989) *The Nature of Social and Educational Inquiry*. Norwood, NJ, Ablex.

Smith, L. M. and Geoffrey, W. (1968) *The Complexities of the Urban Classroom*. New York, Holt, Rinehart and Winston.

Smith, L. T. (2021) *Decolonizing Methodologies: Research and Indigenous Peoples*, 2nd edition. London, Zed Books.

St. Pierre, E. A. (2021) 'Why post qualitative inquiry?', *Qualitative Inquiry*, 27, 2, pp. 163–166.

Swedberg, R. (2021) 'What is a method? On the different uses of the term method in sociology', *Distinktion: Journal of Social Theory*, 22, 1, pp. 108–128.

Tavory, I. and Timmermans, S. (2014) *Abductive Analysis: Theorizing Qualitative Research*. Chicago, IL, University of Chicago Press.

Taylor, C. (1964) *The Explanation of Behaviour*. London, Routledge and Kegan Paul.

Taylor, C. (1971) 'Interpretation and the sciences of man', *Review of Metaphysics*, 25, 1, pp. 3–51.

Thomas, G. (1997) 'What's the use of theory?', *Harvard Education Review*, 67, 1, pp. 75–105.

Thomas, G. (2007) *Education and Theory: Strangers in Paradigms*. Maidenhead, Open University Press.

Truzzi, M. (1974) *Verstehen: Subjective Understanding in the Social Sciences*. Reading, MA, Addison-Wesley.

Tudor, A. (1982) *Beyond Empiricism*. London, Routledge and Kegan Paul.

Tukey, J. W. (1977) *Exploratory Data Analysis*. Reading, MA, Addison-Wesley.

Turner, S. P. (2010) 'Critical essay: webs of belief or practices: the problem of understanding', *Archives Européennes de Sociologie/European Journal of Sociology*, LI, 3, pp. 403–427.

Tyler, S. (1986) 'Post-modern ethnography: from document of the occult to occult document', in Clifford, J. and Marcus, G. (eds.) *Writing Culture*. Berkeley, CA, University of California Press.

Uebel, T. (2010) 'Opposition to 'Verstehen' in orthodox logical empiricism', in U. Feest (ed.), *Historical Perspectives on Erklären und Verstehen*. Dordrecht, Springer, pp. 291–310.

Uebel, T. (2019) 'Neurath on Verstehen', *European Journal of Philosophy*, 27, 4, pp. 912–938.

Vaihinger, H. (1925) *The Philosophy of "As If": A System of the Theoretical, Practical and Religious Fictions of Mankind* (translation of *Die Philosophie des Als Ob* by C. K. Ogden). New York, Harcourt, Brace & Co.

van den Berg, A. and Jeong, T. (2022) 'Cutting off the branch on which we are sitting? On postpositivism, value neutrality, and the "bias paradox"', *Society*, 59, 3.

van Drie, J. and Dekker, R. (2013) 'Theoretical triangulation as an approach for revealing the complexity of a classroom discussion', *British Educational Research Journal*, 39, 2, pp. 338–360.

Van Fraassen, B. (1980) *The Scientific Image*. Oxford, Oxford University Press.

Vincent, A. (2007) *The Nature of Political Theory*. Oxford, Oxford University Press.

von Wright, G. H. (1971) *Explanation and Understanding*. London, Routledge and Kegan Paul.

Warshay, L. and Warshay, D. (2005) 'Social causation: logical, substantive, and ethical considerations', Paper presented at the annual meeting of the American Sociological Association, Marriott Hotel, Loews Philadelphia Hotel, Philadelphia, PA, 12 August.

Watson, G. (1987) 'Make me reflexive, but not yet: strategies for managing essential reflexivity in ethnographic discourse', *Journal of Anthropological Research*, 43, 1, pp. 29–41.

Watson, R. (2005) 'Reflexivity, description and the analysis of social settings', *Ciências Sociais Unisinos*, 41, 1, pp. 1–6.

Webb, E. J., Campbell, D. T., Schwartz, R. D. and Sechrest, L. (1966) *Unobtrusive Measures: Nonreactive Research in the Social Sciences*, Chicago, IL, Rand McNally.

Weber, M. (1949) *The Methodology of the Social Sciences*. New York, The Free Press.

Weber, M. (2012) *Collected Methodological Writings* (Ed. and Trans. H. H. Bruun and S. Whimster). London, Routledge.

Whitaker, E. M. and Atkinson, P. (2021) *Reflexivity in Social Research*. London, SAGE.

Williams, B. (2002) *Truth and Truthfulness*. Princeton, NJ, Princeton University Press.

Williams, M. (2001) *Problems of Knowledge*. Oxford, Oxford University Press.

Winch, P. (1958) *The Idea of a Social Science*. London, Routledge and Kegan Paul. (2nd edition, with a new intro, 1990).

Winch, P. (1964) 'Understanding a primitive society', *American Philosophical Quarterly*, 1, 4, pp. 307–324.

Wittgenstein, L. (1969) *On Certainty*. Oxford, Blackwell.

Wolff, K. H. (ed.) (1950) *The Sociology of Georg Simmel*. Glencoe, IL, Free Press.

Woodward, J. (2003) *Making Things Happen: A Theory of Causal Explanation*. Oxford, Oxford University Press.

Woolgar, S. (ed.) (1988) *Knowledge and Reflexivity: New Frontiers in the Sociology of Knowledge*. London, SAGE.

Ziman, J. (2000) *Real Science*. Cambridge, Cambridge University Press.

Znaniecki, F. (1934) *The Method of Sociology*. New York, Farrar and Rinehart.

Glossary of some philosophical terms

It is not possible here to discuss all of the philosophical terms used within social science today, but I have tried to cover the main ones that have been mentioned in this book. Not all accounts of the meanings of these terms provided in social science methodology texts are entirely accurate. I have tried to make the entries here meet that requirement, while being as clear as possible. The terms discussed are presented alphabetically.

Axiology

In some of the methodological literature, and in this book too, the word 'axiological' is used to refer to those issues that concern the purpose or goal of social research, thereby complementing the terms 'epistemological' and 'ontological', which refer to other sorts of fundamental assumption that underpin its practice. In philosophical usage, 'axiology' traditionally refers to the study of values, so in its adjectival form it can be taken to refer to matters relating to value. The orthodox or traditional conception of the value of research is that it produces knowledge that is worthwhile in itself (intrinsic value), enhancing our understanding of the world, and/or provides knowledge that serves practical purposes (instrumental value). Over the past few decades there has been increasing emphasis on the second function. Indeed, it sometimes seems to be assumed that 'knowledge is power', in the sense that producing knowledge will (or should) automatically bring about practical improvement in the world, either gradual or revolutionary. However, there are good reasons to be doubtful about this assumption: most research publications have little obvious impact, and when they do the desirability of this may be open to question. Their contribution is usually much more mediated and uncertain, at best.

In response to a perceived failure of social research in pursuit of knowledge to have significant effect, some researchers have sought to redefine its goal in immediate practical terms: requiring that it should be designed directly to serve policymaking or practice, challenge the dominant ideology, eliminate social inequalities, or emancipate those subjected to oppression. These practical goals may be regarded as complementary to the pursuit of knowledge, though there has been a tendency for them to supplant it. I argue elsewhere in this book that their inclusion as goals is illegitimate and leads to bias.

It is important to recognise an axiological distinction between the *goal* of research, what it is designed to achieve, and the *motives* that researchers have for engaging in it and for investigating particular topics. We probably all hope that our research will bring about practical improvement in the world, but that is different from trying to design it so as to ensure this outcome. In my view, the first is legitimate, while the second is not.

There has also been questioning of the conventional goal of social research from a different direction. Radical epistemological ideas drawing on relativism and scepticism raise questions about whether the traditional goal of research as producing knowledge is achievable. These ideas have rarely been consistently applied, but some commentators have pushed them far enough effectively to erase any distinction between research, on the one hand, and serving a political agenda or producing imaginative literature, on the other.

Despite the problems associated with them, attempts to redefine the goal of research, or to adopt sceptical or relativist arguments about the possibility of knowledge, touch on important axiological questions about the value both of social research and of the sort of society which it serves.

Constructionism

Constructionism ('constructivism' is sometimes used as a synonym) draws on a range of philosophical ideas, notably those of Kant, Hegel, phenomenology, pragmatism, structuralism, post-structuralism, and postmodernism. Basic to it is rejection of the idea that cognition, or even perception, is a process whereby objects that already exist in the world impress their character upon our understanding. Instead, it is argued that perception and cognition are *active* processes, in which even what is apparently 'given' is actually a product of processes of selection and construction. Another key theme is that these processes are socio-cultural, as well as personal, in character: different cultures or discourses generate divergent experiential worlds and stocks of 'knowledge'. However, while most usage of 'constructionism' involves these assumptions, there is considerable variation in the meaning given to the term. Here I will describe what seems to be the most common usage.

The constructionist idea that different cultures or discourses produce discrepant 'worlds' is similar to *interpretivism* (see later entry), but there remain important differences. Where interpretivists tend to assume that people's behaviour is governed by stable perspectives built up to make sense of and deal with their circumstances, these perspectives reflecting the situations they face, constructionists often view people as constructing particular understandings on particular occasions in a much more fluid way, drawing upon a range of conflicting discourses available to them. Furthermore, constructionists often argue that cultural worlds are brought into existence and sustained in and through the practices in which people engage, and that there is no access to some 'real' world beyond them. This radical interpretation suggests that the focus of inquiry must be on those practices themselves, and perhaps even on how socio-cultural processes position and constitute people as individuals with particular identities in particular contexts. Here constructionism threatens to undercut the possibility of human agency.

For some constructionists, these processes of socio-cultural construction are all that exists or at least that can be studied. This idea has important implications for how research is pursued. The task can no longer be to document the characteristics of various types of object (even mundane ones like children, adults, schools, teachers, hospitals, doctors, etc.) existing in the world – their actions and relationships, the causes and consequences of these, and so forth. It is insisted that we must not be misled by appearances into forgetting that such 'objects' owe their existence and their character to the constitutive processes involved in generating them as perceivable and conceivable phenomena.

An even more radical constructionism recognises that, if applied consistently, it requires researchers to treat the phenomena they study as constructed in and through their own research practices, rather than as existing independently of these. However, only a very few constructionists have adopted this extreme position *and* acknowledged that it undercuts itself.

Critical research

The phrase 'critical research' began as a euphemism for Marxism, in the United States at a time when the latter was anathema, around the middle of the twentieth century. However, the meaning of this label soon came to be extended beyond a concern with capitalism and class conflict to focus on a wider range of social inequalities – to do with sex/gender, race/ethnicity, sexual orientation, and ability/disability. This reflected the rise of social movements focused on these inequalities. Marxism was itself a diverse tradition, with sharp variations in both philosophical and political orientations, the two sometimes linked. However, with the broadening focus an even wider range of ideas about the nature of society and how it should change came to be included under the heading of 'critical research'. A feature they shared was an insistence that, in the words of Marx, the point is not simply to interpret the world but to change it (Thesis Eleven of Marx's *Theses on Feuerbach*). Critical research therefore focuses on documenting what is wrong with existing social arrangements – usually the existence, or worsening, of some form of inequity – and arguing for change. However, there has often been a tension between the pursuit of such research in academic contexts and political struggle. (Indeed, in my view, the two are incompatible.)

Among the most influential sources of critical research was Critical Theory, sometimes also referred to as the Frankfurt School of Marxism. However, its key figures – Horkheimer and Adorno – increasingly deviated from conventional Marxist ideas, coming to mount a fundamental philosophical critique of modernity. In recent times critical research has also been influenced by poststructuralism and postmodernism and, most recently, by 'new materialisms'.

Empiricism

In its main philosophical sense, this term refers to the belief that all knowledge comes via the senses, being based on direct experience; in other words, it is empirical. Historically, this position was at odds with the views of some influential philosophers, notably Plato and Descartes, who believed that knowledge, even of the 'external world', is founded on innate ideas possessed by human beings. More specifically, the term 'empiricism' emerged in the seventeenth and eighteenth centuries as a contrast with 'rationalism', which assumed that the foundations of knowledge are a *priori*, in other words that they are given 'before all experience' and structure that experience. The spread of empiricist ideas was encouraged by the success of natural science, which was widely believed to produce knowledge solely on the basis of empirical analysis. In the early twentieth century, logical empiricism (also referred to as logical positivism) insisted that natural science is the paradigm for all genuine knowledge, and that its findings can be validated through logical inference from sense data or from direct observation of physical objects, their features, and movements. However, not all forms of empiricism take this extreme form (indeed, not even all logical empiricists adopted it).

Within social science, there was a shift in the twentieth century from 'empiricism' being treated as a positive label to it having a more negative connotation, referring to approaches that place excessive weight on the role of empirical (usually quantitative) evidence and that neglect theory. A famous example is C. Wright Mills' criticism of 'abstracted empiricism', which he took to be represented by the largely quantitative, survey-based approach to social research championed by Paul Lazarsfeld; though it should be noted that Mills combined this critique with similarly dismissive criticism of what he called 'grand theory'. Critics of empiricism may stress the need for speculative thought in developing theoretical ideas; for systematic theory in explaining social phenomena; or for the role of interpretation and qualitative data in making sense of social phenomena.

There are several areas of uncertainty at the core of empiricism that are worth mentioning. A first one concerns what counts as experience. There are those who view it as consisting of sense data: distinct impressions on the senses that can be described in terms of the shape, size, movement, and colour of objects. These may or may not be treated as impersonal representations of what is external to the human body. By contrast, others adopt a wider conception of experience, extending beyond sense data, and refuse to treat it as a sequence of separate events. An example is provided by the pragmatist philosopher William James, who labelled his own position 'radical empiricism'. He insisted that experience is not a series of isolated impressions, that it is already structured. Furthermore, experience is the entire stream of consciousness, consisting of everything we feel, or are aware of, and that we 'know', and not just what we attribute to an external reality of physical sights, sounds, and objects. This kind of empiricism necessarily accepts that people's experience may vary significantly, so that all experience is personal; though there is also a sense in which human experience is shared – indeed, this is required for communication. By contrast, within social science there remains a tendency to treat 'empiricism' as assuming that research evidence must be objective and impersonal; and in this respect it is contrasted with reliance on data relating to subjective, personal experience.

A second area of uncertainty concerns the relationship between experience and knowledge; in particular, what form(s) of inference are required for the production of knowledge from empirical evidence? The range of views here extends from those who believe that we cannot go beyond simple inferences from one element of experience to another, for instance that one perception predicts some other type of perception, to those who allow inferences beyond the data to what is taken to lie behind it and may have generated it, or inference to more general categories of other kinds. The first of these positions is closer to the stereotype of the empiricist than the second, and the contrasting position to it is one that stresses the important role of theory or imagination.

A final uncertainty is an ambivalence in ordinary usage of the word 'experience'. Sometimes we treat people's experience as simply reflecting the world, as when we say that someone has more experience of something than other people, implying that they have a better understanding of it. At other times, however, we treat experience as potentially deceptive, drawing on a contrast between appearance and reality. Of course, both can be true: our experience may give us an accurate sense of some aspects of the world, but it may also be misleading in other respects. It is important to recognise both possibilities.

As already noted, among qualitative social scientists 'empiricism' has come to have a predominantly negative connotation, for example as referring to an overemphasis on the use of explicit quantitative measurement procedures, on hypothesis-testing, or simply on documenting the 'facts' of some matter. However, anyone who assigns a significant role to empirical evidence may be accused of empiricism: much like 'positivism', the term has come to be used as an all-purpose means of rejecting views with which one disagrees. While there are many social scientists who would insist on the need for careful attention to evidence, they would usually hesitate to call themselves 'empiricists'.

There is, however, a positive use of the term that has emerged recently that draws on the work of the French philosopher Gilles Deleuze. There are some similarities between his notion of 'transcendental empiricism' and the 'radical empiricism' of James, in that both are concerned to emphasise the 'concrete richness of the sensible' and to resist universalising abstractions in favour of situated particularity. Perhaps the most radical feature of Deleuze's empiricism is to reject any notion of a transcendent self that can gain knowledge, in favour of an immanent account of how self and knowledge are produced within experience. Deleuze's transcendental empiricism has been particularly influential in the context of 'new materialisms' and 'post-qualitative' inquiry.

Epistemology

This is the branch of philosophy concerned with whether knowledge is possible, and if so how it can be gained, as well as what its limits are. Epistemological argument may relate to knowledge in general or to knowledge of particular kinds. Scepticism is one, radical, epistemological view – it questions the very possibility of knowledge; though a sceptic may doubt only some kinds of knowledge not all of them. For example, there are many philosophers who are sceptics about the notion of *ethical* knowledge – concerning what is good, what ought to be done, and so on – but who are not sceptics about factual matters – regarding what types of thing exist in the world, what sorts of relation operate among them, and so on. (This use of 'sceptic' is to be distinguished from the everyday notion of someone who is more than usually doubtful about claims to knowledge, in general or of particular kinds.) Another epistemological disagreement concerns whether or not a distinctive mode of inquiry is required in order to gain knowledge about human psychological and social phenomena, as against the physical phenomena studied by the natural sciences.

While epistemological issues are analytically distinct from ontological ones, they each have implications for the other. Indeed, sometimes it can be difficult to distinguish between them. For example, relativism – the idea that all our understandings of the world are relative to our perceptual and cognitive capacities, our framework of assumptions, our psychological dispositions, or our socio-cultural positions or backgrounds – is sometimes formulated in ontological terms as the belief that there are 'multiple realities'. At other times a contrast is drawn between relativism and this ontological claim (characteristic of what has been referred to as the 'ontological turn'), relativists simply claiming that there are multiple perspectives on a single reality, and that these are fundamentally different in character and not open to independent assessment as regards their validity or value.

It is worth noting that the word 'epistemology' is sometimes used in plural form to refer to different views about the nature of knowledge, whether and how it can be acquired. In this sense, it can be a synonym for methodological 'paradigm', 'philosophy', or 'approach'.

Interpretivism

This term refers to a range of ideas that have been influential across the social sciences. One source of these is the discipline of hermeneutics, which was originally concerned with studying what is involved in interpreting texts from the ancient world, both the Bible and those of ancient Greece and Rome.

A central assumption here is that we cannot understand those who produced these texts, or the people whose character and behaviour are depicted in them, in the same terms that we understand people in our own society today. Instead, it was insisted that there are significant cultural differences between historical periods even within the same society. This argument was later extended beyond the understanding of texts to apply to understanding human behaviour more generally, being applied by twentieth-century anthropologists in thinking about how to understand diverse contemporary cultures, especially non-literate ones very different in character from Western societies. Subsequently, the argument even came to be applied *within* Western societies, by anthropologists, sociologists and others: it was argued that there are subcultures within any large complex society that will differ quite significantly in assumptions about the nature of the world, in what values they prioritise, in sensibility and behaviour.

Interpretivism relies on a conception of human behaviour which insists that, rather than people responding to situations simply on the basis of biological instincts or idiosyncratic patterns of learned response, behaviour is shaped by cultural meanings. What this implies is that any attempt to understand and explain it must rely on some means of accessing those meanings.

Several suggestions have been put forward for how other cultures and subcultures can be understood, such as exercising the psychological capacity of empathy or setting out to learn the culture so that one can internalise 'the native point of view'. Emphasis was also sometimes placed on the idea that we all have the capacity to learn how to read cultural signs, and thereby make sense of others' communications and actions. However, some have argued that understanding other cultures, at least in the manner that they are understood by their members, is impossible. Rather, all interpretation reflects the presuppositions, sensibilities, preferences, of the interpreter. This implies a form of relativism.

Materialism

This term has long been used within philosophy, usually to refer to the ontological view that what exists is made up of matter; or the idea that matter determines the existence and character of all phenomena. The traditional contrast here is with idealism, which assumes that everything is composed of ideas or is spiritual in character, or that it is ideas or discourses that determine everything else. There is also, usually, a contrast between materialism and religious assumptions about the supernatural.

However, there is considerable variation in what 'matter' is taken to mean. It may be conceived at the level of 'medium-sized dry goods' such as tables or chairs, or at that of molecules, atoms, or even subatomic particles. Alternatively, in social science, 'material factors' may refer to technologies, to actual processes of social interaction (as against thoughts and feelings), or to people's desires or interests (as against their values). Clearly, what 'materialism' entails, and the justification for it, will vary according to which of these interpretations is adopted.

Historically, the most influential version of materialism within social science has been that deriving from Marx, which treats technology and the social relations of production as the 'material base' that structures the character of the wider society. This is often referred to as historical, or dialectical, materialism. Marxism is opposed to various kinds of idealism, initially that of Hegel, but subsequently of other kinds too – such as sociological accounts that emphasise the independent role of values in shaping people's behaviour. There has, however, been considerable dispute even amongst Marxists about exactly what is included in the material base, as well as about in what sense and to what degree it determines the character of other parts of society.

Recent 'new materialisms' represent a reaction against an earlier emphasis on discourses as constituting the world. The role of objects in human social life is foregrounded, and agency is ascribed to physical phenomena and animals, not just to humans. (See the Introduction for a more detailed outline.)

Ontology

This term refers to enquiry into, or assumptions or theories about, the nature of what exists, including whether anything can be said to exist at all. One influential area of disagreement concerns whether all phenomena have the same fundamental character, or whether there are multiple kinds of being. A related one is about whether ideas or matter are the true nature of being (idealism versus materialism); or whether both exist and are of equal importance. Often involved are questions about the relationship between mind and body, or mind and society.

Also under this heading would be arguments that the character of social phenomena is fundamentally different from that of the objects and events studied by natural scientists. For example it is insisted by interpretivists that, by contrast with other physical objects, people act on the basis of how they interpret the situations they are in, how they define their own identities, and so on. The epistemological implication often drawn from this is that a distinctive approach is required in order to study human social life, though there are disagreements about what form this should take. In part, this reflects the fact that there are different views about the nature of social phenomena even amongst those who regard their character as distinct from physical phenomena: some see them as constituted by discourses, others as taking a more material form; as being a product of socio-historical forces or micro-processes of social interaction.

The word 'ontology' is sometimes used in the plural to refer to approaches adopting different ontological assumptions. Along the same lines, there is sometimes reference to 'onto-epistemological positions'.

Phenomenology

In general terms, this word refers to the study of how things appear in, or are constituted by, experience (or, occasionally, it means studying the surfaces of things). Its main usage in philosophy stems from the phenomenological movement that was inaugurated by Edmund Husserl. He believed that, in order to resolve traditional philosophical problems, it was necessary to try to describe as carefully and fully as possible how phenomena of different types appear in experience. He rejected the narrow empiricist idea that external objects simply make impressions upon our senses, in other words that the process of perception is a passive matter of reception. Rather, he argued, the things that we experience, whether they are real objects in the world, imaginary ones, or simply ones that are possible, are constituted through perceptual or cognitive activity much of which is normally below the level of consciousness. Only by explicating this activity, Husserl thought, could we come to a true understanding of the world and of our place in it; and thereby provide a sound foundation for mathematics and science, on the one hand, and for ethics and social inquiry, on the other.

Subsequent philosophers have drawn on Husserl's work and developed or transformed it in various directions, these include Stein, Heidegger, Merleau-Ponty, Sartre, and Levinas. While this philosophical work is appealed to by some social researchers, quite diverse lessons have been drawn from it, producing orientations that are at odds with one another; examples would include phenomenography and ethnomethodology. Much social science use of the term 'phenomenology' refers simply to detailed investigation of how people see or experience themselves and their world, as for example in the case of Interpretive Phenomenological Analysis.

Positivism

This is a word that is now used in a largely negative way (which is ironic given that it was originally intended to oppose the 'negativism' of those Enlightenment writers who simply rejected the ideas and institutions of the past as erroneous and worthless). Few researchers today would describe themselves as positivists. Instead, the term is generally employed to dismiss what are regarded as false interpretations of science, the false assumption that natural science should be the model for social research, or other epistemological and ontological views that are rejected.

The term 'positivism' was invented by the early nineteenth-century French philosopher Auguste Comte. He saw science as providing not just sound knowledge of the world but also a new worldview that could be used as a basis for reorganising society in a more rational manner, in line with its inherent process of development. In his view, science was to replace older forms of belief, including Christianity, on which human beings had necessarily relied in the past in making sense of and adapting to their world. He saw science as taking over the social functions of those previously dominant forms of belief – even as forming the basis for a new religion.

In the late nineteenth and early twentieth centuries, the generally accepted meaning of 'positivism' changed, coming to stand for a particular conception of the nature of scientific method, one which involved logically deriving scientific laws from empirical evidence that took the form of observational data. Here its meaning overlaps considerably with that of 'empiricism', as in the case of the early twentieth-century philosophical movement that is often referred to, interchangeably, as 'logical positivism' or 'logical empiricism'. Also frequently involved here is the idea that natural science provides the prime model of rational inquiry and thinking.

Today, within social science the term 'positivism' is often taken to refer to the belief that the phenomena studied have an existence independent of the research process, so that it is effectively a synonym for 'realism'. This is rather confusing since, in the past, some positivists have been anti-realists. Great care is necessary in the use of this term.

Postmodernism

This word has been employed in a variety of ways. While it may be used quite narrowly to refer to the views expressed by the French writer Jean-François Lyotard, who popularised it, frequently its reference is much broader, being employed as a general heading for much influential French philosophical writing of the 1960s and 1970s. So, while Lyotard was distinctive in this context in promoting the term 'postmodern' (whose earlier use can be traced back to architecture and the philosophy of history), the label 'postmodernist' is often now also applied to the work of others who did not employ, or even rejected, the label: Barthes, Baudrillard, Cixous, Derrida, Foucault, Irigaray, Kristeva, and Lacan, for instance. Central to this broader meaning of the term is a rejection of what is identified as Enlightenment or modern thinking, especially its belief in the capacity of Reason to grasp the nature of reality and to provide the basis for a form of social organisation that realises human ideals. Marxism was often taken as the most advanced form of Enlightenment thinking by French writers, and much of what now comes under the heading of postmodernism was a reaction (on the Left) against it, in particular regarding it as responsible for the terror and oppression characteristic of Soviet society under Stalin and for the conservatism of the French Communist Party's reaction to the Algerian war of independence and the 'events' of May 1968.

In more specific terms, the ideas associated with postmodernism in this wider sense include one or more of the following:

- A rejection of teleological meta-narratives, whereby history is portrayed as having an inbuilt goal, for example as going through various phases in order to achieve the progressive or dialectical realisation of authentic human nature.
- Abandonment of the idea that knowledge or understanding come through some Subject – individual or collective – which is capable of grasping the nature of reality. Instead there is emphasis on the role of what is beyond the capacity of Reason, and especially of science, to understand. There is also an insistence on the fragmented or multiple character of individual identities.
- Rejection of those perspectives and orientations that seek to comprehend the world in terms of universal or totalising categories, thereby tending to reduce the other to the same, or what is unknown to the framework of what is known. What is required instead, it is insisted, is an openness to what is different.
- A denial of the assumption that language, or discourse more generally, is a tool or a structure that generates coherent and clear meanings that can capture the essential nature of reality. Instead, discourse is viewed as a force

that speaks through us and constitutes who we are. Moreover, it is unstable, so that meaning is continually shifting, involves internal tensions, and is potentially deceptive, never succeeding in representing what it claims to represent. Closely associated with this is a rejection of binary distinctions.

• Rejection of claims to scientific expertise, and of the model of science as emancipatory and progressive. Scientific knowledge, including that from the psychological and social sciences, is often viewed as playing a repressive role within Western societies, and globally. On this basis, it may be concluded that part of the task of the intellectual should be to subvert scientific or research-based claims to knowledge and expertise. At the same time, there can be appeals to new forms of science which are at odds with that which is institutionally dominant. More usually, art and literature, some kinds of philosophy, and even religious mysticism, are taken as the alternative; however, the distinctions amongst these options, like other distinctions, may be challenged.

These postmodernist ideas draw on (as well as rejecting) what preceded them in French philosophical thought – notably phenomenology, existentialism and structuralism – as well as on nineteenth- and early twentieth-century reactions against, and reworkings of, 'the Enlightenment'; notably the writings of Nietzsche and Heidegger. Such ideas took on a distinctive character in the work of feminists, who portrayed Enlightenment thinking as masculinist.

Poststructuralism

This is often used as a synonym for 'postmodernism', in the broader sense I outlined earlier. It is usually taken to refer to rejection of the idea that there are coherent discourses that generate the phenomena we experience, as claimed by structuralism, in favour of the view that such discourses are unstable and changing, and that they operate in and through power. Nevertheless, poststructuralism inherited from structuralism the idea that language or discourse has a structure that is independent of individual intentions, indeed that it produces what is believed and said, and even who it is that is speaking or writing.

'Poststructuralism' is just as misleading a designation as 'postmodernism', since most of the authors who are usually listed under this heading did not use or even rejected the label. Probably the clearest example of someone whose thinking did indeed emerge out of structuralism is Roland Barthes. But it must be remembered that the work of French philosophers of the generation who came of age in the 1950s, and subsequently to prominence in the 1960s, was shaped by a number of influences, both positively and negatively, not just by structuralism. In particular, 'post-structuralists' reacted against the phenomenology and existentialism of the previous generation of French philosophers, such as Sartre and Merleau-Ponty. At the same time, they retained from existentialism a focus on the concrete, and an emphasis on the contingent character of reality, as well as resistance to the idea that history is moving towards some dialectical end, whether that claimed by Hegel or by Marx. More positive influences, along with structuralism, were the interpretations of Hegel by Wahl, Kojeve, and Hyppolite. Both these sources challenged existentialism by shifting the focus from subjective consciousness to the role of language or discourse as a force which constitutes whatever is experienced. Another important influence, especially on Michel Foucault, was the historical epistemology of Bachelard and Canguilhem. They conceived of science as involving a rupture with commonsense, and as itself differentiated across the various sciences rather than being a single entity. The 'structuralist' Marxism of Althusser also drew on this source and had considerable influence.

Post-structuralism, like postmodernism, is a very mixed bag.

Pragmatism

Aside from the everyday meaning of this term, as a focus on what is practically feasible, it can also refer to a philosophical approach that emerged in the second half of the nineteenth century in the United States, that was very influential in the first half of the twentieth century, and whose influence is still present today. Pragmatism developed from detailed readings of German philosophy, notably the work of Kant and Hegel, though it also drew on the philosophical ideas of the medieval scholastics. The term 'pragmatism' is attributed to Charles Sanders Peirce, who was a practising scientist and mathematician as well as a philosopher. His views are complex, and developed considerably over his lifetime. His starting point was the idea that science involves operationalising the meaning of concepts in terms of the outcomes of experimental inquiry, this enabling conceptual distinctions that are meaningless to be dismissed. So, what was important, according to Peirce, was the practical meaning that a concept had in the context of scientific investigation. At the same time, he did not believe that concepts are simply instruments to be judged by their usefulness, as some subsequent pragmatists have done: he regarded them as producing representations of reality. Indeed, this was why they were effective in dealing with the world: he insisted that concepts will only work if they capture what he referred to as 'reals'.

Later pragmatists, notably William James and John Dewey, developed distinctive versions of pragmatism. Peirce sought to distance his position from that of James, who located the meaning, and the validity, of ideas in terms of their practical value in dealing with the problems of life. Over the course of a long career, Dewey developed a distinctive and comprehensive viewpoint which rejected the 'quest for certainty' that he saw as characteristic of past philosophy, in other words the search for a secure foundation beyond all possible doubt on which knowledge could be based. Instead, he conceptualised scientific inquiry as arising from practical problems, and as concerned with discovering solutions to them. Moreover, he conceived of it as a democratic process, not simply operating within communities of scientists but more widely. As a result, he placed considerable emphasis on the role of education, which he conceived as being properly designed to encourage and facilitate practical inquiry.

More recently, the strongest influence of pragmatism on social research has probably come through the writings of Richard Rorty, who is often portrayed as reinterpreting pragmatism in a postmodernist fashion. However, his interpretation of pragmatism has been sharply challenged, not least by those who treat Peirce as its main source. Later philosophers self-identifying as pragmatists adopt quite diverse positions, for example Haack, Misak, and Brandom.

Realism

There are many different interpretations, and kinds, of realism (an influential one today in some fields of social research is 'critical realism', deriving from the writings of Roy Bhaskar). Broadly speaking, the term 'realism' refers to ontological views about or approaches to research which assume that the phenomena investigated exist and have features that are independent of the process of inquiry. Practically speaking, most research has been realist in this sense. However, there have been those who have raised questions about whether the phenomena to which research texts refer can be said to exist, or have the character they are claimed to have, independently of the particular framework of assumptions or the set of methods employed by the researcher. This is a form of anti-realism, but what that term means always depends upon what kind of realism is being rejected. There are several alternative positions that have been treated as opposites to realism, including relativism (which insists that all accounts reflect the assumptions and commitments of the researcher) and scepticism (which may deny that we can gain knowledge of the world, or at least that we can go beyond immediate appearances). Constructionism draws on both of these.

There are many complications surrounding realism, relating to what is and is not treated as real, and exactly what the word 'real' is taken to mean; what the relationship can be between real phenomena and our descriptions, explanations, and theories about them; and also whether and how we can have knowledge of them. Nevertheless, in broad terms most of us, most of the time, operate on the basis of assumptions that are realist. Indeed, it is hard to see how we could avoid doing this. Often a distinction is drawn between naïve and more subtle conceptions of realism, the latter recognising that realism does not require us to believe that all real phenomena have the same nature as chairs and tables, or that we can have direct knowledge of them. There are also many other adjectives applied to qualify 'realism', including 'indirect', 'metaphysical', 'internal', 'epistemological', as well as 'critical' (and there are at least two versions of critical realism). Like other philosophical terms, this one too must be handled with care.

Relativism

Generally speaking, this term refers to the idea that any knowledge claim necessarily operates within a particular framework of assumptions, and that there are always alternative frameworks from which quite different conclusions could be drawn about what is true or real. Furthermore, according to relativists, there is, and can be, no external, overarching perspective – a 'view from nowhere' or 'god's-eye view' – in terms of which the validity of different frameworks of assumptions could be assessed. These frameworks may be associated with different cultures, though there can be multiple ones within the same society, even within the same academic discipline. They could also be tied to particular social categories or groups. Furthermore, like scepticism, relativism can be global – being applied to all kinds of knowledge, experience, feeling, etc. – or it can be held to apply only to some kinds of knowledge. For example, many people are moral relativists, believing that what is good or right varies between cultures or among individual people (for example, that ethics is a matter of personal interpretation), but they do not necessarily also believe that the truth of factual claims about the world – about what exists, what happened, why, and so on – is framework-relative. As noted in the entry on epistemology, relativism is an epistemological view, but it can also be presented in ontological form, as when people claim that there are 'multiple realities', an idea associated with the 'ontological turn' in anthropology and in Science and Technology Studies. 'Relativism' is sometimes treated as a negative, dismissive label; but there are also those who apply it to their own views and defend the position.

Standpoint epistemology

This is the idea that our understanding of the world varies according to our social location or 'standpoint', *and that one standpoint offers a better basis for gaining knowledge of the social world than others.* In this latter respect it is different from relativism. Its origin lies in the work of Karl Marx, who regarded the working class in Western industrial societies as uniquely placed to understand the nature of capitalism, not just what was wrong with it but also how it operated, and how it could be changed. He drew this conclusion on the basis of a conception of historical development that he derived from Hegel, according to which progress towards the realisation of human ideals occurs through conflict between the perspectives and actions of dominant and subordinate social groups, and the revolutions that bring new groups and their ideologies to power. Marx argued that the working class have direct experience of the exploitation that is at the heart of capitalism – the ruling class's theft of 'profit' from the value produced by labour power. He suggested that, while profit is presented within conventional economics as the result of fair exchange, the working class are able to see through this mystification; whereas, by contrast, this is more difficult for members of the bourgeoisie. Furthermore, he believed that the struggle between these classes would bring an end to the process of historical development, human ideals finally being realised under communism.

Standpoint epistemology was taken up by feminists in the 1970s, and subsequently by representatives of ethnic and sexual minorities and by disability activists. The grounds for epistemic privilege could not, of course, be exactly the same as those put forward by Marx, but various alternatives were offered, these often drawing on the idea that oppression is more visible to those suffering it than to those responsible for it. Another line of argument was that subordinate groups develop a 'double consciousness': they may acquire the dominant ideology alongside the understanding they gain from their own experience of the world, thereby being in a position to interrogate both and to develop more accurate social knowledge.

The notion of 'standpoint' is complex: it refers to a potentiality; it does not necessarily correspond to the actual views of subordinate groups. For example, following Marx, Lenin believed that without leadership from the communist party the working class would not attain the revolutionary consciousness required to bring about major social change. Similarly, feminists have recognised the need for 'consciousness raising' because many women simply accept patriarchy as normal and natural. In other words, if female emancipation is to be achieved, a key role must be played by feminists as an intellectual vanguard. Similar arguments have been developed in relation to the standpoints of other subordinated groups.

Structuralism

Various meanings can be given to this term. In its widest sense, it is used to refer to any form of analysis that identifies structures of some kind that underly and generate surface appearances. This would include the structural-functionalism that was once influential in both anthropology and sociology. However, the main sense of the term refers to a mode of thinking that began in linguistics but spread across the sociocultural sciences during the twentieth century, taking a variety of forms. The primary source was the linguistic theory of Ferdinand de Saussure. Whereas most previous study of language had focused on the historical sources of, and patterns of change in, languages, he insisted that their current structures must also be examined: there should be 'synchronic', not just 'diachronic', investigation. Saussure drew a sharp distinction between 'la langue' and 'la parole', the first being a coherent, underlying linguistic system, whereas the second referred to the contingent, complex, and heterogeneous speech that occurs through its use. He argued that languages operate on the basis of an internal structure made up of contrasts, whereby each element gains its significance through its differences from, and relationships with, others. For instance, at the level of phonology, the sounds deployed by a language are distinguished from one another not by their intrinsic characteristics so much as by the alternatives with which they contrast, these being different in each language. So, in English, the sound corresponding to 'p' contrasts with those associated with 'b' and 't', whereas in other languages these sounds may not be distinguished; while other distinctions among sounds that English neglects *do* have significance. And the relevant sound distinctions retain their meaning irrespective, for example, of loudness or pitch.

Much the same is true of the meaning of words. Saussure insisted that what a word means is not given by the things to which it refers but rather by how the word relates to the meanings of contrasting or related words. So, the word 'table' gets its meaning through contrasts with 'chair', 'sofa', 'stepladder', etc., as well as from relationships with words with which it can be combined – 'sitting at', 'eating at', and so on. In short, a language is not made up of a collection of arbitrary names for various types of object that exist in the world but rather forms a system, and it is the relations making up this system (notably, but not exclusively, contrasts) that determine the meaning of words and thereby of utterances. Saussure believed that this account of the generation of meaning could be extended beyond the field of verbal language, and subsequently a number of linguists and anthropologists sought to show how this could be done, under the headings of 'semiotics' or 'semiology'.

While Saussure did not derive any philosophical conclusions from his account of language, later structuralists have sometimes done so. His argument that, in most languages, sign-vehicles, such as words, do not have any intrinsic relationship with the phenomena to which they relate, that this relationship is arbitrary and varies between languages, has sometimes been taken to imply that the relationship between statements about some set of phenomena and the phenomena themselves is arbitrary, or even that it is meaningless to talk of phenomena as existing independently of their linguistic constitution as phenomena of particular types. One label for this is linguistic determinism: the idea that how we experience the world is determined by the linguistic categories we employ, and the grammatical relations in which these are implicated, so that native speakers of different languages inhabit different experiential worlds. This is an argument frequently ascribed to the anthropologists Edward Sapir and (especially) Benjamin Lee Whorf in the early twentieth century, and it has had considerable influence.

The most significant development of structuralism beyond the field of language was the work of the anthropologist Claude Lévi-Strauss. He analysed both marriage patterns and myths as structured in the manner of language, drawing on the idea that the character of objects derives from the set of relationships in which they are involved and not from their intrinsic qualities taken in isolation. The aim was to identify the underlying generative process, equivalent to Saussure's notion of 'langue', that determines what can and cannot occur: the deep structure lying beneath surface appearances. For Lévi-Strauss this was the structure of the mind itself, as a universal, collective phenomenon, which organises experience and action, rendering meaningful what is, in itself, essentially meaningless.

An important feature of structuralism is that it is sometimes taken to represent a new form of science. Like some other kinds of science, what this claims to offer is discontinuous with the forms of understanding that lay people have: it claims to provide 'un-commonsense knowledge'. However, there have been diverse interpretations of the form this takes: in addition to Lévi-Strauss's structuralist anthropology, there was the structuralist Marxism of Althusser and his students, as well as the earlier 'genetic structuralism' of Piaget in psychology. Subsequently, Lacan developed a form of structuralism within psychoanalysis, claiming that the unconscious is structured in much the same way as language; while Barthes, a literary and cultural analyst, used structuralism to identify how ideological meanings are conveyed via the mass media, for example by photographs but also through mass entertainments like wrestling matches.

Name index

Subject index

For Product Safety Concerns and Information please contact our EU
representative GPSR@taylorandfrancis.com
Taylor & Francis Verlag GmbH, Kaufingerstraße 24, 80331 München, Germany

9 781032 395746